To my darling
Julie

from your loving
Dad

ANCESTRY AND AMALGAMATIONS IN THE BRITISH ARMY

1660 - 2008

An illustrated Guide

GOFF LUMLEY

Published by Partizan Press 2009
100 Baker Road, Newthorpe,
Nottingham, NG16 2DP
Ph/Fx: +44 (0) 1159 382111
Email: ask@caliverbooks.com
www.caliverbooks.com

First published in Great Britain in 2009 by Partizan Press

Layout by Goff Lumley

Cover design by Jay Forster

ISBN: 978-1-85818-592-7

Printed in the UK by The Good News Press Ltd., Ongar, Essex

CONTENTS

INTRODUCTION

Efficient organisations never stand still. They remodel themselves to address deficiencies and they change to adapt to changing circumstances.

The British Army has been doing this throughout it's history. Consequently, our Army's visible facets (it's Regiments and Corps) have changed over time as new units have appeared and old ones merged together.

One would expect such changes to be recorded for bureaucratic and historical reasons but one would also expect them to be recorded for another reason - our emotive relationship with our Regiments and Corps.

The latter were not just organised groups of men (and eventually women). They were men who were intimately involved in the turbulent history and defence of our nation at that violent and often heroic level of life or death. Such involvement breeds a sense of *camaraderie* and *esprit de corps* which imbues not only our serving soldiers but all the soldiers who have gone before. In fact, it goes even wider because there will be few families who do not have some connection with some Regiment or Corps at some time in their past even though they themselves may never have served in our Armed Forces.

Because of these connections, regimental ancestry and amalgamation details have a wide appeal and that appeal has led to the appearance of several books on the subject.

This guide is another.

Why do we need another one, you might ask. Well the first and obvious reason is to address the point made in the opening paragraph which is - change continues. For example, we are only a few years into the 21st century and yet that century has already seen the formation of seven new regiments. They are shown below together with their year of formation. The first six were formed by amalgamation and the last is new. Fresh publications are therefore needed just to keep the records up to date.

The Royal Regiment of Scotland	: 2006
The Duke of Lancaster's Regiment	: 2006
The Yorkshire Regiment	: 2006
The Mercian Regiment	: 2007
The Royal Welsh	: 2006
The Rifles	: 2007
The Special Reconnaissance Regiment	: 2005

My second reason for producing another book is to combine ancestry and amalgamation data with illustrations of evolving regimental cap badges.

This has two advantages.

Regimental cap badges have always been iconic and eye-catching regimental identifiers. Their inclusion will thus breathe life into the dry bones of the ancestral data and their visual impact will make the latter easier to assimilate. That easy assimilation has been assisted by presenting the information as dated family trees with regimental cap badges woven into the trees. Combining the two should make the guide more user-friendly.

The other advantage is also associated with the cap badge illustrations.

Because the badges are woven into family trees, it is easy to find sequences of badges associated with specific regiments. This isn't always possible in some (still admirable) publications where different types of badges (e.g. helmet plate centres and field service cap badges) are presented in different chapters. In addition, this gathering together of related badges makes it easy to see the design connections (or lack of them) between the badges of predecessors and the badges of regiments formed from them. Such connections show how keen constituents of new, composite regiments were to preserve some aspect of their old badge in their new badge. It helps keep the honoured memories of old regiments alive.

Finally, including over a thousand badge illustrations (albeit with some repetition) means the guide is not just a guide to ancestry and amalgamations. It also doubles up as a guide to evolving cap badge designs going back, in this instance, to the time when our infantry regiments were identified by their number in the line.

So – two guides in one book. That can't be bad!

GENERAL NOTES

Regiments and Corps have been listed in this guide (with some exceptions) in the 2008 British Army Order of Precedence. The latter is included in the Appendices. The exceptions are primarily amongst Arms and Services but include other units such as the Parachute Regiment. They have been introduced to group together units which have an ancestral and/or functional relationship even though the individual units may be listed apart in the Order of Precedence. For example, the Royal Horse Artillery and Royal Regiment of Artillery are presented together so one can easily see how the former fits in with the latter.

The dates when regiments were raised plus their evolving regimental names, have also been listed together with dates on which changes occurred. As regiments were often listed under the names of their colonels before 1751, the names of the latter have been included. Knowing a colonel's name does not help you identify his regiment by it's post-1751 title if the name is all you have got. Cross-references have therefore been included in the Appendices to relate colonels names and post-1751 titles.

After 1751, infantry (foot) regiments were known by their number in the line. Many were given territorial designations, in 1782, to add to their number. Subsequently, the Cardwell/Childers reforms of 1881 amalgamated foot regiments in territorially designated pairs and discarded the numbers. These 1881 territorial designations usually tied in with the 1782 territorial designations but there were exceptions. An additional cross-reference has therefore been included in the Appendices to relate 'Regiment of Foot' numbers to both pre- and post-1881 territorial names. A further cross-reference relates post-1881 territorial names to numbers. You can thus go from number to name or name to number.

Ancestral data for cavalry and infantry are presented in subsections which generally pivot around dates relating to major amalgamation events. Thus, cavalry data pivot around 1922 when many amalgamations occurred and infantry data pivot around 1881 when, as has been said, the amalgamations associated with the Cardwell/Childers reforms took place. Attempts have been made to present both sides of the 'pivoted data' on facing pages in the interest of user-friendliness. However, you will note that this has not been achieved in 'The Rifles' section. This is because the section is particularly complex. It has to address, in stages, the ancestry and subsequent amalgamation of no fewer than 21 numbered Regiments of Foot (plus the un-numbered Rifle Brigade) into just one regiment. When you look at such numbers, it really brings home to you just how many of our old regiments have seemingly disappeared!

Two other pivotal points are used in the presentation of infantry data – again relating to major amalgamation events. The first is 1957-58 when the introduction of the 1958 brigade system led to many more amalgamations. The second is 2006-07 when the new regiments mentioned in the introduction were formed. Additional information has been provided on the workings of the 1958 brigade system in the notes at the beginning of the infantry chapter. The information outlines the system's initial effect and it's subsequent influence on the 2006-07 amalgamations.

As for notes on the remaining Regiments, Corps and other items:-

The idiosyncratic nature of some Arms and Services presentations has already been addressed in the opening paragraph. Air, Sea and Special Forces have been given a chapter of their own because they are out of the ordinary as the last name implies. The chapter includes information on WW2 units which were the fore-runners of almost all our current elite forces.

The opportunity has also been taken to include various other war-raised units as well as some disbanded 20th century units like our old Irish regiments.

Badge illustrations generally go back to the fourth quarter of the 19th century. As such, they provide eye-catching identifiers back to the period when infantry regiments were known by numbers. They are, with few exceptions, other rank badges.

References to other eye-catching identifiers have been included for our 18th century infantry. They are the facing colours and lace on the infantry's red coats. Each regiment, at least in it's early days, had it's own colour combination. A concluding subsection in relevant infantry sections provides a list of colours.

Crown changes have been addressed for most of the relevant badges. QVC, KC and QC abbreviations may be used. They refer to Queen Victoria's Crown (pre-1901), King's Crown (1901-1952) and Queen's Crown (1952 onwards). However, it should be noted that the above are simply convenient terms to help differentiate between the three on badges. Individual crown shapes are not strictly reserved for either Kings or Queens.

Finally, the start date for this guide has been chosen as 1660. The date ties in with the restoration of the monarchy, after the Civil War, and the gradual formation of a new Standing Army. The latter eventually evolved into the 'British Army' after the Act of Union with Scotland in 1707.

ACKNOWLEDGEMENTS

This guide evolved from an earlier one which covered the 20th century. The earlier one did not address amalgamations before that period and did not address the ancestry of the regiments involved (although it did address more than just the regular forces). It is highly likely that it would have represented the beginning and end of my little foray into publishing if it had not been for my publisher, David Westwood of MLRS Books. His suggestion that I produce this additional guide and his continued interest and support in the production process are gratefully acknowledged as a significant driving force behind the guide's appearance.

In addition to David, there are other forces which must be acknowledged.

They are the combined ranks of previous authors. Their books provide that rich source of factual information which others can build on. For that, I thank them.

A selected bibliography is given below.

Bibliography

Ascoli, D. A *Companion to The British Army, 1660 -1983 (Harrap, London)*
Barnes, Major R. M. *The Uniforms and History of the Scottish Regiments (Sphere Books Ltd)*
Brereton, J. M. *A Guide to the Regiments and Corps of the British Army on the Regular Establishment (Bodley Head)*
Edwards, Major T. E. R*egimental Badges (Gale & Polden Ltd)*
Frederick, J. B. M. *Lineage Book of the British Army (Hope Farm Press, New York)*
Gaylor, J. *Military Badge Collecting (Leo Cooper, Pen & Sword)*
Griffin, P. D. *Encyclopedia of Modern British Army Regiments (Sutton Publishing)*
Hallows, I. S. *Regiments and Corps of the British Army (Arms and Armour Press)*
Kipling, A.L. & King, H. L. *Head-Dress Badges of the British Army (Volumes 1 and 2)(Muller, Blond & White)*
Lumley, G. *Regiments and Mergers in the British Army, 1907-2007 (MLRS Books)*
Parker, J. *The Gurkhas (Bounty Books)*
Taylor, P. *Allied Special Forces Insignia 1939-1948 (Leo Cooper, Pen & Sword)*
Thompson, J. *The Royal Marines – From Sea Soldiers to a Special Force (Sidgwick and Jackson)*
Usher, G. *Dictionary of British Military History (A & C Black)*
Westlake, R. *English and Welsh Infantry Regiments – An Illustrated Record of Service 1662 -1994 (Spellmount)*

Finally, no guide like this appears overnight - they take ages!

This does mean your wife has to put up with your prolonged pre-occupation during the production process. My wife has not only put up with it, she has been both supportive and understanding. For this, she has my heartfelt thanks.

CAVALRY
(Household Cavalry and Royal Armoured Corps)

THE HOUSEHOLD CAVALRY REGIMENT

1. Pre-1922 Ancestry

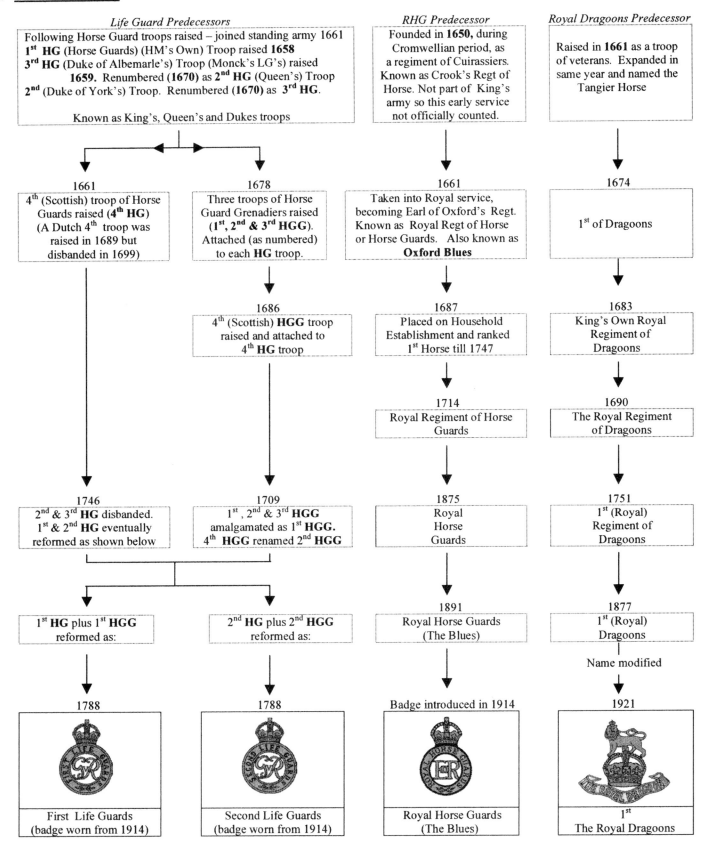

Life Guard Predecessors

Following Horse Guard troops raised – joined standing army 1661
1ˢᵗ **HG** (Horse Guards) (HM's Own) Troop raised **1658**
3ʳᵈ **HG** (Duke of Albemarle's) Troop (Monck's LG's) raised
    1659. Renumbered (**1670**) as 2ⁿᵈ **HG** (Queen's) Troop
2ⁿᵈ (Duke of York's) Troop. Renumbered (**1670**) as 3ʳᵈ **HG**.

Known as King's, Queen's and Dukes troops

RHG Predecessor

Founded in **1650**, during Cromwellian period, as a regiment of Cuirassiers. Known as Crook's Regt of Horse. Not part of King's army so this early service not officially counted.

Royal Dragoons Predecessor

Raised in **1661** as a troop of veterans. Expanded in same year and named the Tangier Horse

1661 — 4ᵗʰ (Scottish) troop of Horse Guards raised (**4ᵗʰ HG**) (A Dutch 4ᵗʰ troop was raised in 1689 but disbanded in 1699)

1678 — Three troops of Horse Guard Grenadiers raised (**1ˢᵗ, 2ⁿᵈ & 3ʳᵈ HGG**). Attached (as numbered) to each **HG** troop.

1661 — Taken into Royal service, becoming Earl of Oxford's Regt. Known as Royal Regt of Horse or Horse Guards. Also known as **Oxford Blues**

1674 — 1ˢᵗ of Dragoons

1686 — 4ᵗʰ (Scottish) **HGG** troop raised and attached to 4ᵗʰ **HG** troop.

1687 — Placed on Household Establishment and ranked 1ˢᵗ Horse till 1747

1683 — King's Own Royal Regiment of Dragoons

1714 — Royal Regiment of Horse Guards

1690 — The Royal Regiment of Dragoons

1746 — 2ⁿᵈ & 3ʳᵈ **HG** disbanded. 1ˢᵗ & 2ⁿᵈ **HG** eventually reformed as shown below

1709 — 1ˢᵗ, 2ⁿᵈ & 3ʳᵈ **HGG** amalgamated as 1ˢᵗ **HGG**. 4ᵗʰ **HGG** renamed 2ⁿᵈ **HGG**

1875 — Royal Horse Guards

1751 — 1ˢᵗ (Royal) Regiment of Dragoons

1ˢᵗ HG plus 1ˢᵗ HGG reformed as:

2ⁿᵈ HG plus 2ⁿᵈ HGG reformed as:

1891 — Royal Horse Guards (The Blues)

1877 — 1ˢᵗ (Royal) Dragoons — Name modified

1788 — First Life Guards (badge worn from 1914)

1788 — Second Life Guards (badge worn from 1914)

Badge introduced in 1914 — Royal Horse Guards (The Blues)

1921 — 1ˢᵗ The Royal Dragoons

The 1ˢᵗ and 2ⁿᵈ Life Guards and the Royal Horse Guards became, respectively, the 1ˢᵗ, 2ⁿᵈ and 3ʳᵈ Bns of the Guards Machine Gun Regiment between February 1918 and March 1919 (the Foot Guards Machine Gun Bn became the 4ᵗʰ). The Household Cavalry regiments continued to wear their own cap badges during that period and resumed their normal functions afterwards (See Foot Guards Section for further details).

2. Post – 1922 Ancestry

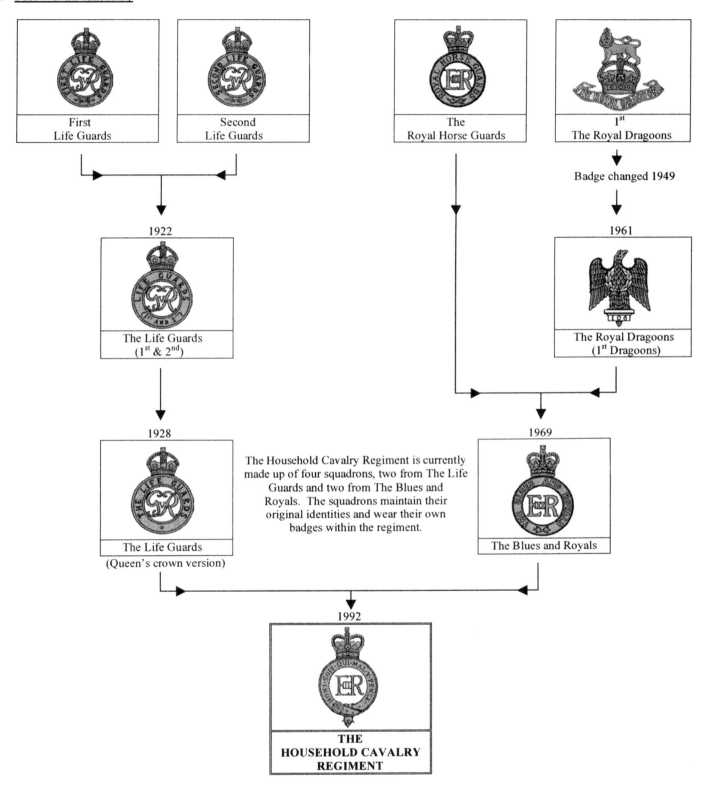

First Life Guards

Second Life Guards

The Royal Horse Guards

1st The Royal Dragoons

Badge changed 1949

1922

The Life Guards (1st & 2nd)

1961

The Royal Dragoons (1st Dragoons)

1928

The Life Guards (Queen's crown version)

The Household Cavalry Regiment is currently made up of four squadrons, two from The Life Guards and two from The Blues and Royals. The squadrons maintain their original identities and wear their own badges within the regiment.

1969

The Blues and Royals

1992

THE HOUSEHOLD CAVALRY REGIMENT

Note The above is a fully operational, fighting regiment. The Household Cavalry's well-known ceremonial duties are carried out by the **Household Cavalry Mounted Regiment**. The latter is made up of Life Guard and Blues and Royals squadrons.

The Household Cavalry Regiment and the Household Cavalry Mounted Regiment, together, make up **THE HOUSEHOLD CAVALRY.**

1st THE QUEEN'S DRAGOON GUARDS

1. Pre - 1900 Ancestry

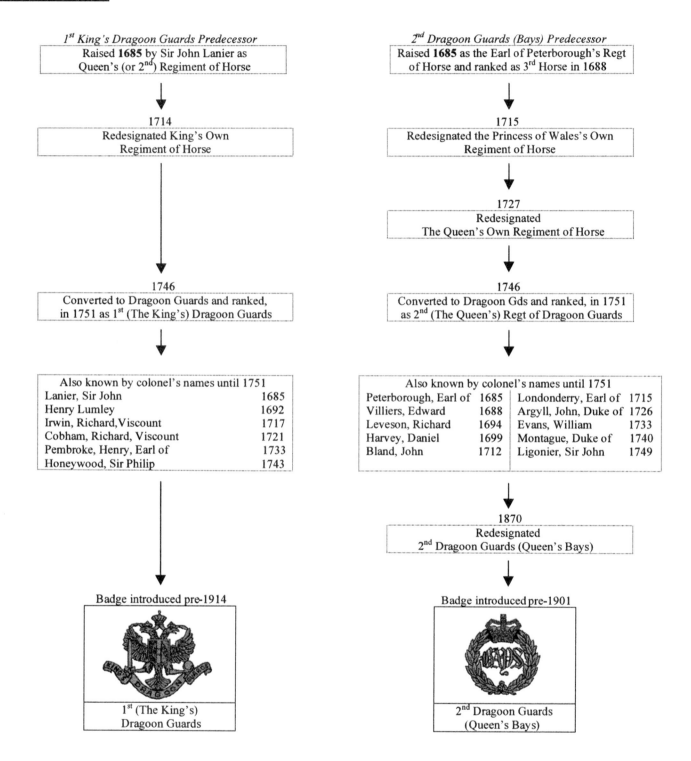

1st King's Dragoon Guards Predecessor

Raised **1685** by Sir John Lanier as
Queen's (or 2nd) Regiment of Horse

↓

1714
Redesignated King's Own
Regiment of Horse

↓

1746
Converted to Dragoon Guards and ranked,
in 1751 as 1st (The King's) Dragoon Guards

↓

Also known by colonel's names until 1751

Lanier, Sir John	1685
Henry Lumley	1692
Irwin, Richard, Viscount	1717
Cobham, Richard, Viscount	1721
Pembroke, Henry, Earl of	1733
Honeywood, Sir Philip	1743

↓

Badge introduced pre-1914

1st (The King's)
Dragoon Guards

2nd Dragoon Guards (Bays) Predecessor

Raised **1685** as the Earl of Peterborough's Regt
of Horse and ranked as 3rd Horse in 1688

↓

1715
Redesignated the Princess of Wales's Own
Regiment of Horse

↓

1727
Redesignated
The Queen's Own Regiment of Horse

↓

1746
Converted to Dragoon Gds and ranked, in 1751
as 2nd (The Queen's) Regt of Dragoon Guards

↓

Also known by colonel's names until 1751

Peterborough, Earl of	1685	Londonderry, Earl of	1715
Villiers, Edward	1688	Argyll, John, Duke of	1726
Leveson, Richard	1694	Evans, William	1733
Harvey, Daniel	1699	Montague, Duke of	1740
Bland, John	1712	Ligonier, Sir John	1749

↓

1870
Redesignated
2nd Dragoon Guards (Queen's Bays)

↓

Badge introduced pre-1901

2nd Dragoon Guards
(Queen's Bays)

4

2. Post - 1900 Ancestry

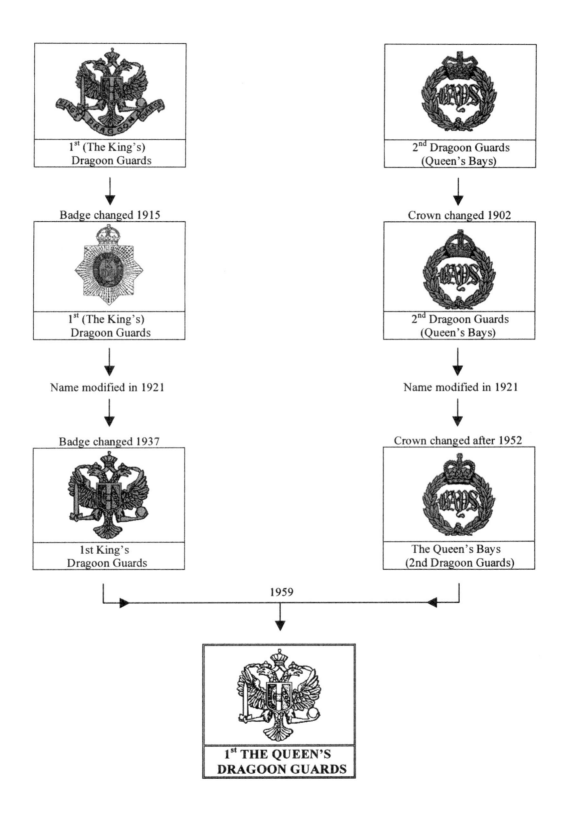

THE ROYAL SCOTS DRAGOON GUARDS
(Carabiniers and Greys)

1. Pre-1922 Formation

Royal Scots Greys Predecessor	*3rd Dragoon Guards Predecessor*	*Carabiniers Predecessor*
Raised **1678** from independent troops and regimented in **1681** as Royal Regt of Scots Dragoons or His Majesty's Regt of Dragoons.	Raised **1685** as the (1st) Earl of Plymouth's Regiment of Horse. Ranked as 4th Horse from 1688	Raised **1685** as the Queen Dowager's Regt of Horse and ranked as 9th Horse from 1688. Re-ranked 8th Horse in 1690.

1688 (Royal Scots Greys)
Ranked 2nd Dragoons, known as Grey Dragoons or Scots Regt of White Horse from 1702

1692 (Carabiniers)
Renamed The King's Regt of Carabiniers then re-ranked 7th Horse in 1694.

Royal Scots Greys — Also known by colonels names until 1751

Dalyell, Lt Gen Tom	1681
Dunmore, Earl of	1685
Livingstone, Sir Thomas	1688
Hay, Lord John	1704
Dalrymple, Lord John	1706
Portmore, Earl of	1714
Campbell, Sir James	1717
Stair, Earl of	1745
Crauford, Earl of	1747
Rothes, John, Earl of	1750

3rd Dragoon Guards — Known by colonels names until 1751

Fenwick, Sir John	1687
Colchester, Viscount	1688
Berkeley, Lord John	1692
Wood, Cornelius	1693
Windsor, Viscount	1712
Wade, George	1717
Howard, Sir Charles	1748

Carabiniers — Also known by colonels names until 1751

Name	Year	Name	Year
Lumley, Viscount	1685	Shannon, Viscount	1721
Talbot, Sir John	1687	Macartney, George	1727
Hewett, Viscount	1688	Deloraine, Earl of	1730
Byerley, Robert	1689	Rich, Sir Robert	1731
Wyndham, Hugh	1692	Cathcart, Lord	1733
Palmes, Francis	1706	Bowles, Phineas	1740
Blackwell, Leigh	1713	Cholmondeley, J	1749
Waring, Richard	1715	Sackville, Lord	1750
		Dejean, Lewis	1750

1737 (Royal Scots Greys)
Also known, from this date as Royal Regiment of North British Dragoons

1746 (3rd Dragoon Guards)
Converted to Dragoon Guards and re-ranked as 3rd Dragoon Guards

1747 (Carabiniers)
Listed as His Majesty's First Regt of Carabiniers and re-ranked 3rd (Irish) Horse.

1751 (Royal Scots Greys)
Officially designated 2nd (Royal North British) Regt of Dragoons

1751 (3rd Dragoon Guards)
Officially named 3rd Regiment of Dragoon Guards

1751 (Carabiniers)
Officially designated 3rd Regiment of Horse

1866 (Royal Scots Greys)
Redesignated 2nd (Royal North British) Dragoons (Royal Scots Greys)

1765 (3rd Dragoon Guards)
Redesignated 3rd (The Prince of Wales's) Dragoon Guards, later simplified to 3rd (Prince of Wales's) Dragoon Guards

1756 (Carabiniers)
Redesignated 3rd Regiment of Horse (Carabiniers)

1877 (Royal Scots Greys)
Redesignated 2nd Dragoons (Royal Scots Greys)

1921 (3rd Dragoon Guards)
Redesignated 3rd Dragoon Guards (Prince of Wales's)

1788 (Carabiniers)
Converted to 6th Regiment of Dragoon Guards

1921 (Royal Scots Greys)
Redesignated The Royal Scots Greys (2nd Dragoons)

1826 (Carabiniers)
Redesignated 6th Regt of D Gs (Carabineers). Spelling changed to 'Carabiniers' in 1840

Badge introduced pre-1901

The Royal Scots Greys
(2nd Dragoons)

Badge introduced pre-1901

3rd Dragoon Guards
(Prince of Wales's)

Modified name/badge pre-1901

The Carabiniers
(6th Dragoon Guards)

2. Post-1922 Ancestry

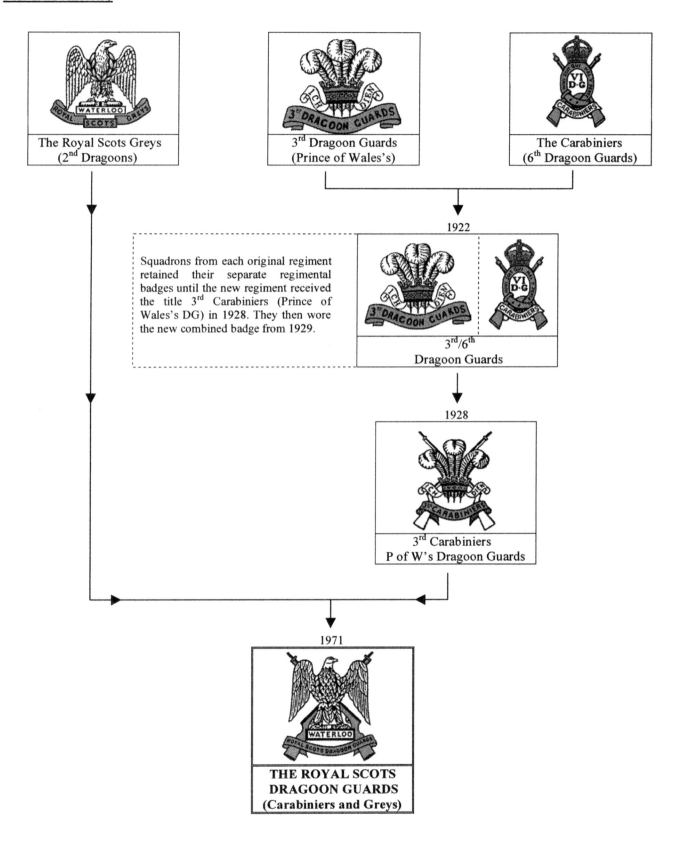

The Royal Scots Greys
(2nd Dragoons)

3rd Dragoon Guards
(Prince of Wales's)

The Carabiniers
(6th Dragoon Guards)

1922

Squadrons from each original regiment retained their separate regimental badges until the new regiment received the title 3rd Carabiniers (Prince of Wales's DG) in 1928. They then wore the new combined badge from 1929.

3rd/6th
Dragoon Guards

1928

3rd Carabiniers
P of W's Dragoon Guards

1971

**THE ROYAL SCOTS
DRAGOON GUARDS
(Carabiniers and Greys)**

THE ROYAL DRAGOON GUARDS

1. Pre-1922 Ancestry

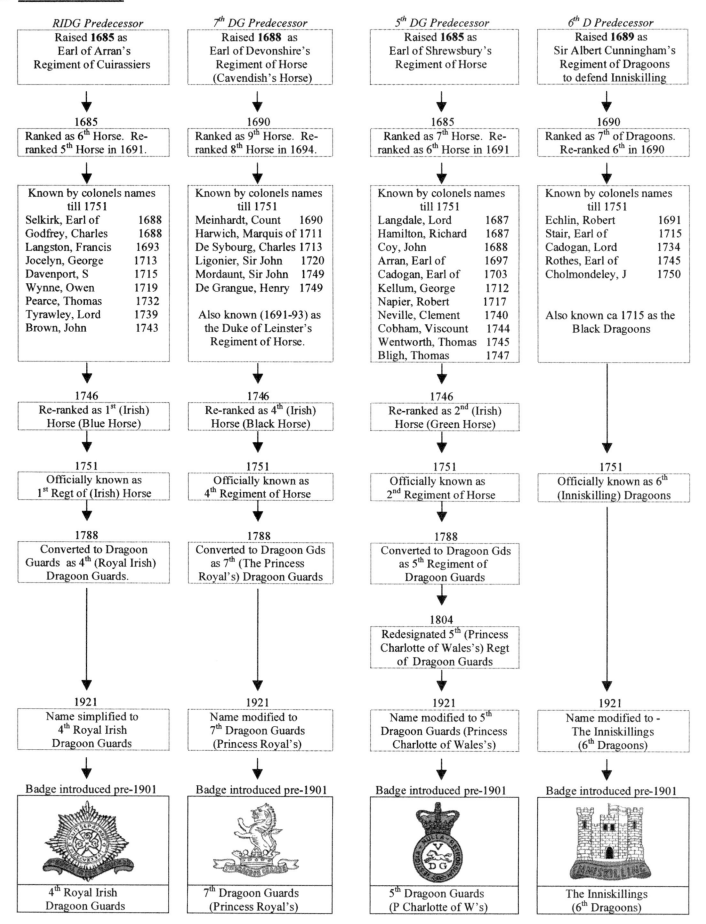

RIDG Predecessor	*7th DG Predecessor*	*5th DG Predecessor*	*6th D Predecessor*
Raised **1685** as Earl of Arran's Regiment of Cuirassiers	Raised **1688** as Earl of Devonshire's Regiment of Horse (Cavendish's Horse)	Raised **1685** as Earl of Shrewsbury's Regiment of Horse	Raised **1689** as Sir Albert Cunningham's Regiment of Dragoons to defend Inniskilling
1685 Ranked as 6th Horse. Re-ranked 5th Horse in 1691.	**1690** Ranked as 9th Horse. Re-ranked 8th Horse in 1694.	**1685** Ranked as 7th Horse. Re-ranked as 6th Horse in 1691	**1690** Ranked as 7th of Dragoons. Re-ranked 6th in 1690

Known by colonels names till 1751

RIDG		*7th DG*		*5th DG*		*6th D*	
Selkirk, Earl of	1688	Meinhardt, Count	1690	Langdale, Lord	1687	Echlin, Robert	1691
Godfrey, Charles	1688	Harwich, Marquis of	1711	Hamilton, Richard	1687	Stair, Earl of	1715
Langston, Francis	1693	De Sybourg, Charles	1713	Coy, John	1688	Cadogan, Lord	1734
Jocelyn, George	1713	Ligonier, Sir John	1720	Arran, Earl of	1697	Rothes, Earl of	1745
Davenport, S	1715	Mordaunt, Sir John	1749	Cadogan, Earl of	1703	Cholmondeley, J	1750
Wynne, Owen	1719	De Grangue, Henry	1749	Kellum, George	1712		
Pearce, Thomas	1732			Napier, Robert	1717		
Tyrawley, Lord	1739	Also known (1691-93) as the Duke of Leinster's Regiment of Horse.		Neville, Clement	1740	Also known ca 1715 as the Black Dragoons	
Brown, John	1743			Cobham, Viscount	1744		
				Wentworth, Thomas	1745		
				Bligh, Thomas	1747		

1746 Re-ranked as 1st (Irish) Horse (Blue Horse)	**1746** Re-ranked as 4th (Irish) Horse (Black Horse)	**1746** Re-ranked as 2nd (Irish) Horse (Green Horse)	
1751 Officially known as 1st Regt of (Irish) Horse	**1751** Officially known as 4th Regiment of Horse	**1751** Officially known as 2nd Regiment of Horse	**1751** Officially known as 6th (Inniskilling) Dragoons
1788 Converted to Dragoon Guards as 4th (Royal Irish) Dragoon Guards.	**1788** Converted to Dragoon Gds as 7th (The Princess Royal's) Dragoon Guards	**1788** Converted to Dragoon Gds as 5th Regiment of Dragoon Guards	
		1804 Redesignated 5th (Princess Charlotte of Wales's) Regt of Dragoon Guards	
1921 Name simplified to 4th Royal Irish Dragoon Guards	**1921** Name modified to 7th Dragoon Guards (Princess Royal's)	**1921** Name modified to 5th Dragoon Guards (Princess Charlotte of Wales's)	**1921** Name modified to - The Inniskillings (6th Dragoons)
Badge introduced pre-1901	Badge introduced pre-1901	Badge introduced pre-1901	Badge introduced pre-1901
4th Royal Irish Dragoon Guards	7th Dragoon Guards (Princess Royal's)	5th Dragoon Guards (P Charlotte of W's)	The Inniskillings (6th Dragoons)

2. Post-1922 Ancestry

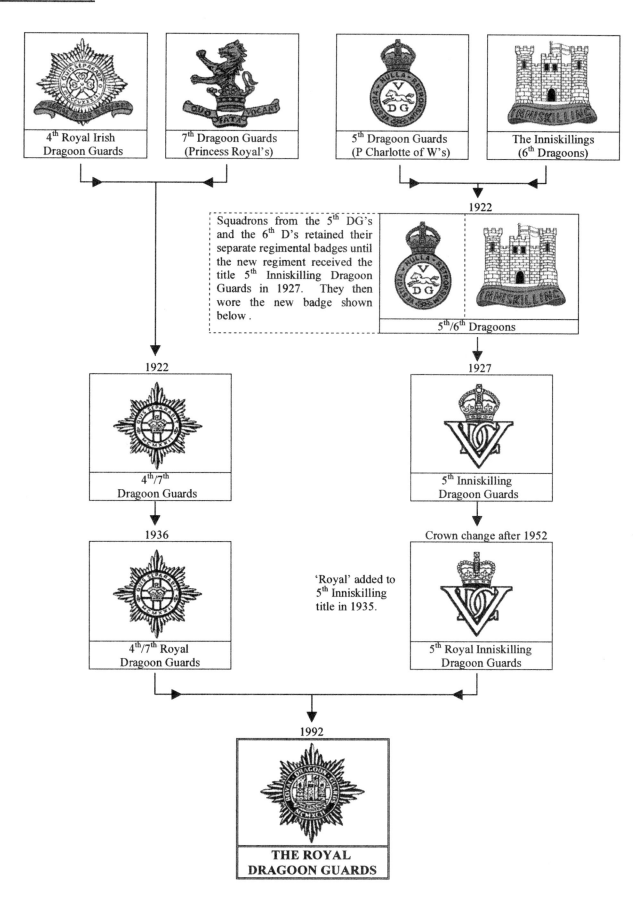

4th Royal Irish Dragoon Guards

7th Dragoon Guards (Princess Royal's)

5th Dragoon Guards (P Charlotte of W's)

The Inniskillings (6th Dragoons)

1922

Squadrons from the 5th DG's and the 6th D's retained their separate regimental badges until the new regiment received the title 5th Inniskilling Dragoon Guards in 1927. They then wore the new badge shown below.

5th/6th Dragoons

1922

4th/7th Dragoon Guards

1927

5th Inniskilling Dragoon Guards

1936

4th/7th Royal Dragoon Guards

'Royal' added to 5th Inniskilling title in 1935.

Crown change after 1952

5th Royal Inniskilling Dragoon Guards

1992

THE ROYAL DRAGOON GUARDS

THE QUEEN'S ROYAL HUSSARS

1. Pre-1922 Ancestry

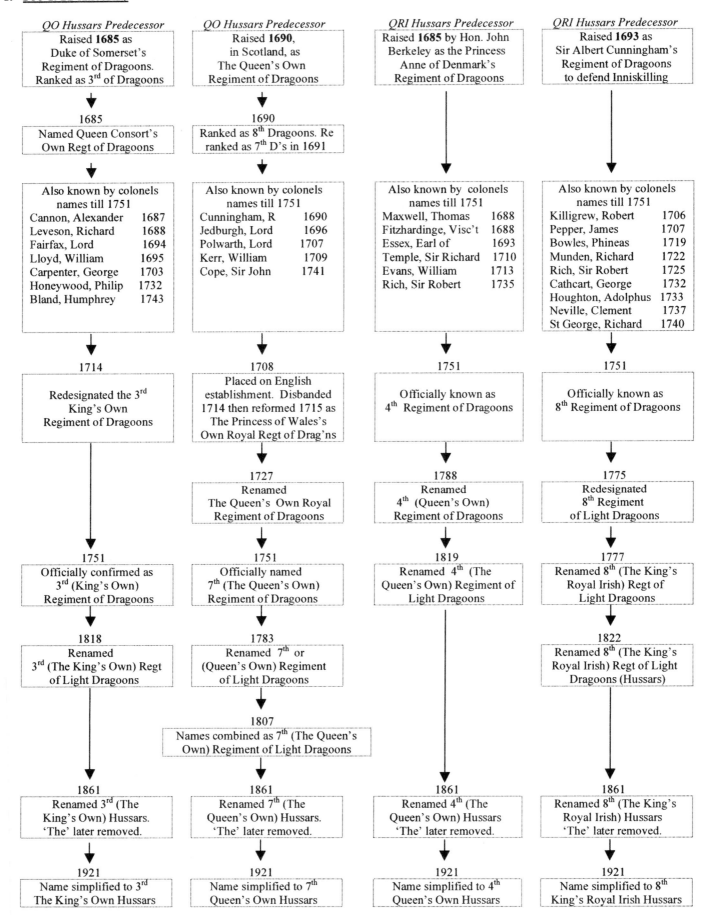

QO Hussars Predecessor

Raised **1685** as Duke of Somerset's Regiment of Dragoons. Ranked as 3rd of Dragoons

↓

1685
Named Queen Consort's Own Regt of Dragoons

↓

Also known by colonels names till 1751
Cannon, Alexander	1687
Leveson, Richard	1688
Fairfax, Lord	1694
Lloyd, William	1695
Carpenter, George	1703
Honeywood, Philip	1732
Bland, Humphrey	1743

↓

1714
Redesignated the 3rd King's Own Regiment of Dragoons

↓

1751
Officially confirmed as 3rd (King's Own) Regiment of Dragoons

↓

1818
Renamed 3rd (The King's Own) Regt of Light Dragoons

↓

1861
Renamed 3rd (The King's Own) Hussars. 'The' later removed.

↓

1921
Name simplified to 3rd The King's Own Hussars

QO Hussars Predecessor

Raised **1690**, in Scotland, as The Queen's Own Regiment of Dragoons

↓

1690
Ranked as 8th Dragoons. Re ranked as 7th D's in 1691

↓

Also known by colonels names till 1751
Cunningham, R	1690
Jedburgh, Lord	1696
Polwarth, Lord	1707
Kerr, William	1709
Cope, Sir John	1741

↓

1708
Placed on English establishment. Disbanded 1714 then reformed 1715 as The Princess of Wales's Own Royal Regt of Drag'ns

↓

1727
Renamed The Queen's Own Royal Regiment of Dragoons

↓

1751
Officially named 7th (The Queen's Own) Regiment of Dragoons

↓

1783
Renamed 7th or (Queen's Own) Regiment of Light Dragoons

↓

1807
Names combined as 7th (The Queen's Own) Regiment of Light Dragoons

↓

1861
Renamed 7th (The Queen's Own) Hussars. 'The' later removed.

↓

1921
Name simplified to 7th Queen's Own Hussars

QRI Hussars Predecessor

Raised **1685** by Hon. John Berkeley as the Princess Anne of Denmark's Regiment of Dragoons

↓

Also known by colonels names till 1751
Maxwell, Thomas	1688
Fitzhardinge, Visc't	1688
Essex, Earl of	1693
Temple, Sir Richard	1710
Evans, William	1713
Rich, Sir Robert	1735

↓

1751
Officially known as 4th Regiment of Dragoons

↓

1788
Renamed 4th (Queen's Own) Regiment of Dragoons

↓

1819
Renamed 4th (The Queen's Own) Regiment of Light Dragoons

↓

1861
Renamed 4th (The Queen's Own) Hussars 'The' later removed.

↓

1921
Name simplified to 4th Queen's Own Hussars

QRI Hussars Predecessor

Raised **1693** as Sir Albert Cunningham's Regiment of Dragoons to defend Inniskilling

↓

Also known by colonels names till 1751
Killigrew, Robert	1706
Pepper, James	1707
Bowles, Phineas	1719
Munden, Richard	1722
Rich, Sir Robert	1725
Cathcart, George	1732
Houghton, Adolphus	1733
Neville, Clement	1737
St George, Richard	1740

↓

1751
Officially known as 8th Regiment of Dragoons

↓

1775
Redesignated 8th Regiment of Light Dragoons

↓

1777
Renamed 8th (The King's Royal Irish) Regt of Light Dragoons

↓

1822
Renamed 8th (The King's Royal Irish) Regt of Light Dragoons (Hussars)

↓

1861
Renamed 8th (The King's Royal Irish) Hussars. 'The' later removed.

↓

1921
Name simplified to 8th King's Royal Irish Hussars

2. Post-1922 Ancestry

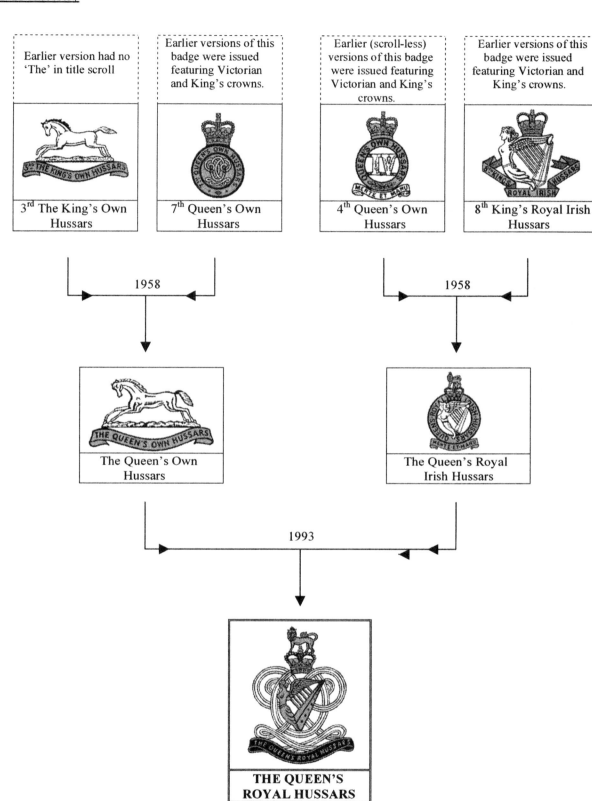

The Queen's Royal Hussars were given the additional sub-title 'The Queen's Own and Royal Irish'.
The latter obviously preserves the names of the original constituents.

THE 9TH /12TH ROYAL LANCERS
(Prince Of Wales's)

1. Pre-1922 Ancestry

9th Lancers Predecessor

Raised **1715** as Maj Gen Owen Wynne's Regiment of Dragoons

Known by colonel's names until 1751
Crofts, James	1719
Molesworth, Viscount	1732
Cope, John	1737
Brown, John	1742
De Grangue, Henry	1743
Reade, George	1749

1751
Ranked as 9th of Dragoons and known by that name from 1751

1783
Redesignated 9th Regt of (Light) Dragoons.
(Lancers) added from 1816

1830
Redesignated
9th
(or Queen's Royal) Lancers

1861
Name confirmed as
9th (The Queen's Royal) Lancers.
'The' prefix later removed.

Badge introduced pre-1901

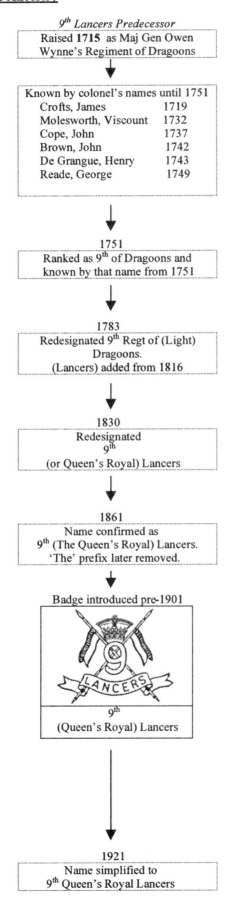

9th
(Queen's Royal) Lancers

1921
Name simplified to
9th Queen's Royal Lancers

12th Lancers Predecessor

Raised **1715** as Col Phineas Bowle's Regiment of Dragoons

Known by colonel's names until 1751
Rose, Alexander	1740
Whitshed, Sir Walter	1743
Bligh, Thomas	1746
Mordaunt, Sir John	1747
Cholmondely, James	1749
Sackville, Lord George	1749
Whiteford, Sir John	1750

1751
Ranked as 12th of Dragoons and known by that name from 1751

1768
Redesignated 12th (The Prince of Wales's) Regiment of (Light) Dragoons

1816
Redesignated 12th (the Prince of Wales's) Regiment of Lancers
'Royal' added 1817

1861
Redesignated
12th (The Prince of Wales's Royal) Lancers.

Badge introduced pre-1903

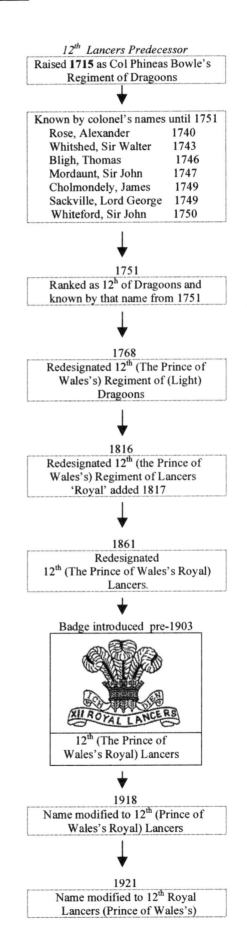

12th (The Prince of Wales's Royal) Lancers

1918
Name modified to 12th (Prince of Wales's Royal) Lancers

1921
Name modified to 12th Royal Lancers (Prince of Wales's)

2. Post-1922 Ancestry

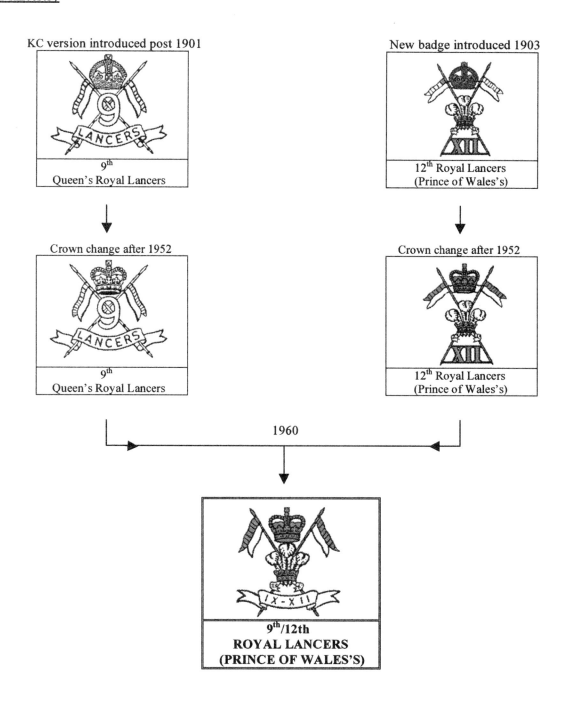

KC version introduced post 1901

9th
Queen's Royal Lancers

New badge introduced 1903

12th Royal Lancers
(Prince of Wales's)

Crown change after 1952

9th
Queen's Royal Lancers

Crown change after 1952

12th Royal Lancers
(Prince of Wales's)

1960

9th/12th
ROYAL LANCERS
(PRINCE OF WALES'S)

THE KING'S ROYAL HUSSARS

1. Pre-1922 Ancestry

10th Hussars Predecessor	*11th Hussars Predecessor*	*14th Hussars Predecessor*	
Raised **1715** as Brig Gen Humphrey Gore's Regt of Dragoons and ranked as 10th Dragoons	Raised **1715** as Phillip Honeywood's Regt of Dragoons and ranked as 11th Dragoons	Raised **1715** as Brig. Gen. James Dormer's Regt of Dragoons and ranked as 14th Dragoons	Three 20th 'LD's existed 1759-1819, 20th Inniskilling LD, 20th LD & 20th Jamaica LD . All were disbanded
Also known by other colonels names till 1751 Churchill, Charles 1723 Cobham, Viscount 1745 Mordaunt, Sir John 1749	**1732 - 1751** Also known during this period as Lord Mark Kerr's Regiment of Dragoons	Also known by other colonels names till 1751 Neville, Clement 1720 Hamilton, Archibald 1737 Tyrawley, Lord 1749	*20th Hussars Predecessor* Raised **1857** by Hon. East India Company as 2nd Bengal European Light Cavalry
1751 Officially known as 10th Regiment of Dragoons	**1751** Officially known as 11th Regiment of Dragoons	**1751** Officially known as 14th Regiment of Dragoons	
1783 Redesignated 10th (or Prince of Wales's Own) Regt of (Light) Dragoons	**1783** Redesignated The 11th Regiment of (Light) Dragoons	**1776** Redesignated 14th Regiment of (Light) Dragoons	
1806 ' Hussars' subtitle added to above title		**1798** Renamed 14th or Duchess of York's Own Regt of (Light) Dragoons	**1861** Taken into the British Army as 20th Regiment of Light Dragoons
1811 Renamed 10th (Prince of Wales's Own Royal) Regt of Light Dragoons (Hussars)	**1840** Renamed 11th (or Prince Albert's Own) Regt of Light Dragoons (Hussars)	**1830** Renamed 14th (The King's) Regiment Of Light Dragoons	**1862** Redesignated 20th Hussars
1861 Renamed 10th (The Prince of Wales's Own Royal) Regt of Hussars 'The' later removed.	**1861** Name simplified to 11th (Prince Albert's Own) Hussars.	**1861** Renamed 14th (The King's) Hussars 'The' later removed.	**1921** Briefly Disbanded??
1921 Name simplified to 10th Royal Hussars (Prince of Wales's Own)	**1921** Name modified to 11h Hussars (Prince Albert's Own)	**1921** Name simplified to 14th King's Hussars	**1922** Reconstituted as a squadron in the amalgamated 14th /20th Hussars
Badge introduced pre-1901	Badge introduced pre-1901	Badge introduced pre-1901	Badge introduced pre-1901
10th Royal Hussars (P of Wales's Own)	11th Hussars (Prince Albert's Own)	14th King's Hussars (Pre-WW1 Eagle)	20th Hussars (Victorian Crown)

2. Post-1922 Ancestry

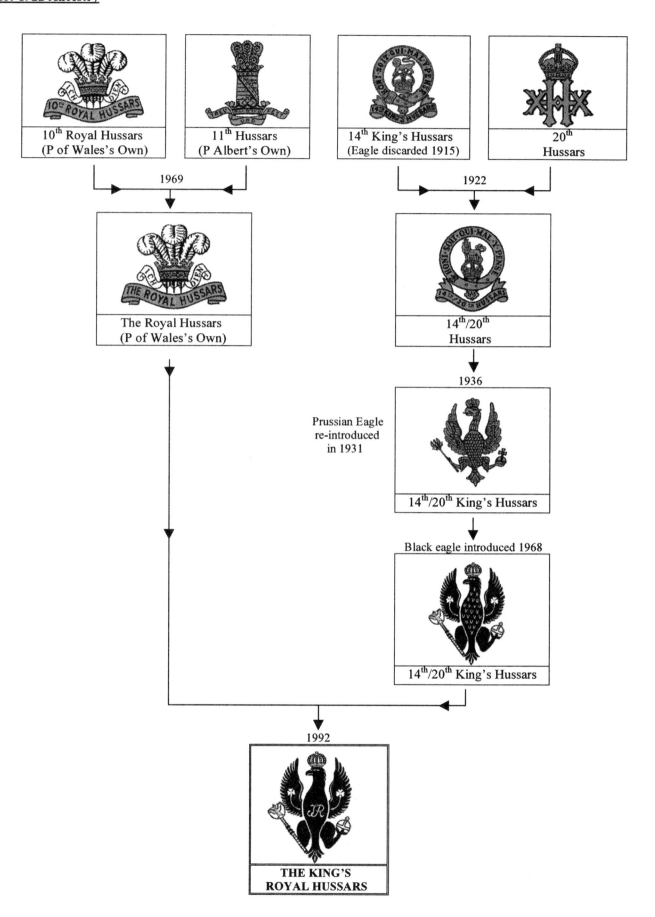

THE LIGHT DRAGOONS

1. Pre-1922 Ancestry

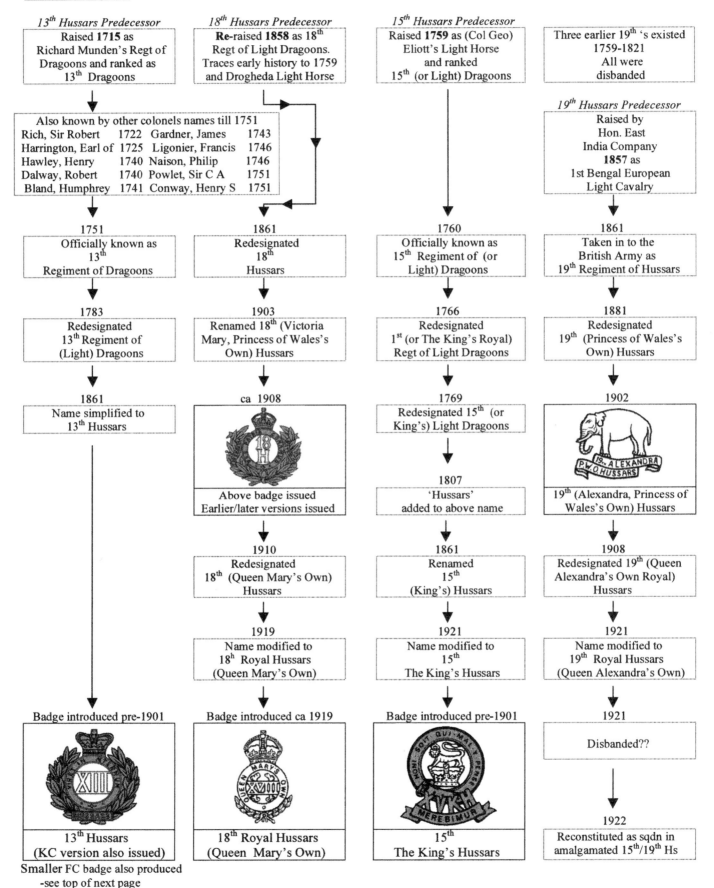

13th Hussars Predecessor	*18th Hussars Predecessor*	*15th Hussars Predecessor*	
Raised **1715** as Richard Munden's Regt of Dragoons and ranked as 13th Dragoons	**Re**-raised **1858** as 18th Regt of Light Dragoons. Traces early history to 1759 and Drogheda Light Horse	Raised **1759** as (Col Geo) Eliott's Light Horse and ranked 15th (or Light) Dragoons	Three earlier 19th 's existed 1759-1821 All were disbanded

Also known by other colonels names till 1751
Rich, Sir Robert   1722   Gardner, James   1743
Harrington, Earl of   1725   Ligonier, Francis   1746
Hawley, Henry   1740   Naison, Philip   1746
Dalway, Robert   1740   Powlet, Sir C A   1751
Bland, Humphrey   1741   Conway, Henry S   1751

19th Hussars Predecessor
Raised by Hon. East India Company **1857** as 1st Bengal European Light Cavalry

1751 Officially known as 13th Regiment of Dragoons

1861 Redesignated 18th Hussars

1760 Officially known as 15th Regiment of (or Light) Dragoons

1861 Taken in to the British Army as 19th Regiment of Hussars

1783 Redesignated 13th Regiment of (Light) Dragoons

1903 Renamed 18th (Victoria Mary, Princess of Wales's Own) Hussars

1766 Redesignated 1st (or The King's Royal) Regt of Light Dragoons

1881 Redesignated 19th (Princess of Wales's Own) Hussars

1861 Name simplified to 13th Hussars

ca 1908

Above badge issued
Earlier/later versions issued

1769 Redesignated 15th (or King's) Light Dragoons

1902

19th (Alexandra, Princess of Wales's Own) Hussars

1910 Redesignated 18th (Queen Mary's Own) Hussars

1807 'Hussars' added to above name

1908 Redesignated 19th (Queen Alexandra's Own Royal) Hussars

1919 Name modified to 18th Royal Hussars (Queen Mary's Own)

1861 Renamed 15th (King's) Hussars

1921 Name modified to 19th Royal Hussars (Queen Alexandra's Own)

1921 Name modified to 15th The King's Hussars

1921

Disbanded??

Badge introduced pre-1901

13th Hussars (KC version also issued)
Smaller FC badge also produced -see top of next page

Badge introduced ca 1919

18th Royal Hussars (Queen Mary's Own)

Badge introduced pre-1901

15th The King's Hussars

1922 Reconstituted as sqdn in amalgamated 15th/19th Hs

16

2. Post-1922 Ancestry

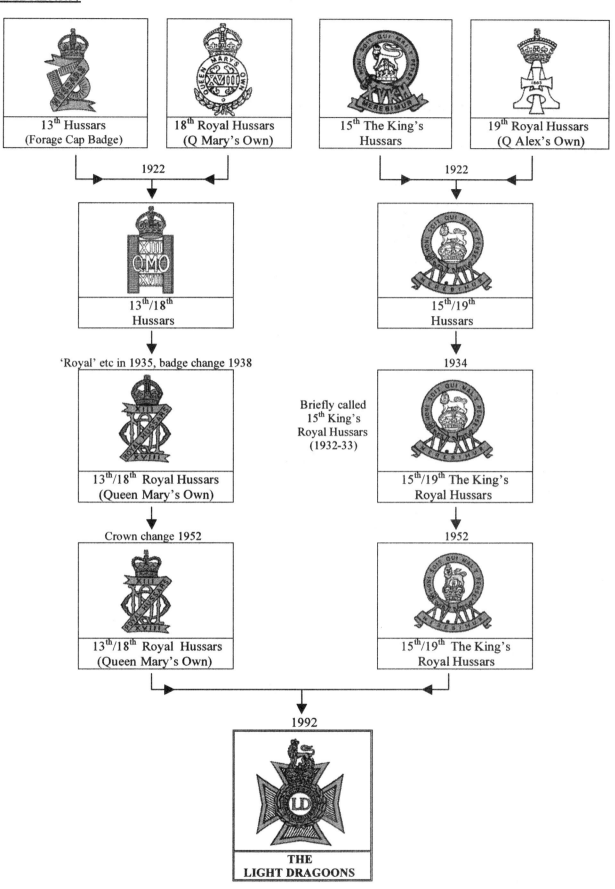

THE QUEEN'S ROYAL LANCERS

1. Pre-1922 Ancestry

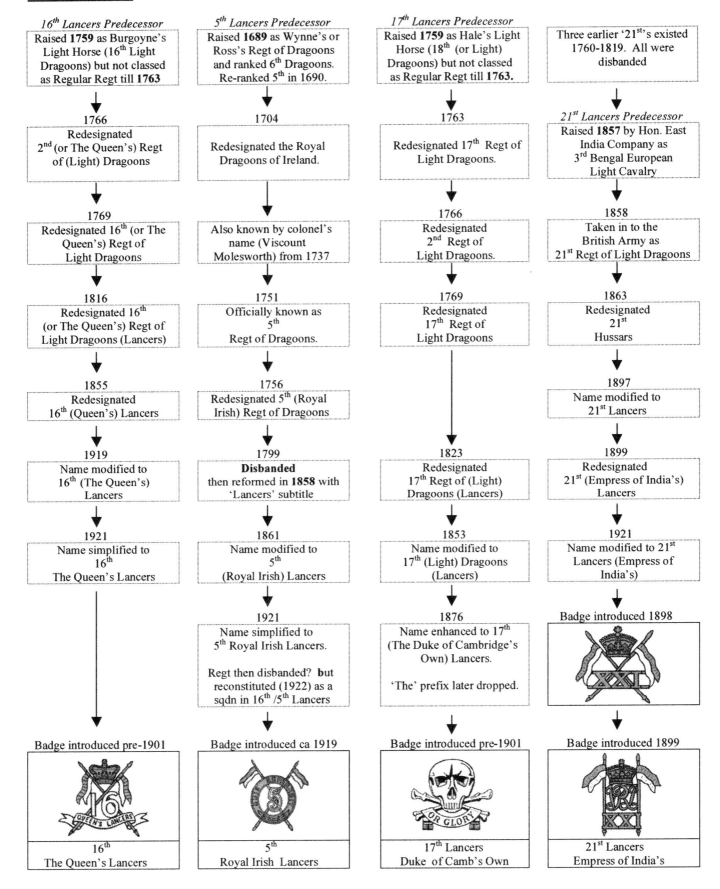

16th Lancers Predecessor

Raised **1759** as Burgoyne's Light Horse (16th Light Dragoons) but not classed as Regular Regt till **1763**

1766
Redesignated 2nd (or The Queen's) Regt of (Light) Dragoons

1769
Redesignated 16th (or The Queen's) Regt of Light Dragoons

1816
Redesignated 16th (or The Queen's) Regt of Light Dragoons (Lancers)

1855
Redesignated 16th (Queen's) Lancers

1919
Name modified to 16th (The Queen's) Lancers

1921
Name simplified to 16th The Queen's Lancers

Badge introduced pre-1901

16th The Queen's Lancers

5th Lancers Predecessor

Raised **1689** as Wynne's or Ross's Regt of Dragoons and ranked 6th Dragoons. Re-ranked 5th in 1690.

1704
Redesignated the Royal Dragoons of Ireland.

Also known by colonel's name (Viscount Molesworth) from 1737

1751
Officially known as 5th Regt of Dragoons.

1756
Redesignated 5th (Royal Irish) Regt of Dragoons

1799
Disbanded then reformed in **1858** with 'Lancers' subtitle

1861
Name modified to 5th (Royal Irish) Lancers

1921
Name simplified to 5th Royal Irish Lancers.

Regt then disbanded? but reconstituted (1922) as a sqdn in 16th /5th Lancers

Badge introduced ca 1919

5th Royal Irish Lancers

17th Lancers Predecessor

Raised **1759** as Hale's Light Horse (18th (or Light) Dragoons) but not classed as Regular Regt till **1763.**

1763
Redesignated 17th Regt of Light Dragoons.

1766
Redesignated 2nd Regt of Light Dragoons.

1769
Redesignated 17th Regt of Light Dragoons

1823
Redesignated 17th Regt of (Light) Dragoons (Lancers)

1853
Name modified to 17th (Light) Dragoons (Lancers)

1876
Name enhanced to 17th (The Duke of Cambridge's Own) Lancers.

'The' prefix later dropped.

Badge introduced pre-1901

17th Lancers Duke of Camb's Own

Three earlier '21st's existed 1760-1819. All were disbanded

21st Lancers Predecessor

Raised **1857** by Hon. East India Company as 3rd Bengal European Light Cavalry

1858
Taken in to the British Army as 21st Regt of Light Dragoons

1863
Redesignated 21st Hussars

1897
Name modified to 21st Lancers

1899
Redesignated 21st (Empress of India's) Lancers

1921
Name modified to 21st Lancers (Empress of India's)

Badge introduced 1898

Badge introduced 1899

21st Lancers Empress of India's

2. Post-1922 Ancestry

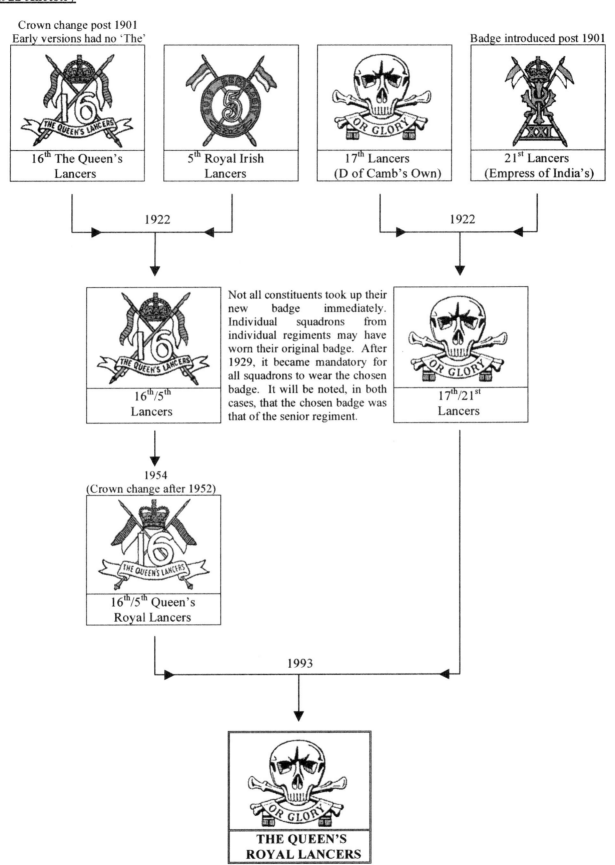

Crown change post 1901
Early versions had no 'The'

Badge introduced post 1901

16th The Queen's Lancers

5th Royal Irish Lancers

17th Lancers (D of Camb's Own)

21st Lancers (Empress of India's)

1922

1922

16th/5th Lancers

Not all constituents took up their new badge immediately. Individual squadrons from individual regiments may have worn their original badge. After 1929, it became mandatory for all squadrons to wear the chosen badge. It will be noted, in both cases, that the chosen badge was that of the senior regiment.

17th/21st Lancers

1954
(Crown change after 1952)

16th/5th Queen's Royal Lancers

1993

THE QUEEN'S ROYAL LANCERS

THE ROYAL TANK REGIMENT

1 Ancestry

The initial predecessor to the Royal Tank Regiment was formed in **Feb 1916** as a secret tank detachment and formally designated an Armoured Car Section, Motor Machine Gun Service, Machine Gun Corps in **March 1916**.

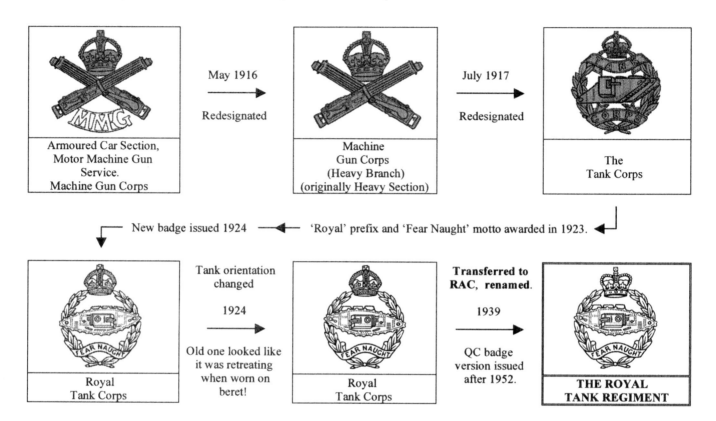

2 Other Information (including cavalry/infantry naming conventions)

Historically, a regiment was a body of men (either infantry or cavalry) which was raised, trained, equipped and commanded by it's colonel. In the infantry, the regiment could have one or more battalions and the cavalry could have several squadrons. In battle, cavalry squadrons usually fought together as one regiment whilst infantry battalions from the same regiment often fought separately. Cavalry regiments thus became both the administrative and the tactical unit whilst the infantry regiments became principally administrative – the battalion being the tactical unit.

This led to a difference in naming conventions for tactical units. Infantry would refer to battalions whilst cavalry would refer to regiments.

The Royal Tank Regiment shows this difference. It's predecessor, the Royal Tank Corps started life as an off-shoot of an infantry organisation (The Machine Gun Corps) as shown above. As the tactical units within the corps expanded, they were called battalions and differentiated by number. One would thus come across the 1st Bn, Royal Tank Corps; 2nd Bn, Royal Tank Corps and so on. When the Royal Tank Corps joined the mechanised cavalry regiments in 1939 to form the Royal Armoured Corps (changing it's name in the process) the battalion reference was gradually discontinued till, by 1945 all were called regiments in the cavalry fashion. Thereafter one would come across the 1st Royal Tank Regiment, the 2nd Royal Tank Regiment and so on.

Many battalions/regiments were formed including those raised using personnel from territorial infantry units. In addition, various independent Armoured Car Companies were formed.

Currently (2008) there are only two regiments still operational – The 1st Royal Tank Regiment and The 2nd Royal Tank Regiment.

THE ROYAL ARMOURED CORPS

1 FORMATION AND ORGANISATION

The Royal Armoured Corps (RAC) came into existence on the **4th April 1939**. It's creation was in response to the growing importance of mechanised warfare. Initially it grouped together all mechanised cavalry units and the Royal Tank Corps – the latter's name being changed to Royal Tank Regiment to avoid confusion. During World War 2, many other regiments formally became part of the RAC as they became mechanised. These included various yeomanry regiments as well as regular cavalry regiments. The Reconnaissance Corps was absorbed in 1944 (see Reconnaissance Corps subsection).

Individual constituents have changed over the years as a consequence of amalgamations and disbandments etc but the Royal Armoured Corps, with the exception of the Household Cavalry, still encompasses our armoured units.

The Household Cavalry did not formally become part of the RAC. They were classed as a Corps in their own right. However, operationally, they are treated as part of the RAC.

Units within the RAC keep their individual identities. They wear their own uniforms and cap badges and have their own unique traditions. The RAC thus provides an umbrella management organisation rather than a 'family'. As such it differs from other large organisations like the Royal Regiment of Artillery.

However, the RAC did have a cap badge but it tended to be worn only by personnel within training units. The trainees would then take up the badge of their new regiment after assignment. The badge, in it's evolving form, is shown below.

1939

Royal Armoured Corps

Badge changed 1942

Royal Armoured Corps

Crown change after 1952

Royal Armoured Corps

WAR-RAISED CAVALRY

1 SOUTH AFRICA 1899-1902

1.1 Her Majesty's Reserve Regiments

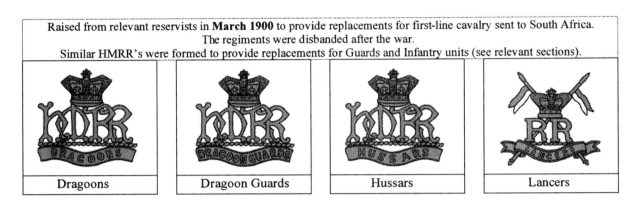

Raised from relevant reservists in **March 1900** to provide replacements for first-line cavalry sent to South Africa. The regiments were disbanded after the war.
Similar HMRR's were formed to provide replacements for Guards and Infantry units (see relevant sections).

Dragoons   Dragoon Guards   Hussars   Lancers

2 WORLD WAR TWO 1939-45

2.1 22nd Dragoons, 23rd Hussars and 24th Lancers

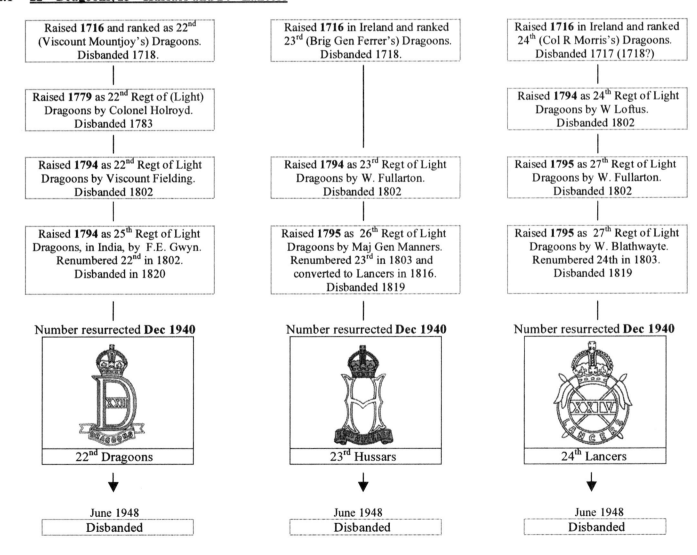

Raised **1716** and ranked as 22nd (Viscount Mountjoy's) Dragoons. Disbanded 1718.

Raised **1779** as 22nd Regt of (Light) Dragoons by Colonel Holroyd. Disbanded 1783

Raised **1794** as 22nd Regt of Light Dragoons by Viscount Fielding. Disbanded 1802

Raised **1794** as 25th Regt of Light Dragoons, in India, by F.E. Gwyn. Renumbered 22nd in 1802. Disbanded in 1820

Number resurrected **Dec 1940**

22nd Dragoons

June 1948 Disbanded

Raised **1716** in Ireland and ranked 23rd (Brig Gen Ferrer's) Dragoons. Disbanded 1718.

Raised **1794** as 23rd Regt of Light Dragoons by W. Fullarton. Disbanded 1802

Raised **1795** as 26th Regt of Light Dragoons by Maj Gen Manners. Renumbered 23rd in 1803 and converted to Lancers in 1816. Disbanded 1819

Number resurrected **Dec 1940**

23rd Hussars

June 1948 Disbanded

Raised **1716** in Ireland and ranked 24th (Col R Morris's) Dragoons. Disbanded 1717 (1718?)

Raised **1794** as 24th Regt of Light Dragoons by W Loftus. Disbanded 1802

Raised **1795** as 27th Regt of Light Dragoons by W. Fullarton. Disbanded 1802

Raised **1795** as 27th Regt of Light Dragoons by W. Blathwayte. Renumbered 24th in 1803. Disbanded 1819

Number resurrected **Dec 1940**

24th Lancers

June 1948 Disbanded

2.2   25th Dragoons, 26th Hussars and 27th Lancers

Raised **1716** and ranked as
25th (Col La Bouchetiere's)
Regt of Dragoons.
Disbanded 1718.

Raised **1795** as 27th Regt of Light
Dragoons by W. Blathwayte.
Renumbered 24th in 1803.
Disbanded 1819

Raised **1795** as 25th Regt of (Light)
Dragoons by Lord Heathfield.
Disbanded 1783

Raised **1794** as 22nd Regt of Light
Dragoons by Viscount Fielding.
Disbanded 1802

Raised **1795** as 29th Regt of Light
Dragoons, in India, by Lord
Heathfield. Renumbered 22nd in
1802. Disbanded in 1818

Raised, in India, from a cadre of
14th /20th King's Hussars. This
presumably influenced the
26th Hussars badge design.

Old 27th Regt itemised above won
elephant head motif in Mahratta
War of 1803. Elephant's head
resurrected for new 27th Lancers.

Number resurrected **Dec 1940**

Number resurrected **Dec 1940**

Number resurrected **Dec 1940**

25th Dragoons

26th Hussars

27th Lancers

June 1948
Disbanded

June 1948
Disbanded

June 1948
Disbanded

2.3   Reconnaissance Corps

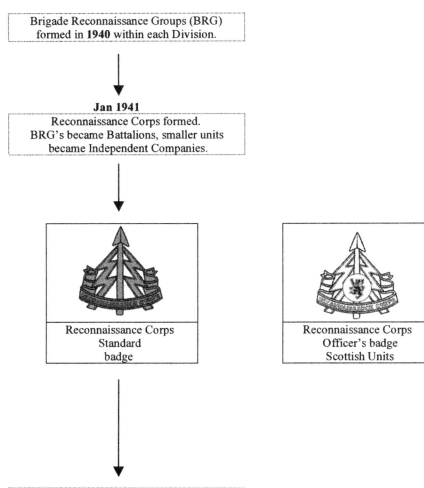

Brigade Reconnaissance Groups (BRG)
formed in **1940** within each Division.

Jan 1941
Reconnaissance Corps formed.
BRG's became Battalions, smaller units
became Independent Companies.

Reconnaissance Corps
49th (West Riding)
Division badge

Reconnaissance Corps
Standard
badge

Reconnaissance Corps
Officer's badge
Scottish Units

Became part of the Royal Armoured Corps
in 1944 then disbanded in August 1946

REGULAR INFANTRY
(including Guards and Gurkhas)

REGULAR INFANTRY NOTES

Cap badge illustrations add visual spice to regimental family trees but their use introduces complications when dealing with the infantry. The complications arise because of the effects associated with the 1958 brigade system.

This system grouped regular infantry regiments into geographically or functionally-related brigades but wasn't popular because many saw it as a first step towards major amalgamations – a concern that later proved justified.

It was viewed with suspicion because the Ministry of Defence (MoD) insisted that all participating regiments (or at least their regular battalions) must give up their individual cap badges and wear, instead, the specially-designed badges of the brigades to which they were assigned. Many saw this as an attempt to wean regiments away from their individual cap badges so subsequent amalgamations would be easier.

The following tables indicate how successful that amalgamation exercise was. By the time the brigade system was abandoned (1964-70 depending on the brigade) the constituents of six brigades had merged into six 'super' regiments. The constituents of the remaining brigades avoided forming 'super' regiments and were able to go back to wearing their own cap badges. Unfortunately, this did not last because the second table strongly suggests that the MoD believed in that old adage – 'if at first you don't succeed, try, try again'.

'Super' Regiments initially formed from the constituents of 1958 Brigades		'Super' Regiments formed from 1958 Brigade Survivors (and descendants)	
1958 Brigade	**Resultant Regiment**	**1958 Brigade**	**Resultant 21st Century Regiment**
Home Counties	Queen's Regiment	Highland plus Lowland	Royal Regiment of Scotland
Fusilier	Royal Regiment of Fusiliers	Lancastrian	Duke of Lancaster's Regiment
East Anglian	Royal Anglians	Mercian	Mercian Regiment
Light Infantry	Light Infantry	Welsh	Royal Welsh
North Irish	Royal Irish Rangers	Yorkshire	Yorkshire Regiment
Green Jacket	Royal Green Jackets	Most of Wessex *	The Rifles

* Plus Light Infantry & the Royal Green Jackets as detailed in The Rifles Section.

The introduction of the 1958 brigade system was thus an important factor in infantry amalgamations. Brigade formation details, their badges and subsequent dissolutions have therefore been woven into relevant family trees even though they complicate the picture. To help you find your way through the complications, please bear the following in mind.

- Some regiments which initially escaped merging into 'super' brigade-related regiments did not revert to their original cap badges. This is because they were involved in smaller-scale amalgamations whilst within the brigade system itself. If they merged around the time the system was initiated, then the resultant new regiments will appear in family tree flow-charts with their new names and relevant *brigade* cap badges. If they then survive the brigade system without further change they re-emerge but, this time, they are shown with their own (new) cap badge. This keeps the cap badge sequence correct.

- Some regiments merged at the start of the brigade system then merged again when the brigade system was disbanded. Regular battalions of the regiments formed after the first merger would only have worn their *brigade* cap badges before taking up badges of the regiments formed after the second merger. In other words, they would not have worn a cap badge of their own. If one **was** designed then the point made in the first paragraph is ignored and the new badge is shown at the beginning of the brigade sequence with an explanatory note.

- All participating regiments were expected to wear their brigade badge from 1958. That date is therefore shown at the start of the brigade sequences in the flow charts. Some regiments merged after taking up their brigade badge (i.e. after 1958). In such cases, two dates are shown at the start of the sequences. The first (1958) is the date the brigade badge was adopted. The second is the date when the relevant regiments merged whilst within the brigade system. If there is only one date then the merger (if one is indicated) occurred in 1958.

GUARDS DIVISION

1. INTRODUCTION

The Guards Division currently contains one regular battalion of each of the following Foot Guard regiments. The first three have been around since the mid 17th century whilst the last two are 20th century newcomers (assuming you are not too strict about accepting the Irish Guards start date of 1900 as part of the 20th century).

The Grenadier and Coldstream Guards both started life before the re-introduction of the monarchy in 1660. The Grenadier Guard predecessor was part of the Royalist Army whilst the Coldstream Guards predecessor was part of the Parliamentary Army. The Scots Guards came into being just as the monarchy was re-established.

As has already been indicated, the Irish Guards came into being in 1900 whilst the Welsh Guards were formed in 1915 to specifically give our Welsh Principality a presence in the (then) Brigade of Guards.

Grenadier Guards

Coldstream Guards

Scots Guards

Irish Guards

Welsh Guards

The Guards are a conservative lot as far as cap badges go and all the above badges have remained virtually unchanged since their initial appearance. They represent 'other rank' badges. However, the Guards have tended to produce badge variants for different non-commissioned ranks, unlike many infantry regiments. These and other badge variants have therefore been included in the ancestral details to enhance the visual interest.

2. GRENADIER GUARDS, COLDSTREAM GUARDS AND SCOTS GUARDS

2.1 ANCESTRY

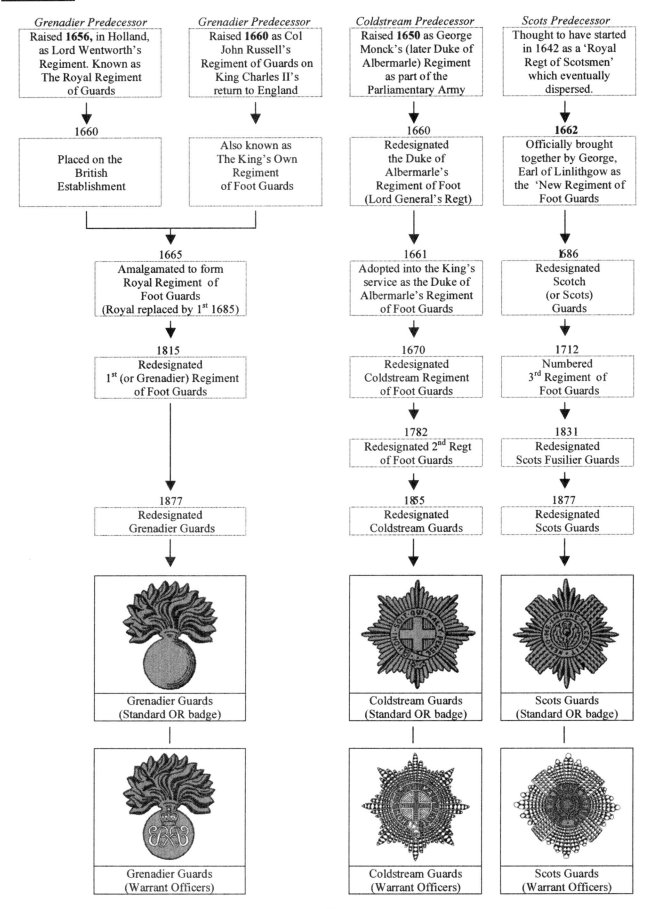

Grenadier Predecessor

Raised **1656,** in Holland, as Lord Wentworth's Regiment. Known as The Royal Regiment of Guards

Grenadier Predecessor

Raised **1660** as Col John Russell's Regiment of Guards on King Charles II's return to England

Coldstream Predecessor

Raised **1650** as George Monck's (later Duke of Albermarle) Regiment as part of the Parliamentary Army

Scots Predecessor

Thought to have started in 1642 as a 'Royal Regt of Scotsmen' which eventually dispersed.

1660

Placed on the British Establishment

Also known as The King's Own Regiment of Foot Guards

1660

Redesignated the Duke of Albermarle's Regiment of Foot (Lord General's Regt)

1662

Officially brought together by George, Earl of Linlithgow as the 'New Regiment of Foot Guards

1665

Amalgamated to form Royal Regiment of Foot Guards (Royal replaced by 1st 1685)

1661

Adopted into the King's service as the Duke of Albermarle's Regiment of Foot Guards

1686

Redesignated Scotch (or Scots) Guards

1815

Redesignated 1st (or Grenadier) Regiment of Foot Guards

1670

Redesignated Coldstream Regiment of Foot Guards

1712

Numbered 3rd Regiment of Foot Guards

1782

Redesignated 2nd Regt of Foot Guards

1831

Redesignated Scots Fusilier Guards

1877

Redesignated Grenadier Guards

1855

Redesignated Coldstream Guards

1877

Redesignated Scots Guards

Grenadier Guards (Standard OR badge)

Coldstream Guards (Standard OR badge)

Scots Guards (Standard OR badge)

Grenadier Guards (Warrant Officers)

Coldstream Guards (Warrant Officers)

Scots Guards (Warrant Officers)

3.   IRISH GUARDS AND WELSH GUARDS

3.1   ANCESTRY

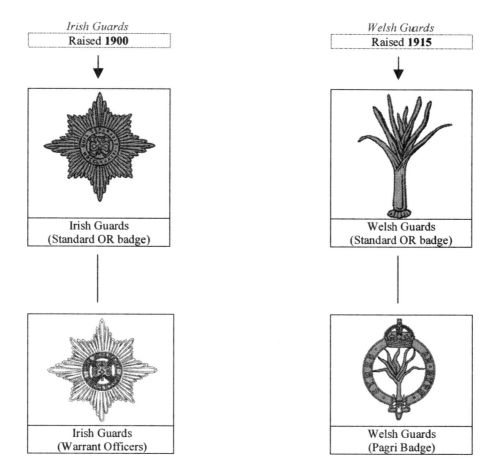

The Welsh Guards do not appear to have any significant variants of their standard, other-ranks cap badge. A pagri badge has therefore been included to balance the presentation.

4. OTHER INFORMATION

The Guards produced a number of war-raised off-shoots. They provided Guard battalions of Her Majesty's Reserve Regiments (HMRRs) during the Boer War and various other units during WW1 and WW2. The HMRR battalions used standard Guard cap badges, unlike cavalry and infantry HMRRs (see relevant sections). A Guards Machine Gun Regiment and Battalion were formed during WW1 and a Parachute Company during WW2. The latter wore a standard Parachute Regiment badge with a striped red and blue backing. The evolutionary pathways for the Machine Gun units are outlined below. You will note that the initial Guards Machine Gun Regiment encompassed both Mounted and Foot Guards before briefly becoming a Foot Guard Regiment alone.

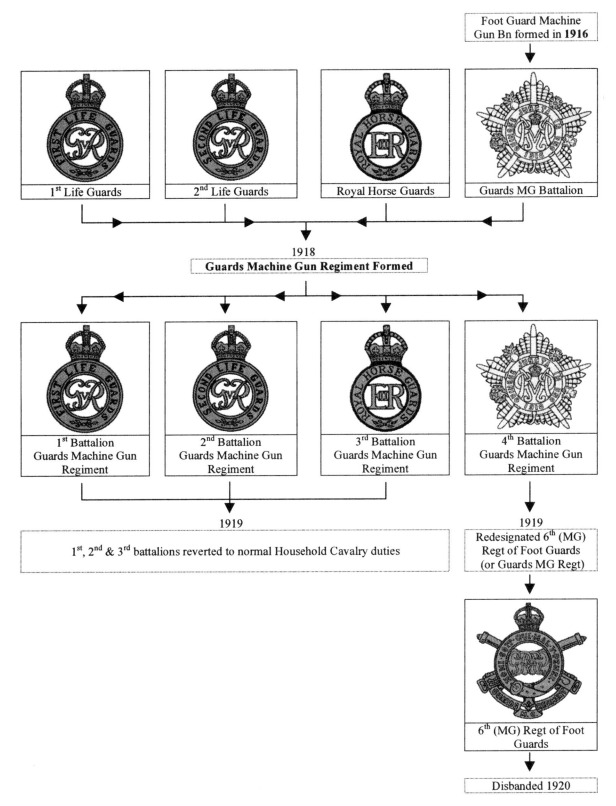

THE ROYAL REGIMENT OF SCOTLAND

1. FORMATION (in 2006)

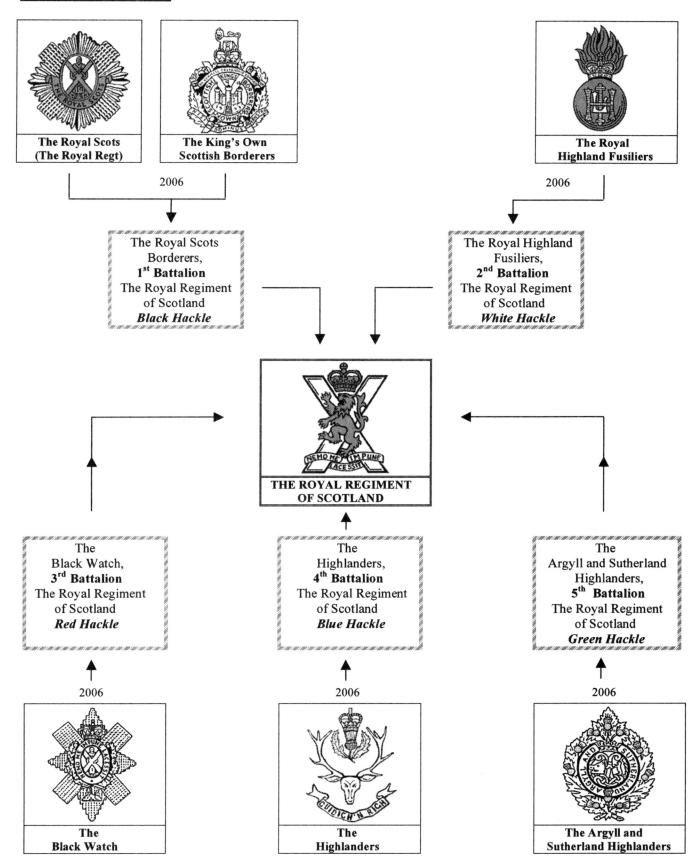

The cap badge is accompanied by a hackle whose colour (as indicated) differentiates the different battalions.

2. 'LOWLAND BRIGADE' COMPONENTS (and their post-1957 lineage)

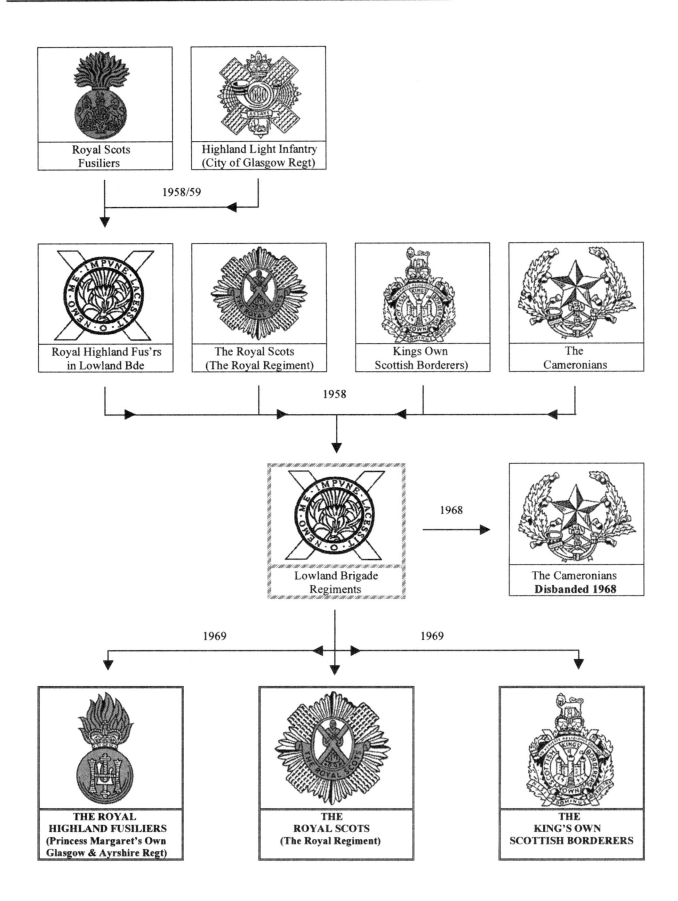

3. <u>'HIGHLAND BRIGADE' COMPONENTS (and their post-1957 lineage)</u>

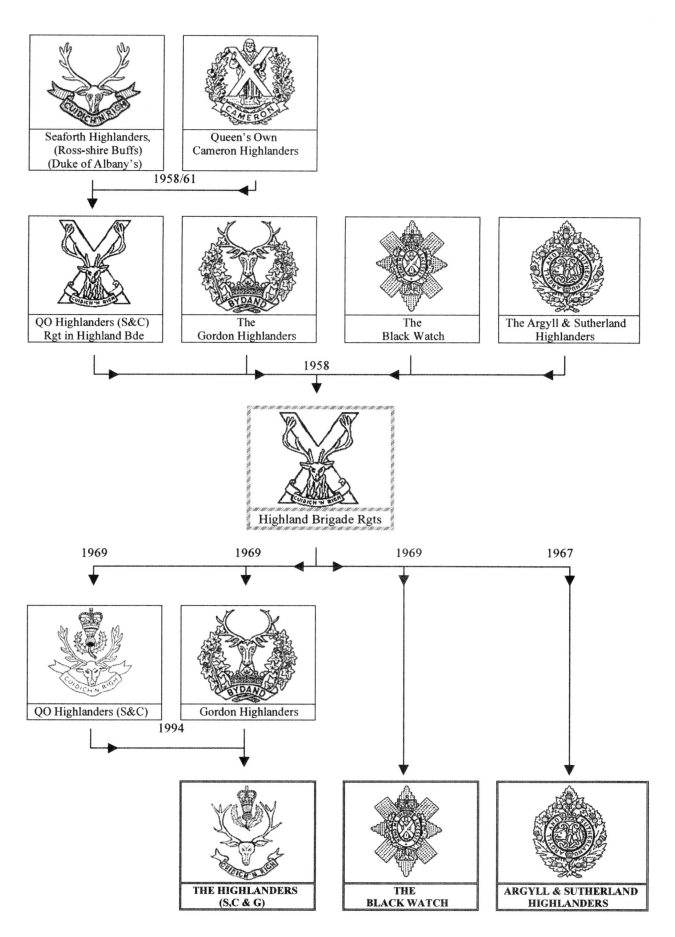

4. INDIVIDUAL 'LOWLAND BRIGADE' REGIMENTS

4.1 Royal Scots, Highland Light Infantry, Royal Scots Fusiliers : PRE - 1881 ANCESTRY

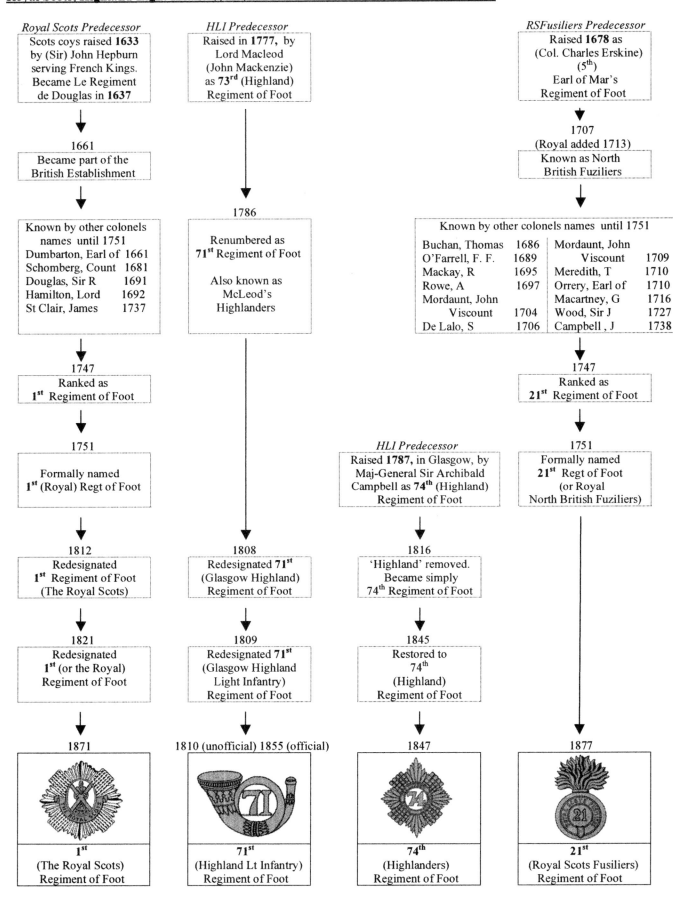

Royal Scots Predecessor

Scots coys raised **1633** by (Sir) John Hepburn serving French Kings. Became Le Regiment de Douglas in **1637**

↓

1661
Became part of the British Establishment

↓

Known by other colonels names until 1751
Dumbarton, Earl of 1661
Schomberg, Count 1681
Douglas, Sir R 1691
Hamilton, Lord 1692
St Clair, James 1737

↓

1747
Ranked as
1st Regiment of Foot

↓

1751
Formally named
1st (Royal) Regt of Foot

↓

1812
Redesignated
1st Regiment of Foot
(The Royal Scots)

↓

1821
Redesignated
1st (or the Royal)
Regiment of Foot

↓

1871

1st
(The Royal Scots)
Regiment of Foot

HLI Predecessor

Raised in **1777**, by Lord Macleod (John Mackenzie) as **73rd** (Highland) Regiment of Foot

↓

1786
Renumbered as
71st Regiment of Foot

Also known as
McLeod's
Highlanders

↓

1808
Redesignated 71st
(Glasgow Highland)
Regiment of Foot

↓

1809
Redesignated 71st
(Glasgow Highland
Light Infantry)
Regiment of Foot

↓

1810 (unofficial) 1855 (official)

71st
(Highland Lt Infantry)
Regiment of Foot

HLI Predecessor

Raised **1787**, in Glasgow, by Maj-General Sir Archibald Campbell as **74th** (Highland) Regiment of Foot

↓

1816
'Highland' removed.
Became simply
74th Regiment of Foot

↓

1845
Restored to
74th
(Highland)
Regiment of Foot

↓

1847

74th
(Highlanders)
Regiment of Foot

RSFusiliers Predecessor

Raised **1678** as (Col. Charles Erskine) (5th) Earl of Mar's Regiment of Foot

↓

1707
(Royal added 1713)
Known as North
British Fuziliers

↓

Known by other colonels names until 1751

Buchan, Thomas	1686	Mordaunt, John	
O'Farrell, F. F.	1689	Viscount	1709
Mackay, R	1695	Meredith, T	1710
Rowe, A	1697	Orrery, Earl of	1710
Mordaunt, John		Macartney, G	1716
Viscount	1704	Wood, Sir J	1727
De Lalo, S	1706	Campbell, J	1738

↓

1747
Ranked as
21st Regiment of Foot

↓

1751
Formally named
21st Regt of Foot
(or Royal
North British Fuziliers)

↓

1877

21st
(Royal Scots Fusiliers)
Regiment of Foot

4.2 Royal Scots, Highland Light Infantry and Royal Scots Fusiliers : 1881 – 1957 ANCESTRY

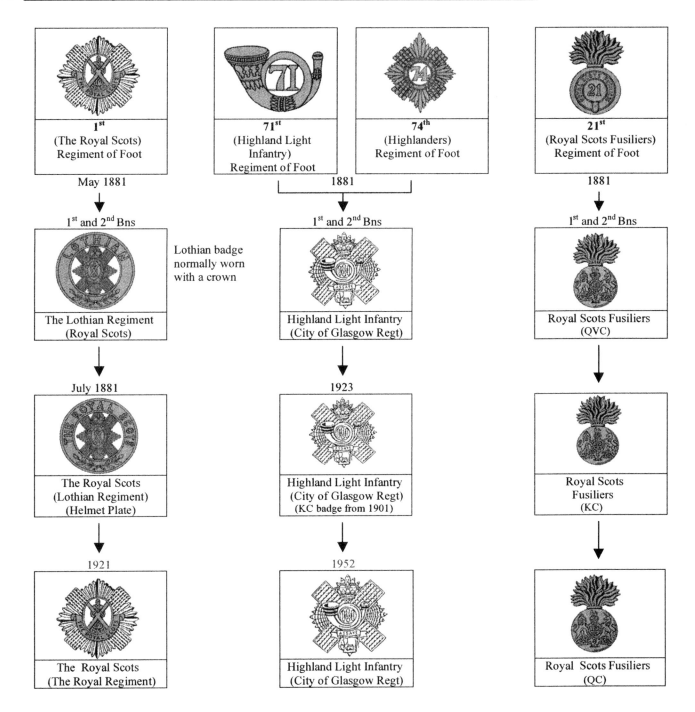

Notes on Regular Battalions

Royal Scots

1st and 2nd battalions amalgamated in 1949 to form 1st Bn

Highland Light Infantry

1st and 2nd battalions amalgamated in 1948 to form 1st Bn

Royal Scots Fusiliers

2nd Battalion disbanded in 1948.

4.3   King's Own Scottish Borderers and Cameronians : PRE - 1881 ANCESTRY

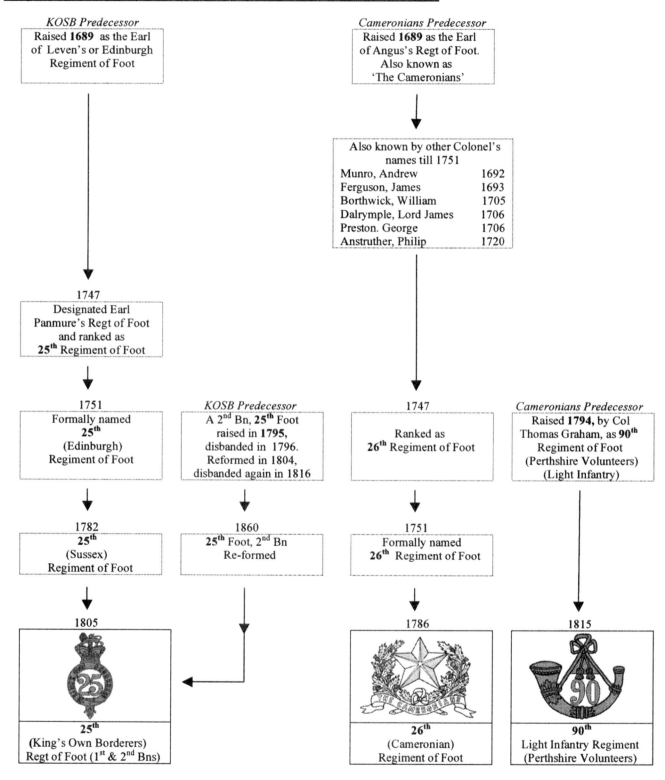

KOSB Predecessor

Raised **1689** as the Earl of Leven's or Edinburgh Regiment of Foot

Cameronians Predecessor

Raised **1689** as the Earl of Angus's Regt of Foot. Also known as 'The Cameronians'

Also known by other Colonel's names till 1751
Munro, Andrew	1692
Ferguson, James	1693
Borthwick, William	1705
Dalrymple, Lord James	1706
Preston. George	1706
Anstruther, Philip	1720

1747
Designated Earl Panmure's Regt of Foot and ranked as **25th** Regiment of Foot

1751
Formally named **25th** (Edinburgh) Regiment of Foot

KOSB Predecessor

A 2nd Bn, **25th** Foot raised in **1795**, disbanded in 1796. Reformed in 1804, disbanded again in 1816

1747
Ranked as **26th** Regiment of Foot

Cameronians Predecessor

Raised **1794,** by Col Thomas Graham, as **90th** Regiment of Foot (Perthshire Volunteers) (Light Infantry)

1782
25th (Sussex) Regiment of Foot

1860
25th Foot, 2nd Bn Re-formed

1751
Formally named **26th** Regiment of Foot

1805
25th (King's Own Borderers) Regt of Foot (1st & 2nd Bns)

1786
26th (Cameronian) Regiment of Foot

1815
90th Light Infantry Regiment (Perthshire Volunteers)

4.4   <u>King's Own Scottish Borderers and Cameronians : 1881 – 1957 ANCESTRY</u>

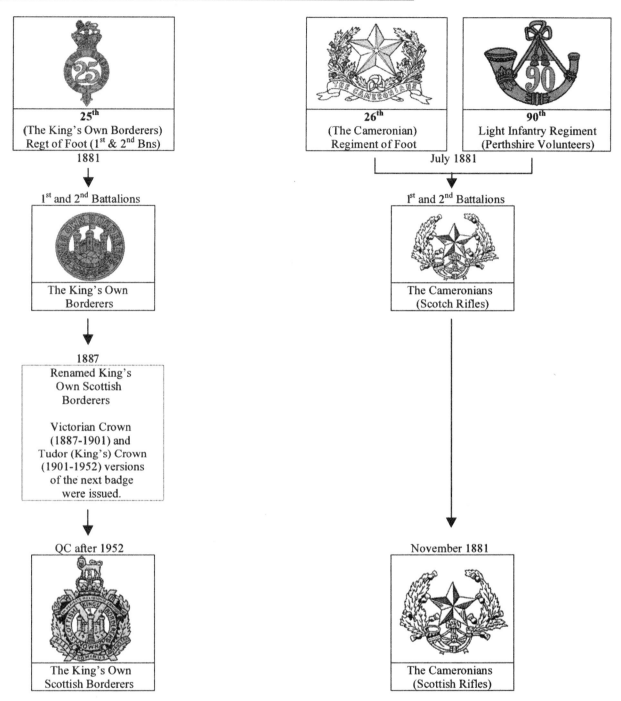

Notes on Regular Battalions

King's Own Scottish Borderers

2nd battalion disbanded in 1948.

Cameronians (Scottish Rifles)

1st and 2nd battalions amalgamated in 1948 to form 1st Bn.

5. INDIVIDUAL 'HIGHLAND BRIGADE' REGIMENTS

5.1 Seaforth Highlanders, Cameron Highlanders and Gordon Highlanders : PRE - 1881 ANCESTRY

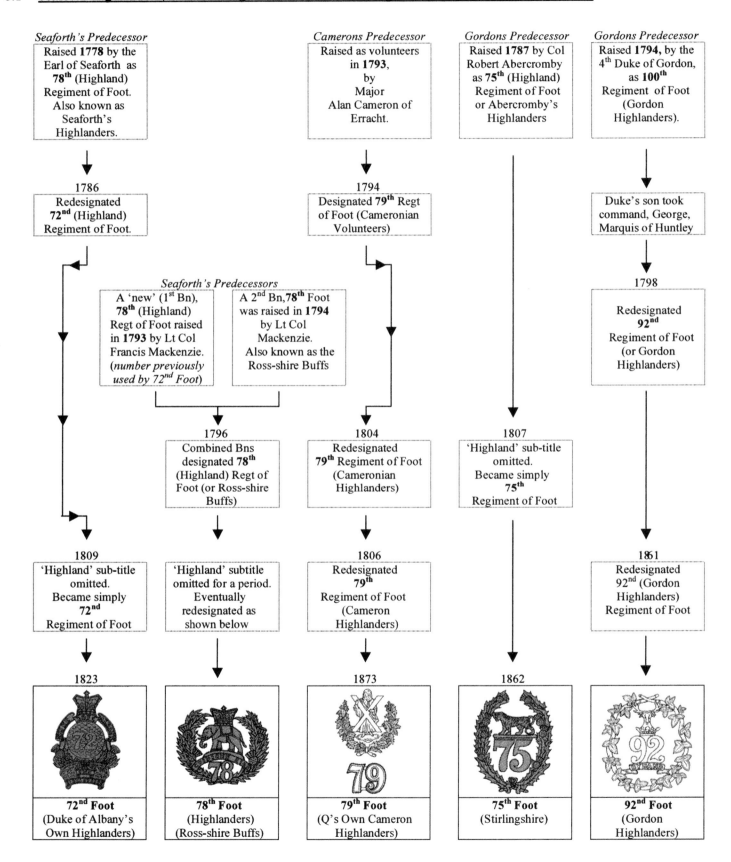

5.2   Seaforth Highlanders, Cameron Highlanders and Gordon Highlanders : 1881 – 1957 ANCESTRY

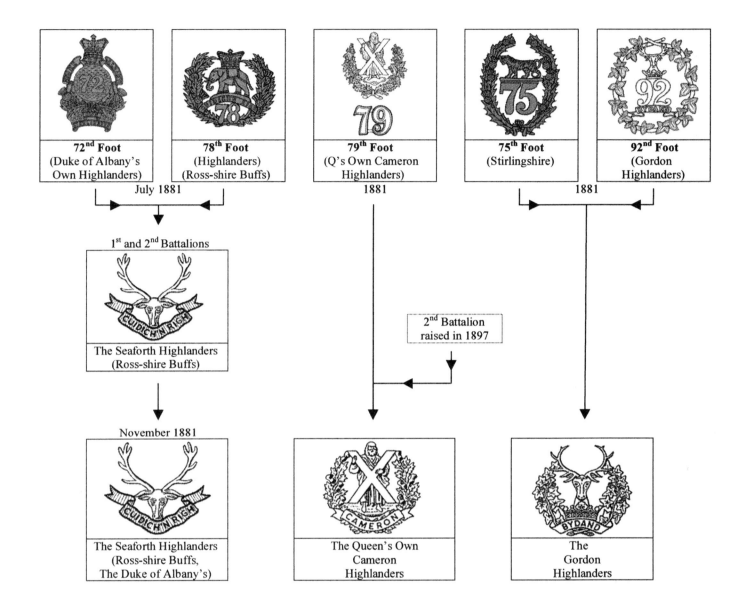

Notes on Regular Battalions

Seaforth Highlanders

1st and 2nd battalions amalgamated in 1948 to form 1st Bn

Cameron Highlanders

2nd Battalion disbanded in 1948.

Gordon Highlanders

1st and 2nd battalions amalgamated in 1948 to form 1st Bn

5.3   <u>**Black Watch and Argyll & Sutherland Highlanders : PRE - 1881 ANCESTRY**</u>

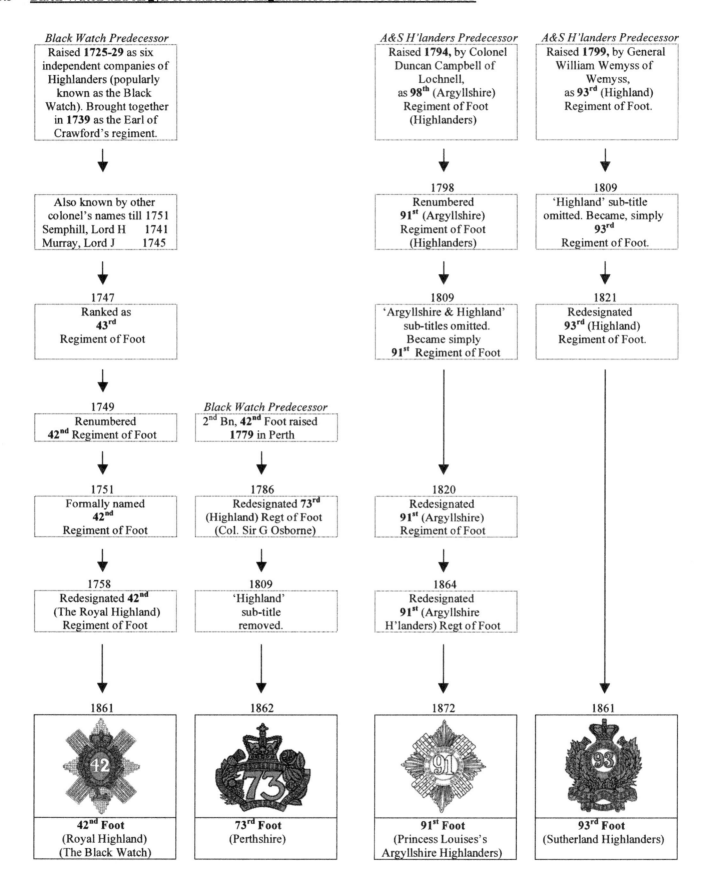

Black Watch Predecessor

Raised **1725-29** as six independent companies of Highlanders (popularly known as the Black Watch). Brought together in **1739** as the Earl of Crawford's regiment.

↓

Also known by other colonel's names till 1751
Semphill, Lord H   1741
Murray, Lord J   1745

↓

1747
Ranked as
43rd
Regiment of Foot

↓

1749
Renumbered
42nd Regiment of Foot

↓

1751
Formally named
42nd
Regiment of Foot

↓

1758
Redesignated **42nd**
(The Royal Highland)
Regiment of Foot

↓

1861

42nd Foot
(Royal Highland)
(The Black Watch)

Black Watch Predecessor
2nd Bn, **42nd** Foot raised
1779 in Perth

↓

1786
Redesignated **73rd**
(Highland) Regt of Foot
(Col. Sir G Osborne)

↓

1809
'Highland'
sub-title
removed.

↓

1862

73rd Foot
(Perthshire)

A&S H'landers Predecessor
Raised **1794**, by Colonel Duncan Campbell of Lochnell,
as **98th** (Argyllshire) Regiment of Foot
(Highlanders)

↓

1798
Renumbered
91st (Argyllshire)
Regiment of Foot
(Highlanders)

↓

1809
'Argyllshire & Highland'
sub-titles omitted.
Became simply
91st Regiment of Foot

↓

1820
Redesignated
91st (Argyllshire)
Regiment of Foot

↓

1864
Redesignated
91st (Argyllshire
H'landers) Regt of Foot

↓

1872

91st Foot
(Princess Louises's
Argyllshire Highlanders)

A&S H'landers Predecessor
Raised **1799**, by General William Wemyss of Wemyss,
as **93rd** (Highland) Regiment of Foot.

↓

1809
'Highland' sub-title omitted. Became, simply
93rd
Regiment of Foot.

↓

1821
Redesignated
93rd (Highland)
Regiment of Foot.

↓

1861

93rd Foot
(Sutherland Highlanders)

40

5.4   Black Watch and Argyll & Sutherland Highlanders : 1881 – 1957 ANCESTRY

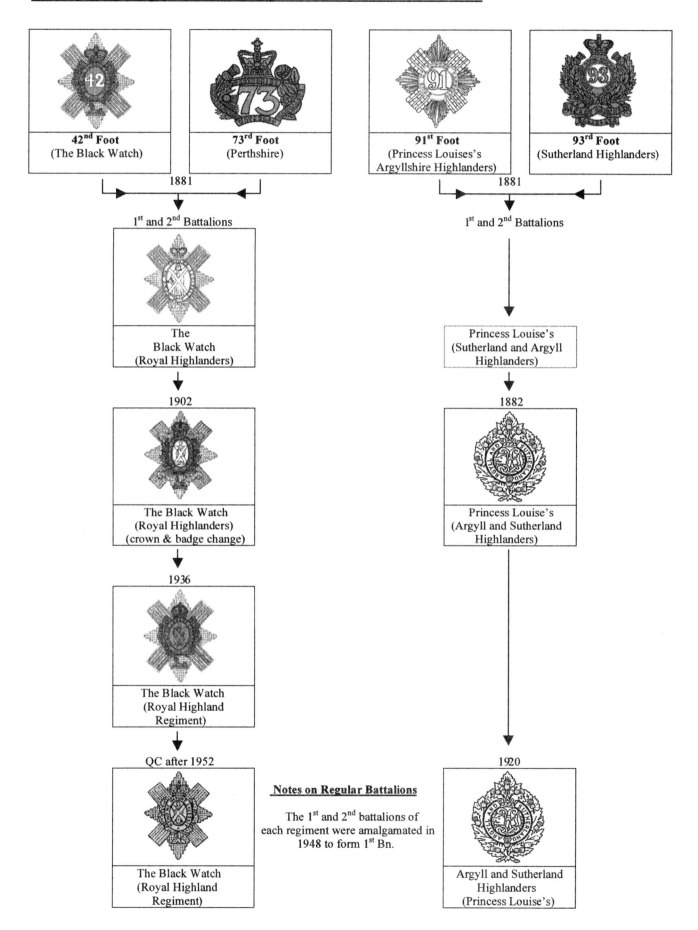

42nd Foot
(The Black Watch)

73rd Foot
(Perthshire)

91st Foot
(Princess Louises's
Argyllshire Highlanders)

93rd Foot
(Sutherland Highlanders)

1881

1881

1st and 2nd Battalions

1st and 2nd Battalions

The
Black Watch
(Royal Highlanders)

Princess Louise's
(Sutherland and Argyll
Highlanders)

1902

1882

The Black Watch
(Royal Highlanders)
(crown & badge change)

Princess Louise's
(Argyll and Sutherland
Highlanders)

1936

The Black Watch
(Royal Highland
Regiment)

QC after 1952

1920

The Black Watch
(Royal Highland
Regiment)

Notes on Regular Battalions

The 1st and 2nd battalions of
each regiment were amalgamated in
1948 to form 1st Bn.

Argyll and Sutherland
Highlanders
(Princess Louise's)

41

6. OTHER INFORMATION

UNIFORM COAT COLOURS (Used to differentiate Regiments of Foot in this section in 1768)				
	Foot No.	Post 1881 Identity	Facing Colour	Lace Colour
	1	Royal Scots (1st & 2nd Bns)	Blue	White with a blue double worm
	21	R Scots Fus's (1st & 2nd Bns)	Blue	White with a blue stripe
	25	KO(S) Borderers (1st & 2nd Bns)	Yellow	White with a blue, yellow and red stripe
	26	Cameronians (1st Bn)	Yellow	White with one blue and two yellow stripes
	42	Black Watch (1st Bn)	Blue	White with a red stripe
	71	Highland LI (1st Bn)	Buff	White with silver lace
	72	Seaforth H'landers (1st Bn)	Yellow	White with silver lace
	73	Black Watch (2nd Bn)	Green	White with gold lace
	74	Highland LI (2nd Bn)	White	White with gold lace
	75	Gordon H'landers (1st Bn)	Yellow	White with silver lace
	78	Seaforth H'landers (2nd Bn)	Buff	White with gold lace
	79	Cameron H'ders (1st & 2nd Bns)	Green	White with gold lace
	90	Cameronians (2nd Bn)	Buff	White with gold lace
	91	A & S H'landers (1st Bn)	Yellow	White with silver lace
	92	Gordon H'landers (2nd Bn)	Yellow	White with silver lace (wore different tartan to above)
	93	A & S H'landers (2nd Bn)	Yellow	White with silver lace (wore same tartan as '91')
	Note: Facings and lace for 71-93 in above list are those in use in 1800.			

18th Century coat example indicates colour placings. Be aware, however, that tailoring differences exist between regiments. **After 1881, facing colours were standardised but some regts were allowed to re-introduce historic colours. The standardised colours were WHITE for English and Welsh regts, YELLOW for Scottish, GREEN for Irish and BLUE for 'Royal' regts.**

THE PRINCESS OF WALES'S ROYAL REGIMENT
(Queen's and Royal Hampshires)

1. FORMATION (and Home Counties Brigade Lineage)

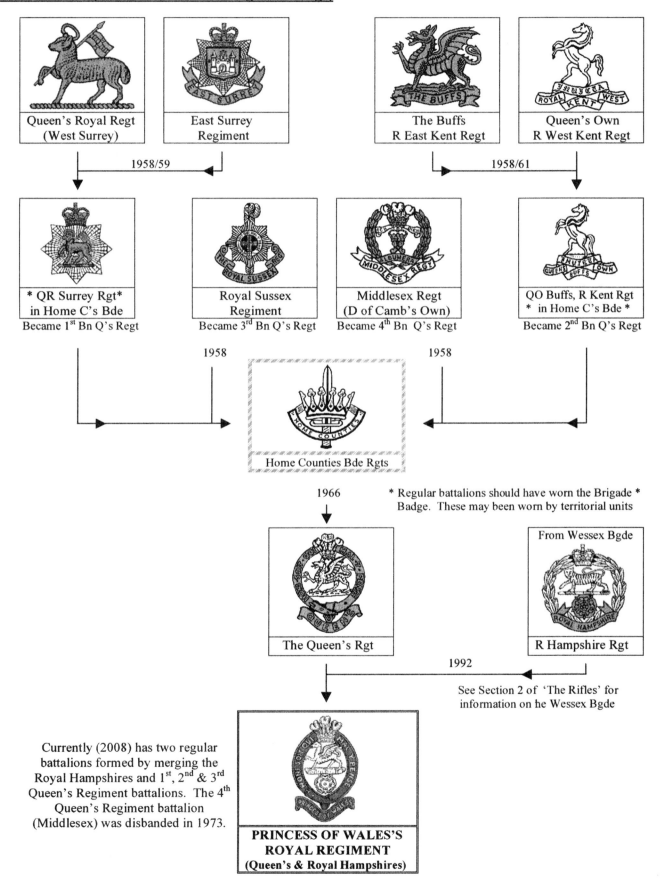

2. SURREY COMPONENTS

2.1 Pre - 1881 Ancestry

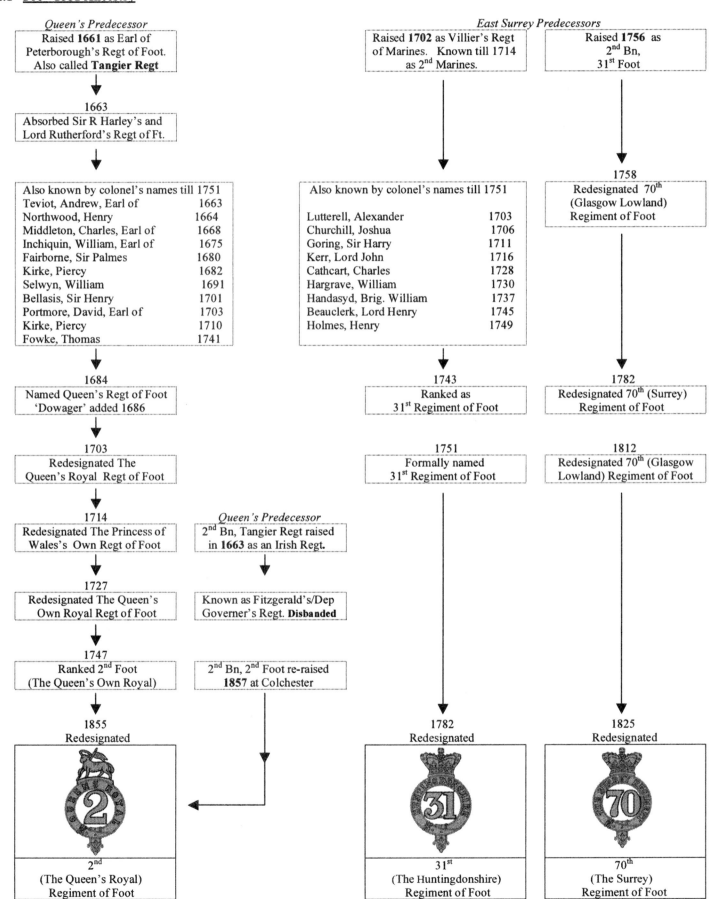

2.2 1881-1957 Ancestry

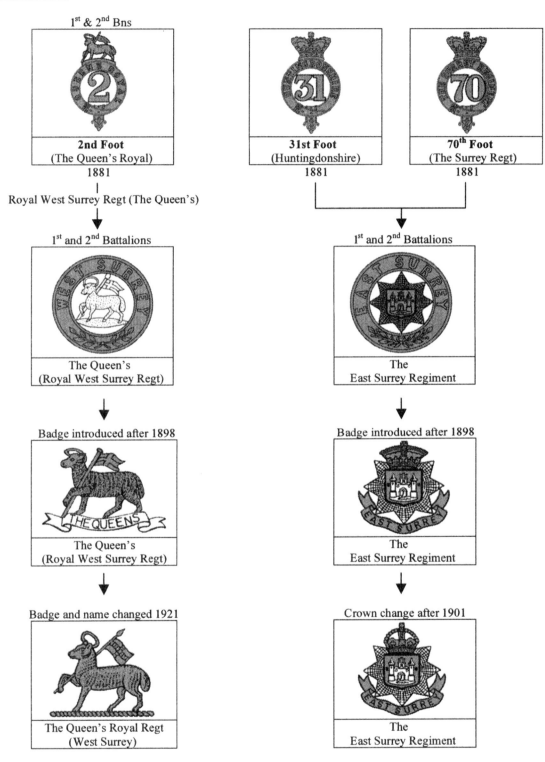

1st & 2nd Bns

2nd Foot
(The Queen's Royal)
1881

Royal West Surrey Regt (The Queen's)

1st and 2nd Battalions

The Queen's
(Royal West Surrey Regt)

Badge introduced after 1898

The Queen's
(Royal West Surrey Regt)

Badge and name changed 1921

The Queen's Royal Regt
(West Surrey)

31st Foot
(Huntingdonshire)
1881

70th Foot
(The Surrey Regt)
1881

1st and 2nd Battalions

The
East Surrey Regiment

Badge introduced after 1898

The
East Surrey Regiment

Crown change after 1901

The
East Surrey Regiment

Notes on Regular Battalions

Queen's (Royal West Surrey) Regiment

2nd Battalion temporarily merged with 2nd Bn, Leicestershire Regt, in 1941, to form The British Battalion which was captured by the Japanese in Singapore. Was reconstituted as 2nd Bn, Leicesters then disbanded in 1948.

East Surrey Regiment

1st and 2nd Battalions amalgamated in 1948 to form 1st Battalion

3. KENT COMPONENTS

3.1 Pre - 1881 Ancestry

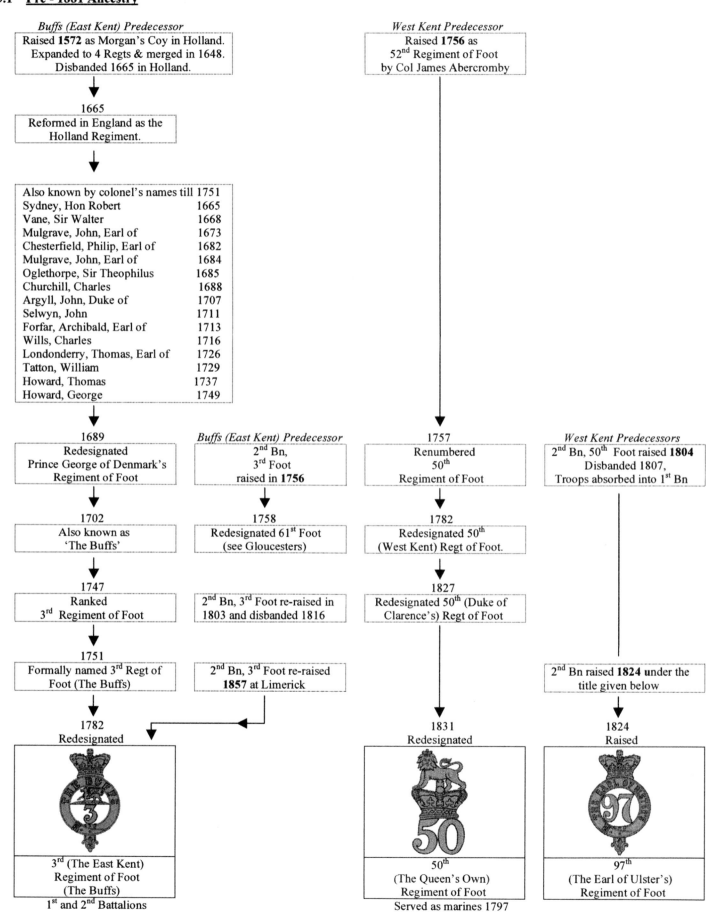

Buffs (East Kent) Predecessor

Raised **1572** as Morgan's Coy in Holland. Expanded to 4 Regts & merged in 1648. Disbanded 1665 in Holland.

West Kent Predecessor

Raised **1756** as 52nd Regiment of Foot by Col James Abercromby

1665
Reformed in England as the Holland Regiment.

Also known by colonel's names till 1751
Sydney, Hon Robert — 1665
Vane, Sir Walter — 1668
Mulgrave, John, Earl of — 1673
Chesterfield, Philip, Earl of — 1682
Mulgrave, John, Earl of — 1684
Oglethorpe, Sir Theophilus — 1685
Churchill, Charles — 1688
Argyll, John, Duke of — 1707
Selwyn, John — 1711
Forfar, Archibald, Earl of — 1713
Wills, Charles — 1716
Londonderry, Thomas, Earl of — 1726
Tatton, William — 1729
Howard, Thomas — 1737
Howard, George — 1749

1689
Redesignated Prince George of Denmark's Regiment of Foot

Buffs (East Kent) Predecessor
2nd Bn, 3rd Foot raised in **1756**

1757
Renumbered 50th Regiment of Foot

West Kent Predecessors
2nd Bn, 50th Foot raised **1804** Disbanded 1807, Troops absorbed into 1st Bn

1702
Also known as 'The Buffs'

1758
Redesignated 61st Foot (see Gloucesters)

1782
Redesignated 50th (West Kent) Regt of Foot.

1747
Ranked 3rd Regiment of Foot

2nd Bn, 3rd Foot re-raised in 1803 and disbanded 1816

1827
Redesignated 50th (Duke of Clarence's) Regt of Foot

1751
Formally named 3rd Regt of Foot (The Buffs)

2nd Bn, 3rd Foot re-raised **1857** at Limerick

2nd Bn raised **1824** under the title given below

1782
Redesignated

1831
Redesignated

1824
Raised

3rd (The East Kent) Regiment of Foot (The Buffs)
1st and 2nd Battalions

50th (The Queen's Own) Regiment of Foot
Served as marines 1797

97th (The Earl of Ulster's) Regiment of Foot

3.2 1881-1957 Ancestry

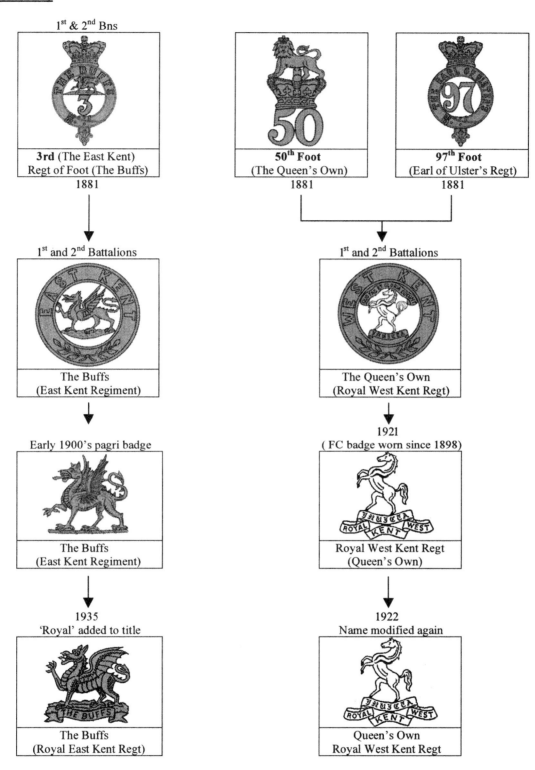

1st & 2nd Bns

3rd (The East Kent)
Regt of Foot (The Buffs)
1881

50th Foot
(The Queen's Own)
1881

97th Foot
(Earl of Ulster's Regt)
1881

1st and 2nd Battalions

The Buffs
(East Kent Regiment)

Early 1900's pagri badge

The Buffs
(East Kent Regiment)

1935
'Royal' added to title

The Buffs
(Royal East Kent Regt)

1st and 2nd Battalions

The Queen's Own
(Royal West Kent Regt)

1921
(FC badge worn since 1898)

Royal West Kent Regt
(Queen's Own)

1922
Name modified again

Queen's Own
Royal West Kent Regt

Notes on Regular Battalions

Queen's (Royal West Surrey) Regiment

2nd Battalion temporarily merged with 2nd Bn, Leicestershire Regt, in 1941, to form The British Battalion which was captured by the Japanese in Singapore. Was reconstituted but then disbanded in 1948.

East Surrey Regiment

1st and 2nd Battalions amalgamated in 1948 to form 1st battalion

4. SUSSEX AND MIDDLESEX COMPONENTS

4.1 Pre - 1881 Ancestry

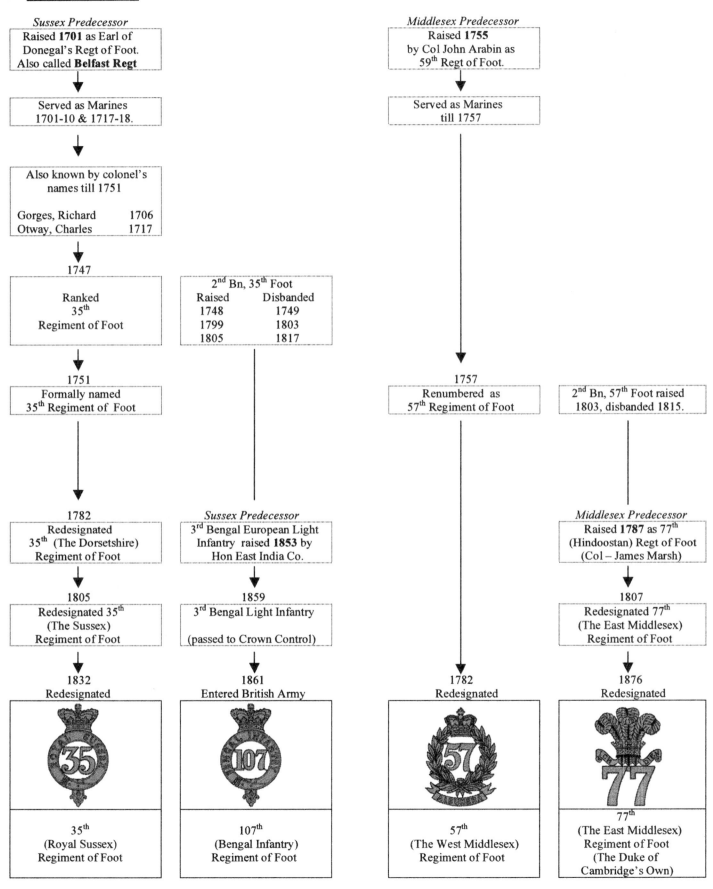

Sussex Predecessor

Raised **1701** as Earl of Donegal's Regt of Foot. Also called **Belfast Regt**

↓

Served as Marines 1701-10 & 1717-18.

↓

Also known by colonel's names till 1751

| Gorges, Richard | 1706 |
| Otway, Charles | 1717 |

↓

1747

Ranked 35th Regiment of Foot

↓

1751

Formally named 35th Regiment of Foot

↓

1782

Redesignated 35th (The Dorsetshire) Regiment of Foot

↓

1805

Redesignated 35th (The Sussex) Regiment of Foot

↓

1832 Redesignated

35th (Royal Sussex) Regiment of Foot

2nd Bn, 35th Foot

Raised	Disbanded
1748	1749
1799	1803
1805	1817

Sussex Predecessor

3rd Bengal European Light Infantry raised **1853** by Hon East India Co.

↓

1859

3rd Bengal Light Infantry (passed to Crown Control)

↓

1861 Entered British Army

107th (Bengal Infantry) Regiment of Foot

Middlesex Predecessor

Raised **1755** by Col John Arabin as 59th Regt of Foot.

↓

Served as Marines till 1757

↓

1757 Renumbered as 57th Regiment of Foot

↓

1782 Redesignated

57th (The West Middlesex) Regiment of Foot

2nd Bn, 57th Foot raised 1803, disbanded 1815.

Middlesex Predecessor

Raised **1787** as 77th (Hindoostan) Regt of Foot (Col – James Marsh)

↓

1807

Redesignated 77th (The East Middlesex) Regiment of Foot

↓

1876 Redesignated

77th (The East Middlesex) Regiment of Foot (The Duke of Cambridge's Own)

4.2   1881-1957 Ancestry

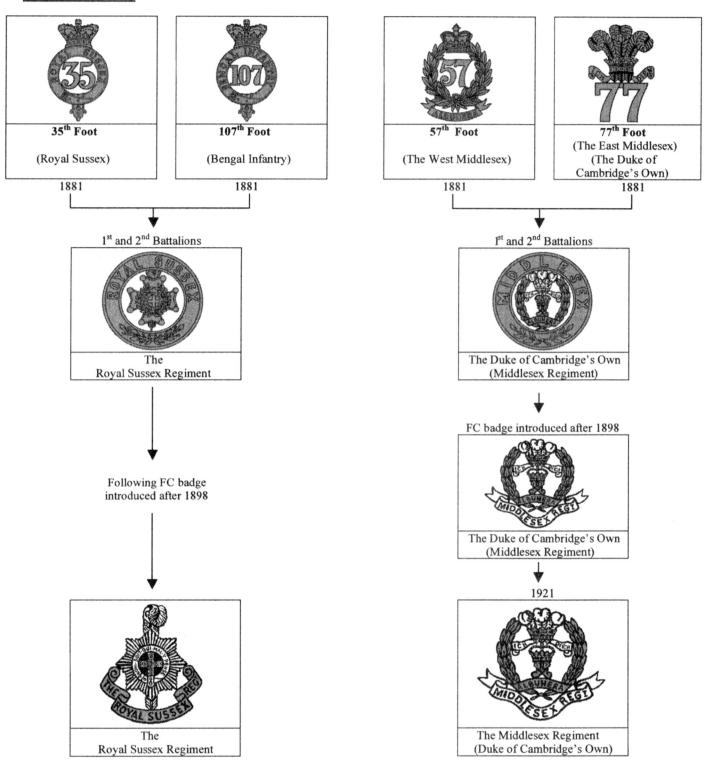

35th Foot

(Royal Sussex)

1881

107th Foot

(Bengal Infantry)

1881

57th Foot

(The West Middlesex)

1881

77th Foot
(The East Middlesex)
(The Duke of
Cambridge's Own)

1881

1st and 2nd Battalions

The
Royal Sussex Regiment

1st and 2nd Battalions

The Duke of Cambridge's Own
(Middlesex Regiment)

Following FC badge
introduced after 1898

FC badge introduced after 1898

The Duke of Cambridge's Own
(Middlesex Regiment)

1921

The
Royal Sussex Regiment

The Middlesex Regiment
(Duke of Cambridge's Own)

Notes on Regular Battalions

The Royal Sussex Regiment

1st and 2nd Battalions amalgamated in 1948 to form 1st Battalion.

The Middlesex Regiment

1st and 2nd Battalions amalgamated in 1948 to form 1st Battalion. The battalion, as the 4th Bn , Queen's Regt was disbanded in 1972.

5. ROYAL HAMPSHIRE COMPONENT

5.1 Pre - 1881 Ancestry

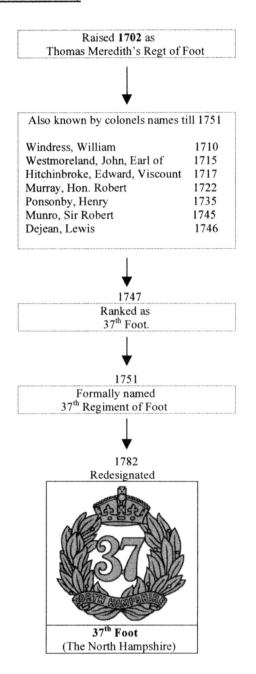

Raised **1702** as
Thomas Meredith's Regt of Foot

↓

Also known by colonels names till 1751

Windress, William	1710
Westmoreland, John, Earl of	1715
Hitchinbroke, Edward, Viscount	1717
Murray, Hon. Robert	1722
Ponsonby, Henry	1735
Munro, Sir Robert	1745
Dejean, Lewis	1746

↓

1747
Ranked as
37th Foot.

↓

1751
Formally named
37th Regiment of Foot

↓

1782
Redesignated

37th Foot
(The North Hampshire)

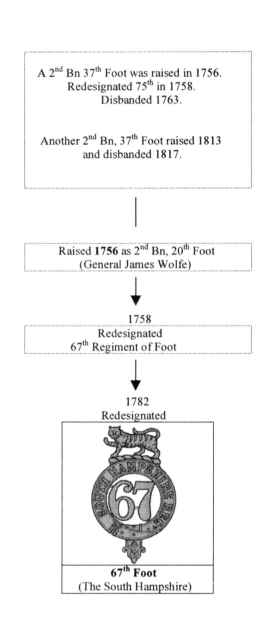

A 2nd Bn 37th Foot was raised in 1756.
Redesignated 75th in 1758.
Disbanded 1763.

Another 2nd Bn, 37th Foot raised 1813
and disbanded 1817.

↓

Raised **1756** as 2nd Bn, 20th Foot
(General James Wolfe)

↓

1758
Redesignated
67th Regiment of Foot

↓

1782
Redesignated

67th Foot
(The South Hampshire)

5.2 1881-1957 Ancestry

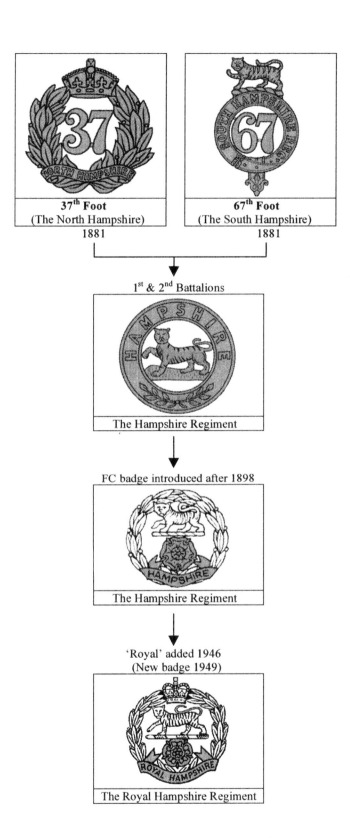

37th Foot
(The North Hampshire)
1881

67th Foot
(The South Hampshire)
1881

1st & 2nd Battalions

The Hampshire Regiment

FC badge introduced after 1898

The Hampshire Regiment

'Royal' added 1946
(New badge 1949)

The Royal Hampshire Regiment

Notes on Regular Battalions

The 2nd battalion was merged with the 1st in 1948.

6. OTHER INFORMATION

This first item is a record of a merger that did **not** happen but got so close that a new badge was produced and disseminated. The Gloucesters and Hampshires were scheduled to merge in 1970. However, a change in Government at around that time disrupted the merger plans and the two regiments obtained a reprieve. This didn't last, as can be seen in details given in the Hampshire regiment section and in the Section addressing The Rifles. Mergers did eventually occur but involved different pathways. In the schematic route below, the Hampshire badge is an officer's badge. The other-ranks badge can be seen in Sub-section 1. The officer's badge has been inserted because the star and the rose within it would seem the obvious source of the star and rose in the composite badge. The sphinx in the latter obviously comes from the Gloucestershire badge.

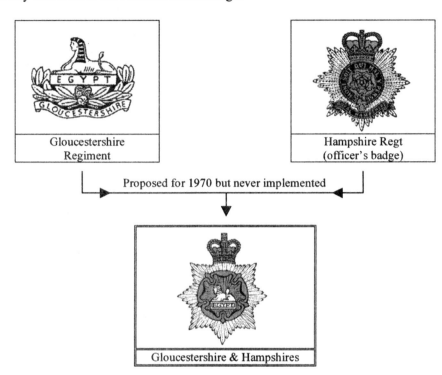

| Gloucestershire Regiment | Hampshire Regt (officer's badge) |

Proposed for 1970 but never implemented

Gloucestershire & Hampshires

UNIFORM COAT COLOURS			
(Used to differentiate Regiments of Foot in this section in 1768)			
Foot No.	Post 1881 Identity	Facing Colour	Lace Colour
2	Queen's (Royal West Surreys) (1st & 2nd Bns)	Blue	White with blue stripe
3	'Buffs' (East Kents) (1st & 2nd Bns)	Buff	White with yellow, black and red stripes
31	East Surreys (1st Bn)	Buff	White with a blue and yellow worm and small red stripe
35	Sussex (1st Bn)	Orange^	White with a yellow stripe
37	Hampshires (1st Bn)	Yellow	White with red and yellow stripes
50	West Kents (1st Bn)	Black^	White with red stripe
57	Middlesex (1st Bn)	Yellow	White with black stripe
67	Hampshires (2nd Bn)	Yellow	White with yellow, purple and green stripes
70	East Surreys (2nd Bn)	Black	White with narrow black worm stripe
77*	Middlesex (2nd Bn)	Yellow	-
97*	West Kents (2nd Bn)	Blue	-
107*	Sussex (2nd Bn)	White	-
	* colours not mentioned in 1768 Warrant?	^ blue after 1831/2	

FACINGS

LACE

REST OF COAT IS RED

18th Century coat example indicates colour placings. Be aware, however, that tailoring differences exist between regiments. **After 1881, facing colours were standardised but some regts were allowed to re-introduce historic colours. The standardised colours were WHITE for English and Welsh regts, YELLOW for Scottish, GREEN for Irish and BLUE for 'Royal' regts.**

THE DUKE OF LANCASTER'S REGIMENT
(King's, Lancashire and Border)

1. FORMATION

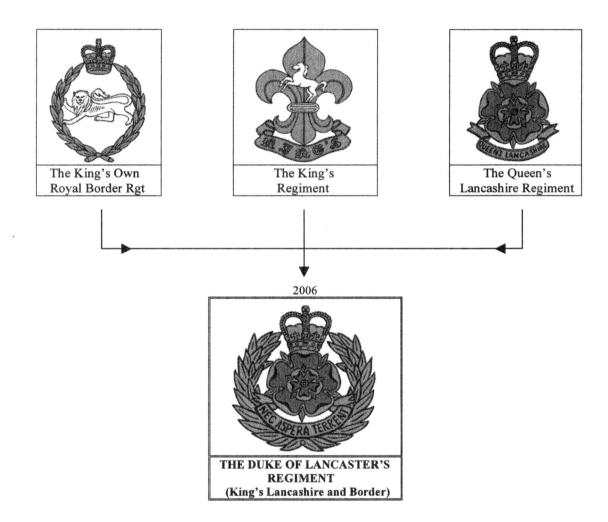

The Duke of Lancaster's Regiment was formed from Lancastrian Brigade ancestors.

The three component regiments, shown above, were expected to form three regular battalions within the Duke of Lancaster's Regiment. However, battalion numbers were reduced to two. Elements from all three component regiments went into the formation of the two.

The Lancastrian and Cumbrian Volunteers (plus the King's elements from the King's and Cheshire Regiment) formed what was initially going to be a 4th (TA) battalion. However, when the regular battalion numbers were reduced, the TA battalion was ranked as the 3rd (TA) battalion.

2. LANCASTRIAN BRIGADE LINEAGE

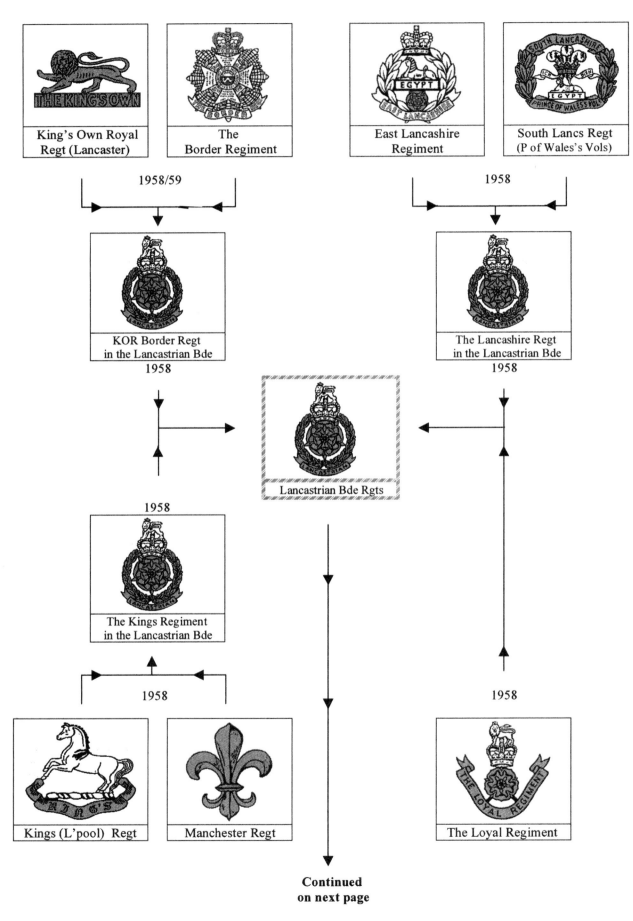

King's Own Royal Regt (Lancaster)

The Border Regiment

East Lancashire Regiment

South Lancs Regt (P of Wales's Vols)

1958/59

1958

KOR Border Regt in the Lancastrian Bde
1958

The Lancashire Regt in the Lancastrian Bde
1958

Lancastrian Bde Rgts

1958

The Kings Regiment in the Lancastrian Bde

1958

Kings (L'pool) Regt

Manchester Regt

1958

The Loyal Regiment

Continued on next page

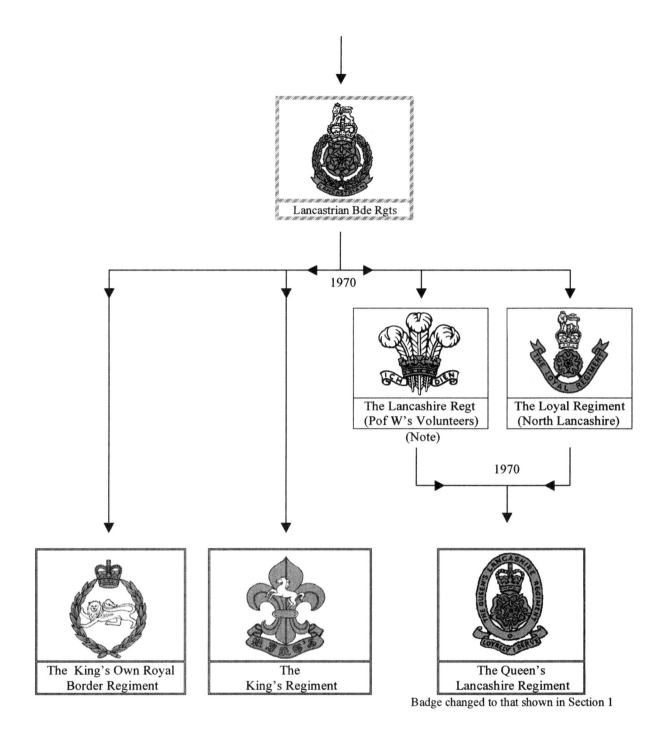

The Lancashire Regt
(Pof W's Volunteers)
(Note)

The Loyal Regiment
(North Lancashire)

The King's Own Royal
Border Regiment

The
King's Regiment

The Queen's
Lancashire Regiment

Badge changed to that shown in Section 1

Note:
The Lancashire Regiment only existed as a regiment in the Lancastrian Brigade. Thus, the regular
battalion should only have worn the Brigade cap badge. The badge shown here may have been worn by
a territorial battalion.

3. KING'S OWN ROYAL REGIMENT (LANCASTER) AND THE BORDER REGIMENT

3.1 Pre-1881 Ancestry

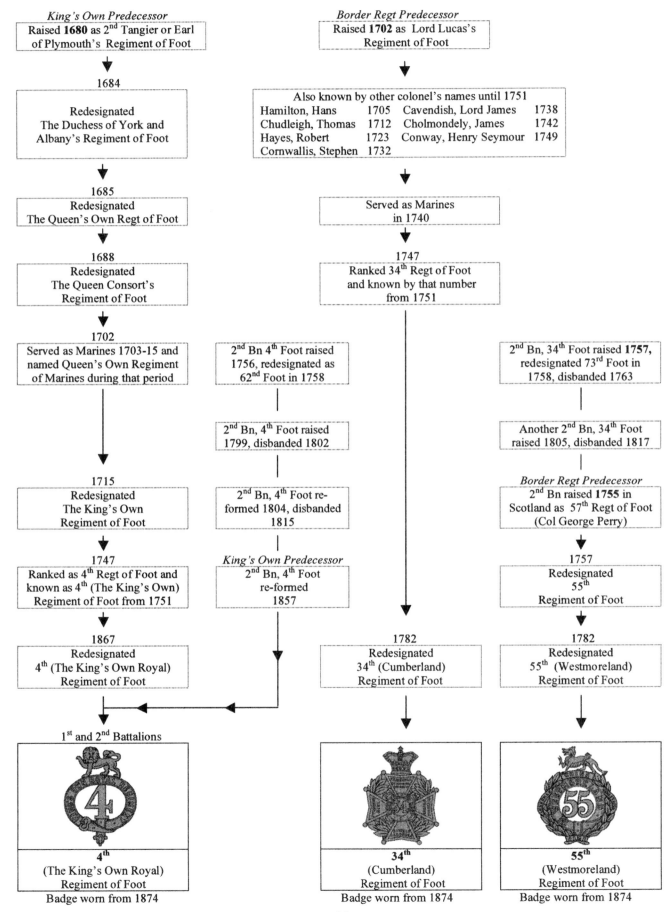

3.2   1881 – 1958 Ancestry

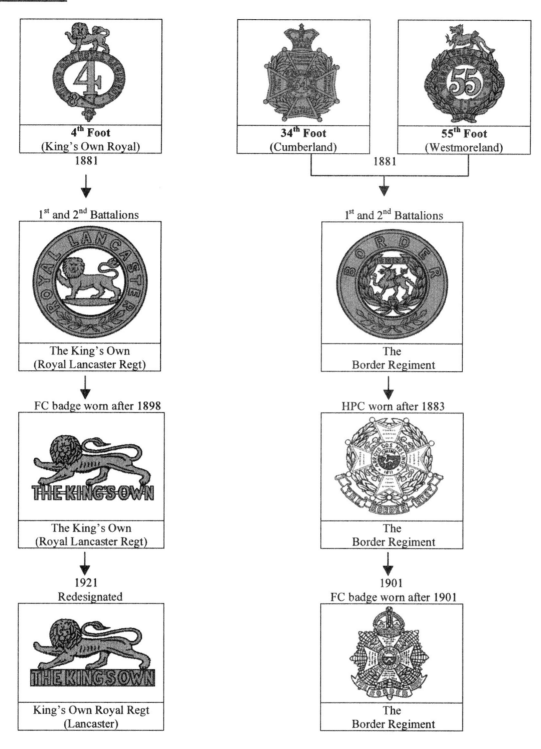

4th Foot
(King's Own Royal)
1881

34th Foot
(Cumberland)

55th Foot
(Westmoreland)
1881

1st and 2nd Battalions

1st and 2nd Battalions

The King's Own
(Royal Lancaster Regt)

The
Border Regiment

FC badge worn after 1898

HPC worn after 1883

The King's Own
(Royal Lancaster Regt)

The
Border Regiment

1921
Redesignated

1901
FC badge worn after 1901

King's Own Royal Regt
(Lancaster)

The
Border Regiment

Notes on Regular Battalions

King's Own Royal Regiment (Lancaster)

The 1st and 2nd battalions were merged in 1949 to form a composite 1st battalion.

The Border Regiment

The 1st and 2nd battalions were merged in 1950 to form a composite 1st battalion.

4. EAST LANCASHIRE AND SOUTH LANCASHIRE REGIMENTS

4.1 Pre -1881 Ancestry

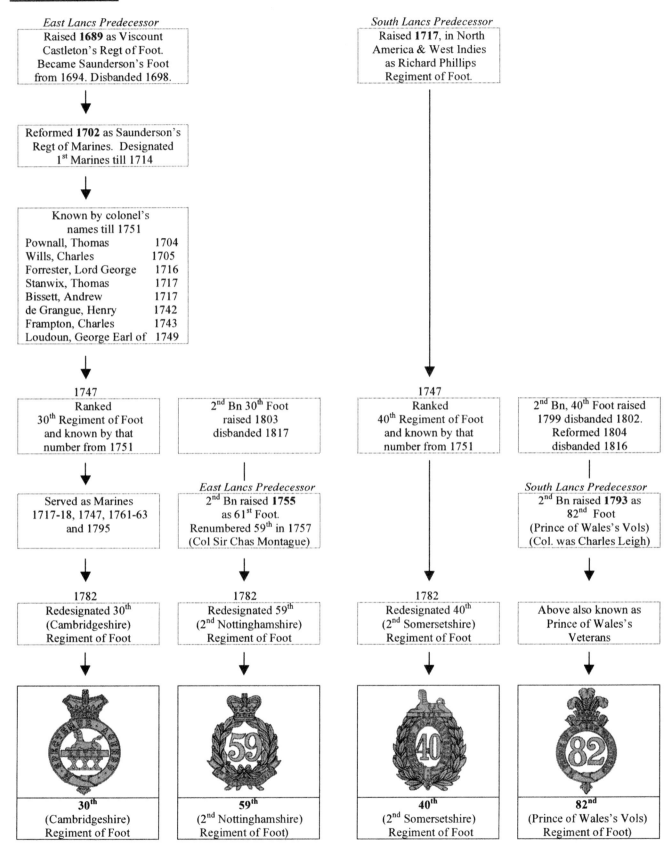

4.2   1881 – 1958 Ancestry

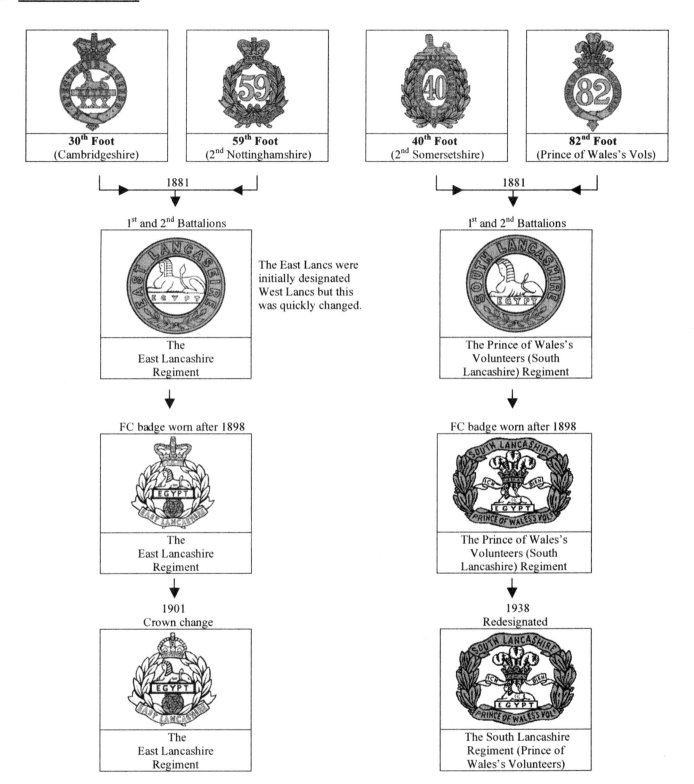

The East Lancs were initially designated West Lancs but this was quickly changed.

Notes on Regular Battalions

East Lancashire Regiment

The 1st and 2nd battalions were merged in 1948 to form a composite 1st battalion.

South Lancashire Regiment

The 1st and 2nd battalions were merged in 1948 to form a composite 1st battalion.

5. KINGS (LIVERPOOL) AND MANCHESTER REGIMENTS

5.1 Pre -1881 Ancestry

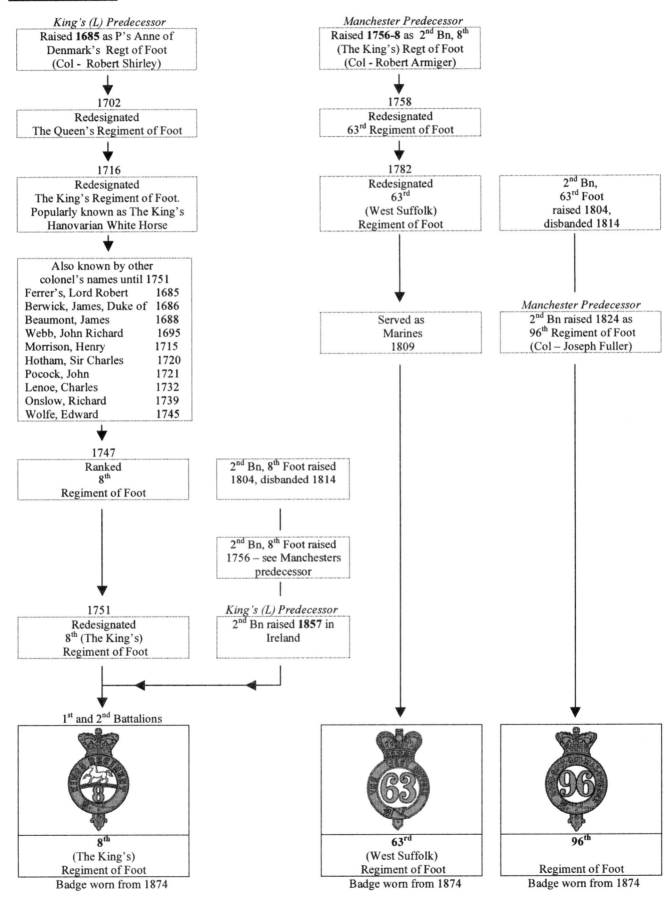

King's (L) Predecessor
Raised **1685** as P's Anne of Denmark's Regt of Foot
(Col - Robert Shirley)

Manchester Predecessor
Raised **1756-8** as 2nd Bn, 8th (The King's) Regt of Foot
(Col - Robert Armiger)

1702
Redesignated
The Queen's Regiment of Foot

1758
Redesignated
63rd Regiment of Foot

1716
Redesignated
The King's Regiment of Foot.
Popularly known as The King's Hanovarian White Horse

1782
Redesignated
63rd
(West Suffolk)
Regiment of Foot

2nd Bn,
63rd Foot
raised 1804,
disbanded 1814

Also known by other colonel's names until 1751
Ferrer's, Lord Robert	1685
Berwick, James, Duke of	1686
Beaumont, James	1688
Webb, John Richard	1695
Morrison, Henry	1715
Hotham, Sir Charles	1720
Pocock, John	1721
Lenoe, Charles	1732
Onslow, Richard	1739
Wolfe, Edward	1745

Served as
Marines
1809

Manchester Predecessor
2nd Bn raised 1824 as
96th Regiment of Foot
(Col – Joseph Fuller)

1747
Ranked
8th
Regiment of Foot

2nd Bn, 8th Foot raised 1804, disbanded 1814

2nd Bn, 8th Foot raised 1756 – see Manchesters predecessor

1751
Redesignated
8th (The King's)
Regiment of Foot

King's (L) Predecessor
2nd Bn raised **1857** in Ireland

1st and 2nd Battalions

8th
(The King's)
Regiment of Foot
Badge worn from 1874

63rd
(West Suffolk)
Regiment of Foot
Badge worn from 1874

96th
Regiment of Foot
Badge worn from 1874

5.2   <u>1881 – 1958 Ancestry</u>

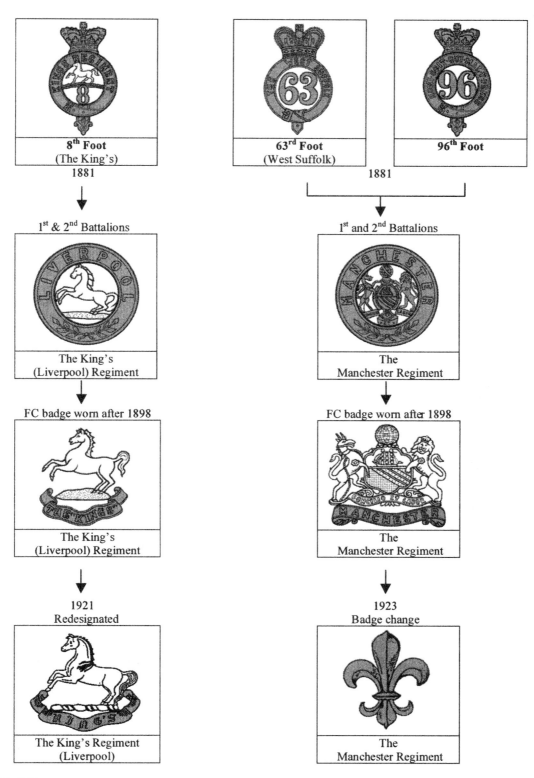

Notes on Regular Battalions

The King's Regiment (Liverpool)

The 1st and 2nd battalions were merged in 1948 to form a composite 1st battalion.

The Manchester Regiment

The 1st and 2nd battalions were merged in 1948 to form a composite 1st battalion.

6. THE LOYAL REGIMENT (NORTH LANCASHIRE)

6.1 Pre -1881 Ancestry

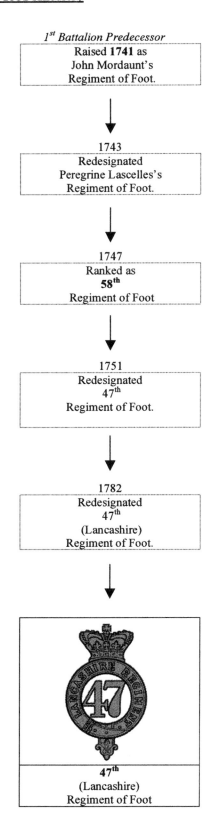

1st Battalion Predecessor

Raised **1741** as
John Mordaunt's
Regiment of Foot.

↓

1743
Redesignated
Peregrine Lascelles's
Regiment of Foot.

↓

1747
Ranked as
58th
Regiment of Foot

↓

1751
Redesignated
47th
Regiment of Foot.

↓

1782
Redesignated
47th
(Lancashire)
Regiment of Foot.

↓

47th
(Lancashire)
Regiment of Foot

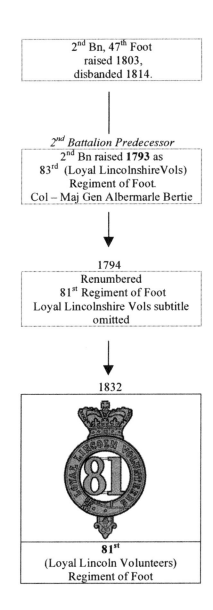

2nd Bn, 47th Foot
raised 1803,
disbanded 1814.

|

2nd Battalion Predecessor

2nd Bn raised **1793** as
83rd (Loyal LincolnshireVols)
Regiment of Foot.
Col – Maj Gen Albermarle Bertie

↓

1794
Renumbered
81st Regiment of Foot
Loyal Lincolnshire Vols subtitle
omitted

↓

1832

81st
(Loyal Lincoln Volunteers)
Regiment of Foot

6.2   1881 – 1958 Ancestry

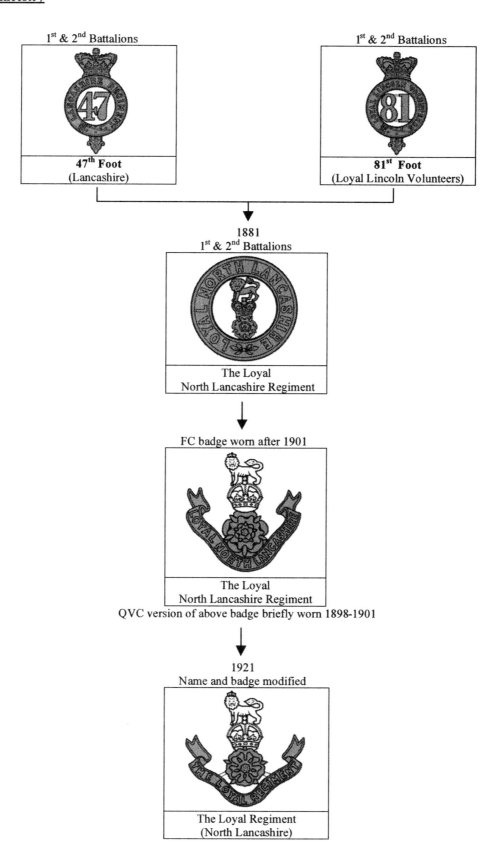

1st & 2nd Battalions

47th Foot
(Lancashire)

1st & 2nd Battalions

81st Foot
(Loyal Lincoln Volunteers)

1881
1st & 2nd Battalions

The Loyal
North Lancashire Regiment

FC badge worn after 1901

The Loyal
North Lancashire Regiment

QVC version of above badge briefly worn 1898-1901

1921
Name and badge modified

The Loyal Regiment
(North Lancashire)

Notes on Regular Battalions

The 1st and 2nd battalions were merged in 1949 to form a composite 1st battalion.

7. OTHER INFORMATION

	Foot No.	Post 1881 Identity	Facing Colour	Lace Colour
		UNIFORM COAT COLOURS (Used to differentiate Regiments of Foot in this section in 1768)		
	4	King's Own Royal (Lancaster) (1st & 2nd Bns)	Blue	White with blue stripe
	8	King's (Liverpool) (1st & 2nd Bns)	Blue	White with a blue and a yellow stripe
	30	East Lancs (1st Bn)	Yellow	White with sky-blue stripe
	34	Border Regt (1st Bn)	Yellow	White with a blue and yellow worm and red stripe
	40	South Lancs (1st Bn)	Buff	White with a red and a black stripe
	47	Loyal Regt (1st Bn)	White	White with one red and two black stripes
	55	Border Regt (2nd Bn)	Green	White with two green stripes
	59	East Lancs (2nd Bn)	Red	White with a red and a yellow stripe
	63	Manchester Regt (1st Bn)	Green	White with small green stripe
	81*	Loyal Regt (2nd Bn)	Buff	-
	82*	South Lancs (2nd Bn)	Yellow	-
	96*	Manchester Regt (2nd Bn)	Yellow	-
		* colours not mentioned in 1768 Warrant?		

FACINGS

LACE

REST OF COAT IS RED

18th Century coat example indicates colour placings. Be aware, however, that tailoring differences exist between regiments.
After 1881, facing colours were standardised but some regts were allowed to re-introduce historic colours. The standardised colours were WHITE for English and Welsh regts, YELLOW for Scottish, GREEN for Irish and BLUE for 'Royal' regts.

THE ROYAL REGIMENT OF FUSILIERS

1. FORMATION (and Fusilier Brigade Lineage)

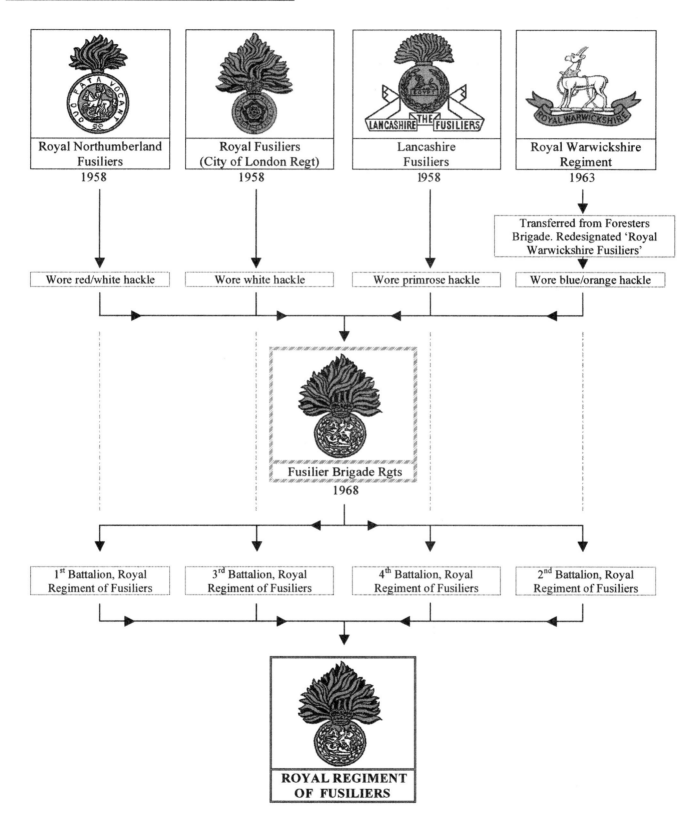

The Royal Regiment of Fusiliers wear the red over white hackle inherited from the Royal Northumberland Fusiliers. The four regular battalions have now been reduced to two.

2. ROYAL NORTHUMBERLAND FUSILIER AND ROYAL WARWICKSHIRE FUSILIER COMPONENTS

2.1 Pre - 1881 Ancestry

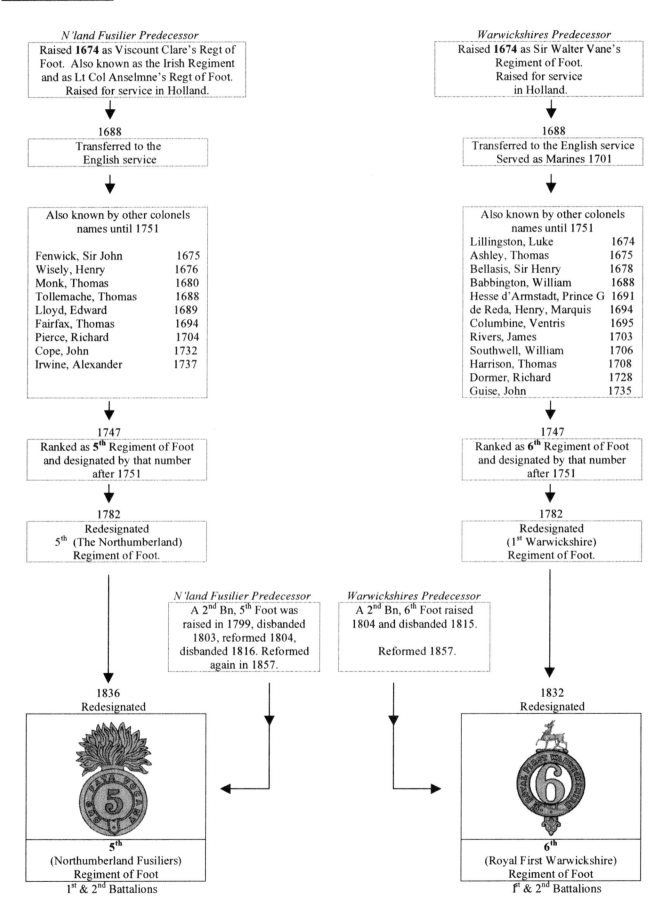

N'land Fusilier Predecessor
Raised **1674** as Viscount Clare's Regt of Foot. Also known as the Irish Regiment and as Lt Col Anselmne's Regt of Foot. Raised for service in Holland.

1688
Transferred to the English service

Also known by other colonels names until 1751

Fenwick, Sir John	1675
Wisely, Henry	1676
Monk, Thomas	1680
Tollemache, Thomas	1688
Lloyd, Edward	1689
Fairfax, Thomas	1694
Pierce, Richard	1704
Cope, John	1732
Irwine, Alexander	1737

1747
Ranked as **5th** Regiment of Foot and designated by that number after 1751

1782
Redesignated
5th (The Northumberland) Regiment of Foot.

N'land Fusilier Predecessor
A 2nd Bn, 5th Foot was raised in 1799, disbanded 1803, reformed 1804, disbanded 1816. Reformed again in 1857.

1836
Redesignated

5th
(Northumberland Fusiliers)
Regiment of Foot
1st & 2nd Battalions

Warwickshires Predecessor
Raised **1674** as Sir Walter Vane's Regiment of Foot. Raised for service in Holland.

1688
Transferred to the English service
Served as Marines 1701

Also known by other colonels names until 1751

Lillingston, Luke	1674
Ashley, Thomas	1675
Bellasis, Sir Henry	1678
Babbington, William	1688
Hesse d'Armstadt, Prince G	1691
de Reda, Henry, Marquis	1694
Columbine, Ventris	1695
Rivers, James	1703
Southwell, William	1706
Harrison, Thomas	1708
Dormer, Richard	1728
Guise, John	1735

1747
Ranked as **6th** Regiment of Foot and designated by that number after 1751

1782
Redesignated
(1st Warwickshire) Regiment of Foot.

Warwickshires Predecessor
A 2nd Bn, 6th Foot raised 1804 and disbanded 1815.

Reformed 1857.

1832
Redesignated

6th
(Royal First Warwickshire)
Regiment of Foot
1st & 2nd Battalions

2.2   1881 - 1957 Ancestry

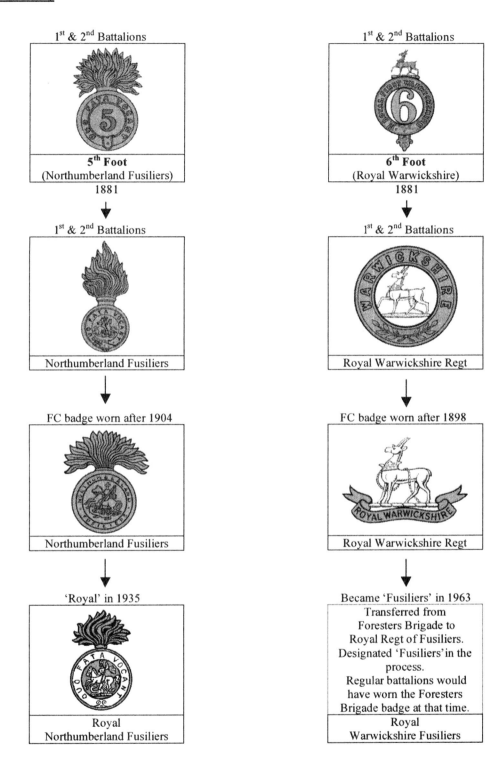

1st & 2nd Battalions

5th Foot
(Northumberland Fusiliers)
1881

1st & 2nd Battalions

Northumberland Fusiliers

FC badge worn after 1904

Northumberland Fusiliers

'Royal' in 1935

Royal
Northumberland Fusiliers

1st & 2nd Battalions

6th Foot
(Royal Warwickshire)
1881

1st & 2nd Battalions

Royal Warwickshire Regt

FC badge worn after 1898

Royal Warwickshire Regt

Became 'Fusiliers' in 1963
Transferred from
Foresters Brigade to
Royal Regt of Fusiliers.
Designated 'Fusiliers' in the
process.
Regular battalions would
have worn the Foresters
Brigade badge at that time.

Royal
Warwickshire Fusiliers

Notes on Regular Battalions

Royal Northumberland Fusiliers

The 2nd Bn was disbanded in 1948.

Royal Warwickshire Regiment

The 2nd Bn was amalgamated with the 1st in 1948.

3. ROYAL FUSILIER AND LANCASHIRE FUSILIER COMPONENTS

3.1 Pre - 1881 Ancestry

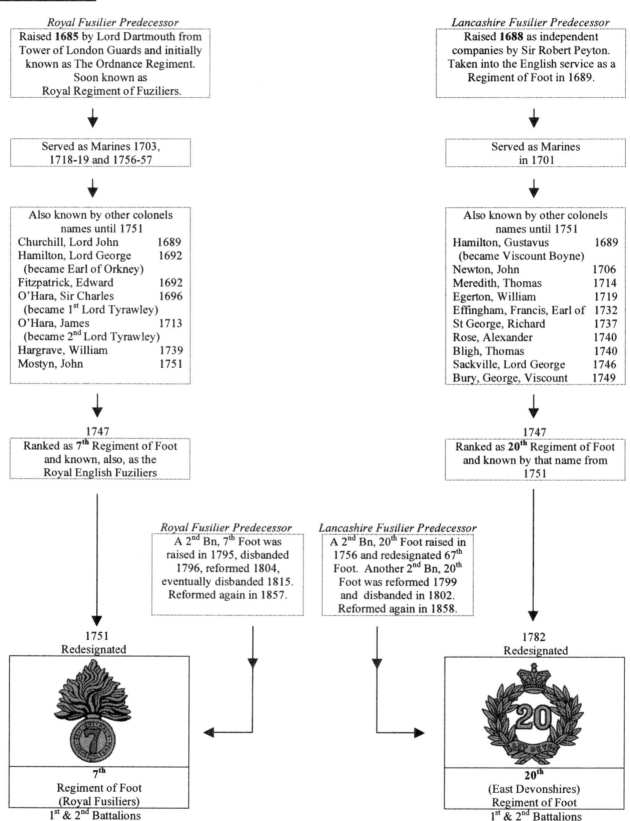

Royal Fusilier Predecessor

Raised **1685** by Lord Dartmouth from Tower of London Guards and initially known as The Ordnance Regiment. Soon known as Royal Regiment of Fuziliers.

Lancashire Fusilier Predecessor

Raised **1688** as independent companies by Sir Robert Peyton. Taken into the English service as a Regiment of Foot in 1689.

Served as Marines 1703, 1718-19 and 1756-57

Served as Marines in 1701

Also known by other colonels names until 1751

Churchill, Lord John	1689
Hamilton, Lord George (became Earl of Orkney)	1692
Fitzpatrick, Edward	1692
O'Hara, Sir Charles (became 1st Lord Tyrawley)	1696
O'Hara, James (became 2nd Lord Tyrawley)	1713
Hargrave, William	1739
Mostyn, John	1751

Also known by other colonels names until 1751

Hamilton, Gustavus (became Viscount Boyne)	1689
Newton, John	1706
Meredith, Thomas	1714
Egerton, William	1719
Effingham, Francis, Earl of	1732
St George, Richard	1737
Rose, Alexander	1740
Bligh, Thomas	1740
Sackville, Lord George	1746
Bury, George, Viscount	1749

1747

Ranked as 7th Regiment of Foot and known, also, as the Royal English Fuziliers

1747

Ranked as **20th** Regiment of Foot and known by that name from 1751

Royal Fusilier Predecessor

A 2nd Bn, 7th Foot was raised in 1795, disbanded 1796, reformed 1804, eventually disbanded 1815. Reformed again in 1857.

Lancashire Fusilier Predecessor

A 2nd Bn, 20th Foot raised in 1756 and redesignated 67th Foot. Another 2nd Bn, 20th Foot was reformed 1799 and disbanded in 1802. Reformed again in 1858.

1751
Redesignated

7th
Regiment of Foot
(Royal Fusiliers)
1st & 2nd Battalions

1782
Redesignated

20th
(East Devonshires)
Regiment of Foot
1st & 2nd Battalions

Many Regiments of Foot were given county titles in 1782 to add to their numbers. The 7th (Royal Fusiliers) were seemingly included in this process and given the county designation 'Derbyshire'. The designation appears to have been resisted and was eventually bestowed on the 95th Regiment of Foot (a Sherwood Foresters predecessor) in 1825.

3.2 <u>1881 - 1957 Ancestry</u>

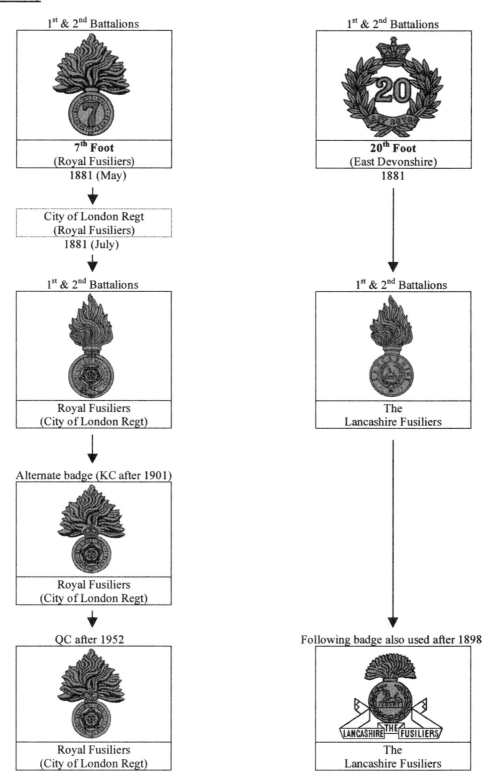

1st & 2nd Battalions

7th Foot
(Royal Fusiliers)
1881 (May)

City of London Regt
(Royal Fusiliers)
1881 (July)

1st & 2nd Battalions

Royal Fusiliers
(City of London Regt)

Alternate badge (KC after 1901)

Royal Fusiliers
(City of London Regt)

QC after 1952

Royal Fusiliers
(City of London Regt)

1st & 2nd Battalions

20th Foot
(East Devonshire)
1881

1st & 2nd Battalions

The
Lancashire Fusiliers

Following badge also used after 1898

The
Lancashire Fusiliers

<u>Notes on Regular Battalions</u>

<u>Royal Fusiliers</u>

The 2nd Bn was disbanded in 1948.

<u>Lancashire Fusiliers</u>

The 2nd Bn was amalgamated with the 1st in 1948.
The 1st Bn successor (4th Bn, RRF) was disbanded in 1969.

4. OTHER INFORMATION

The Royal Regiment of Fusiliers did not absorb Scottish, Irish or Welsh Fusilier regiments. The latter were absorbed, instead, into 'large' Scottish, Irish and Welsh regiments.

The Royal Scots Fusiliers were absorbed into the 'Royal Regiment of Scotland'; the Royal Welch Fusiliers into the 'Royal Welsh' and the Royal Irish Fusiliers and Royal Inniskilling Fusiliers into the 'Royal Irish Regiment'. Information on these fusilier regiments can be found in the sections addressing their relevant 'large' regiment.

There are two other Irish fusilier regiments that deserve a mention. They are the Royal Dublin Fusiliers and the Royal Munster Fusiliers. They were disbanded in 1922 when the Irish Free State was formed (along with other 'Southern' Irish regiments) but were part of the British Army establishment before that time. Information on them and other disbanded Irish regiments have been provided in a section headed 'Old Irish Regiments'.

UNIFORM COAT COLOURS
(Used to differentiate Regiments of Foot in this section in 1768)

Foot No.	Post 1881 Identity	Facing Colour	Lace Colour
5	Northumberland Fusiliers (1st & 2nd Bn)	Green	White with two red stripes
6	Warwicks (1st & 2nd Bns)	Yellow	White with yellow and red stripes
7	Royal Fusiliers (1st & 2nd Bns)	Blue	White with blue stripes
20	Lancashire Fusiliers (1st & 2nd Bns)	Yellow	White with a red and a black stripe

FACINGS

LACE

REST OF COAT IS RED

18th Century coat example indicates colour placings. Be aware, however, that tailoring differences exist between regiments. **After 1881, facing colours were standardised but some regts were allowed to re-introduce historic colours. The standardised colours were WHITE for English and Welsh regts, YELLOW for Scottish, GREEN for Irish and BLUE for 'Royal' regts.**

THE ROYAL ANGLIAN REGIMENT

1. FORMATION (and East Anglian Brigade Lineage)

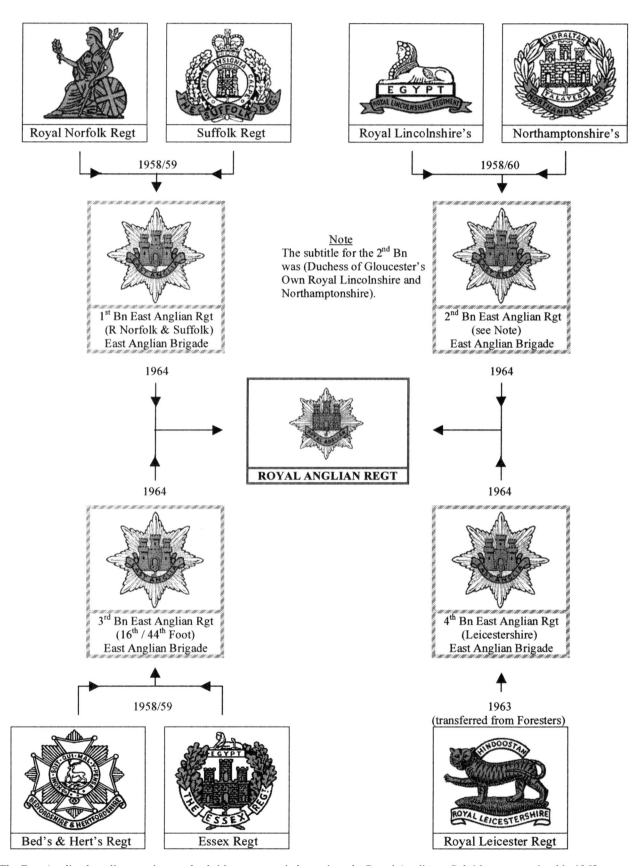

The East Anglian battalion numbers and subtitles were carried over into the Royal Anglians. Subtitles were omitted in 1968. The **4th battalion** (Leicestershires) was **disbanded in 1975**. The **3rd battalion** (16th/44th Foot) was **disbanded in 1992**.

2. ROYAL NORFOLK AND SUFFOLK COMPONENTS

2.1 Pre - 1881 Ancestry

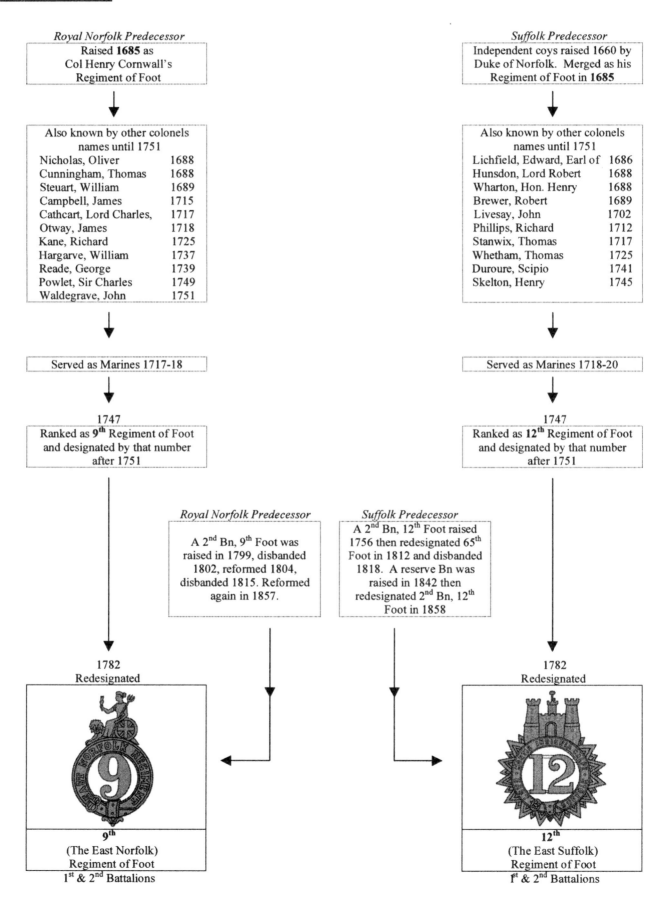

Royal Norfolk Predecessor

Raised **1685** as
Col Henry Cornwall's
Regiment of Foot

Suffolk Predecessor

Independent coys raised 1660 by
Duke of Norfolk. Merged as his
Regiment of Foot in **1685**

Also known by other colonels
names until 1751

Nicholas, Oliver	1688
Cunningham, Thomas	1688
Steuart, William	1689
Campbell, James	1715
Cathcart, Lord Charles,	1717
Otway, James	1718
Kane, Richard	1725
Hargarve, William	1737
Reade, George	1739
Powlet, Sir Charles	1749
Waldegrave, John	1751

Also known by other colonels
names until 1751

Lichfield, Edward, Earl of	1686
Hunsdon, Lord Robert	1688
Wharton, Hon. Henry	1688
Brewer, Robert	1689
Livesay, John	1702
Phillips, Richard	1712
Stanwix, Thomas	1717
Whetham, Thomas	1725
Duroure, Scipio	1741
Skelton, Henry	1745

Served as Marines 1717-18

Served as Marines 1718-20

1747
Ranked as 9th Regiment of Foot
and designated by that number
after 1751

1747
Ranked as 12th Regiment of Foot
and designated by that number
after 1751

Royal Norfolk Predecessor

A 2nd Bn, 9th Foot was
raised in 1799, disbanded
1802, reformed 1804,
disbanded 1815. Reformed
again in 1857.

Suffolk Predecessor

A 2nd Bn, 12th Foot raised
1756 then redesignated 65th
Foot in 1812 and disbanded
1818. A reserve Bn was
raised in 1842 then
redesignated 2nd Bn, 12th
Foot in 1858

1782
Redesignated

1782
Redesignated

9th
(The East Norfolk)
Regiment of Foot
1st & 2nd Battalions

12th
(The East Suffolk)
Regiment of Foot
1st & 2nd Battalions

2.2   1881 - 1957 Ancestry

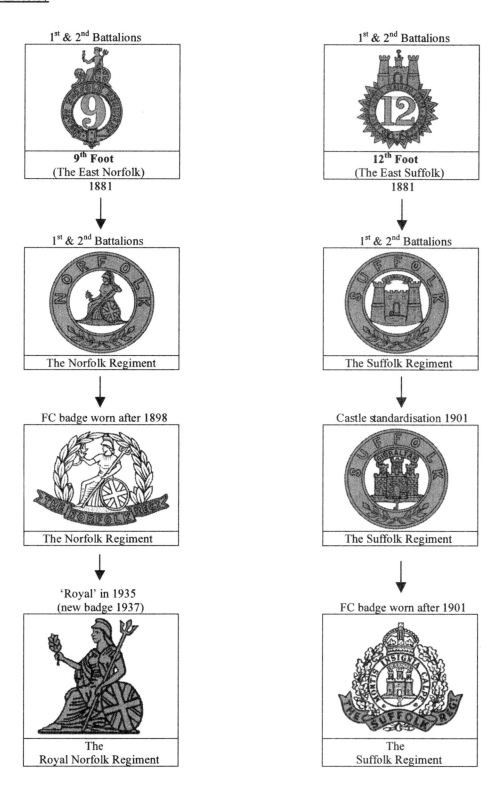

1st & 2nd Battalions

9th Foot
(The East Norfolk)
1881

1st & 2nd Battalions

The Norfolk Regiment

FC badge worn after 1898

The Norfolk Regiment

'Royal' in 1935
(new badge 1937)

The
Royal Norfolk Regiment

1st & 2nd Battalions

12th Foot
(The East Suffolk)
1881

1st & 2nd Battalions

The Suffolk Regiment

Castle standardisation 1901

The Suffolk Regiment

FC badge worn after 1901

The
Suffolk Regiment

Notes on Regular Battalions

Royal Norfolk Regiment

The 2nd Bn was disbanded in 1948.

Suffolk Regiment

The 2nd Bn was amalgamated with the 1st in 1948.

3. ROYAL LINCOLNSHIRE AND NOTHAMPTONSHIRE COMPONENTS

3.1 Pre - 1881 Ancestry

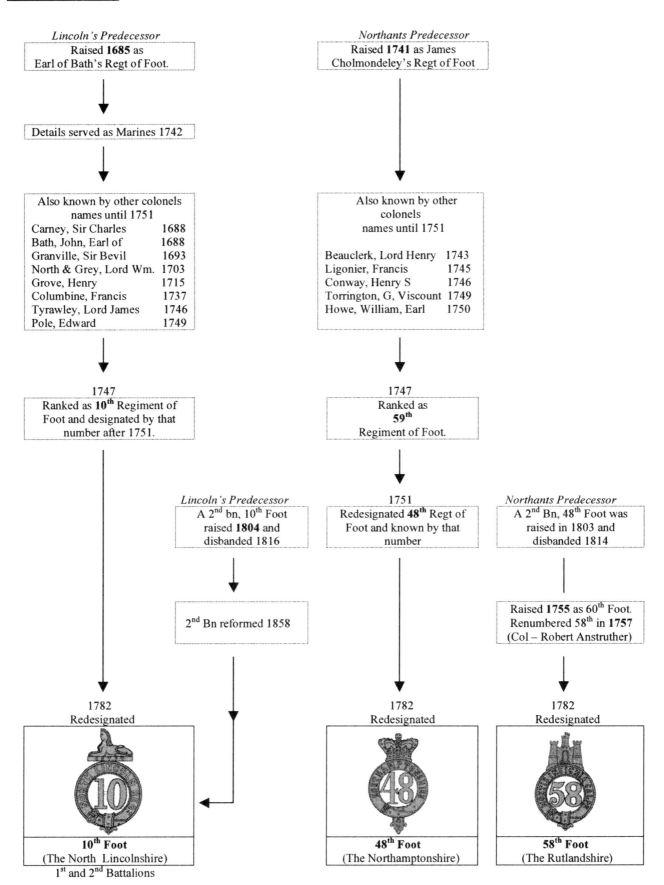

Lincoln's Predecessor
Raised **1685** as
Earl of Bath's Regt of Foot.

Northants Predecessor
Raised **1741** as James
Cholmondeley's Regt of Foot

Details served as Marines 1742

Also known by other colonels
names until 1751
Carney, Sir Charles   1688
Bath, John, Earl of   1688
Granville, Sir Bevil   1693
North & Grey, Lord Wm.   1703
Grove, Henry   1715
Columbine, Francis   1737
Tyrawley, Lord James   1746
Pole, Edward   1749

Also known by other
colonels
names until 1751

Beauclerk, Lord Henry   1743
Ligonier, Francis   1745
Conway, Henry S   1746
Torrington, G, Viscount   1749
Howe, William, Earl   1750

1747
Ranked as **10**th Regiment of
Foot and designated by that
number after 1751.

1747
Ranked as
59th
Regiment of Foot.

Lincoln's Predecessor
A 2nd bn, 10th Foot
raised **1804** and
disbanded 1816

1751
Redesignated **48**th Regt of
Foot and known by that
number

Northants Predecessor
A 2nd Bn, 48th Foot was
raised in 1803 and
disbanded 1814

2nd Bn reformed 1858

Raised **1755** as 60th Foot.
Renumbered 58th in **1757**
(Col – Robert Anstruther)

1782
Redesignated

1782
Redesignated

1782
Redesignated

10th **Foot**
(The North Lincolnshire)
1st and 2nd Battalions

48th **Foot**
(The Northamptonshire)

58th **Foot**
(The Rutlandshire)

3.2 1881 - 1957 Ancestry

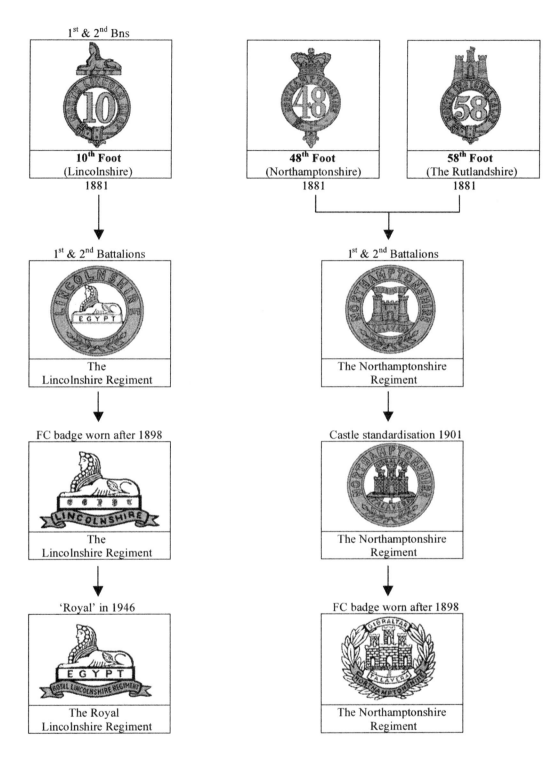

Notes on Regular Battalions

Royal Lincolnshire Regiment

The 2nd Bn was amalgamated with the 1st in 1948.

Northamptonshire Regiment

The 2nd Bn was amalgamated with the 1st in 1948.

4. BEDFORDSHIRE & HERTFORDSHIRE AND ESSEX COMPONENTS

4.1 Pre - 1881 Ancestry

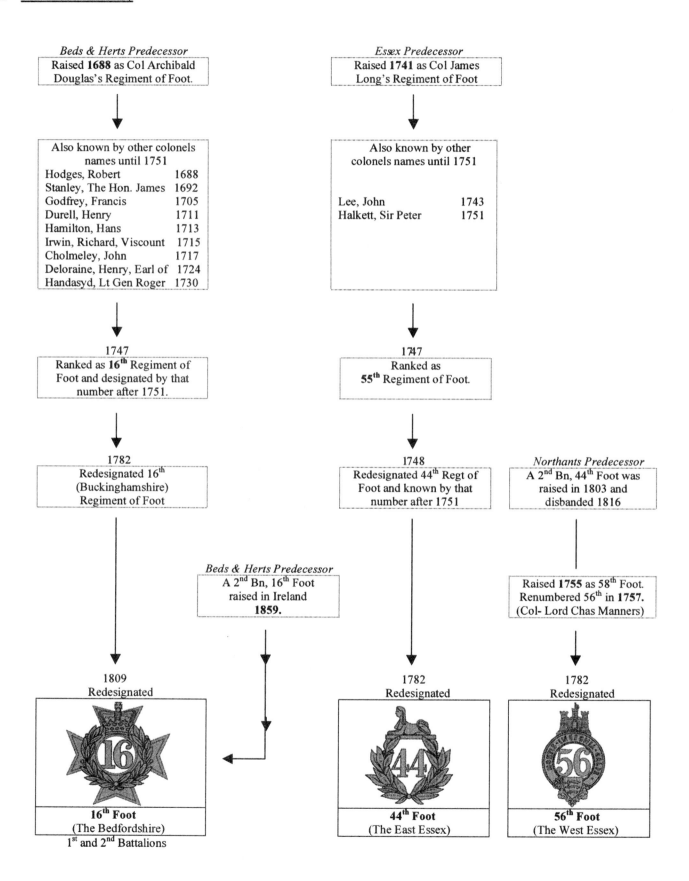

4.2   1881 - 1957 Ancestry

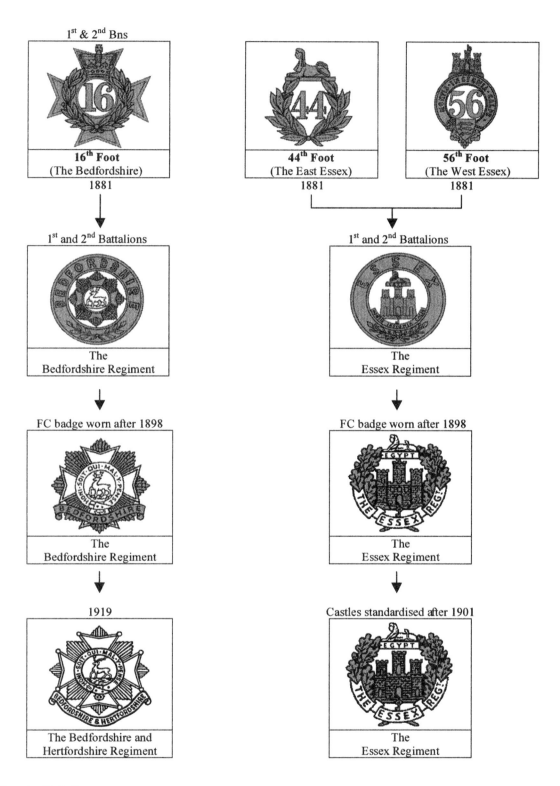

Notes on Regular Battalions

The Bedfordshire & Hertfordshire Regiment

The 2nd Bn was amalgamated with the 1st in 1948.

The Essex Regiment

The 2nd Bn was amalgamated with the 1st in 1948.

5. ROYAL LEICESTERSHIRE COMPONENTS

5.1 Pre - 1881 Ancestry

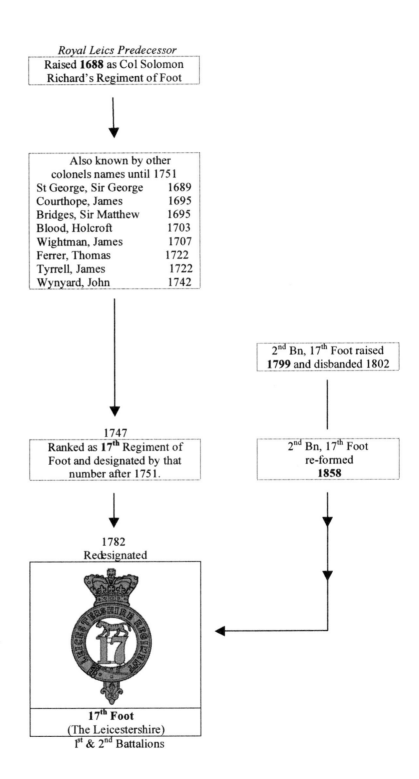

Royal Leics Predecessor

Raised **1688** as Col Solomon
Richard's Regiment of Foot

Also known by other
colonels names until 1751

St George, Sir George	1689
Courthope, James	1695
Bridges, Sir Matthew	1695
Blood, Holcroft	1703
Wightman, James	1707
Ferrer, Thomas	1722
Tyrrell, James	1722
Wynyard, John	1742

2nd Bn, 17th Foot raised
1799 and disbanded 1802

1747
Ranked as **17th** Regiment of
Foot and designated by that
number after 1751.

2nd Bn, 17th Foot
re-formed
1858

1782
Redesignated

17th Foot
(The Leicestershire)
1st & 2nd Battalions

5.2 1881 - 1957 Ancestry

1st & 2nd Battalions

17th Foot
(The Leicestershire)
1881

1st & 2nd Battalions

17th Foot
(The Leicestershire)

FC badge worn after 1898

The
Leicestershire Regiment

'Royal' in 1946

The Royal Leicestershire
Regiment

Notes on Regular Battalions

The Royal Leicestershire Regiment

The 2nd Bn was amalgamated with the 1st in 1948.

6. OTHER INFORMATION

				UNIFORM COAT COLOURS		
				(Used to differentiate Regiments of Foot in this section in 1768)		
		Foot No.	Post 1881 Identity	Facing Colour	Lace Colour	
		9	Norfolks (1st & 2nd Bns)	Yellow	White with two black stripes	
		10	Lincolns (1st & 2nd Bns)	Yellow	White with a blue stripe	
		12	Suffolks (1st & 2nd Bns)	Yellow	White with yellow, crimson and black stripes	
		16	Bedfordshires (1st & 2nd Bns)	Yellow	White with a crimson stripe	
		17	Leicestershires (1st & 2nd Bns)	White	White with two blue and one yellow stripe	
		44	Essex (1st Bn)	Yellow	white with blue, yellow and black stripes	
		48	Northamptonshires (1st Bn)	Buff	White with a black and a red stripe	
		56	Essex (2nd Bn)	Purple	White with a pink-coloured stripe	
		58	Northamptonshires (2nd Bn)	Black	White with a red stripe	

FACINGS

LACE

REST OF COAT IS RED

18th Century coat example indicates colour placings. Be aware, however, that tailoring differences exist between regiments.
After 1881, facing colours were standardised but some regts were allowed to re-introduce historic colours. The standardised colours were WHITE for English and Welsh regts, YELLOW for Scottish, GREEN for Irish and BLUE for 'Royal' regts.

THE YORKSHIRE REGIMENT

1. FORMATION (and Yorkshire Brigade Lineage)

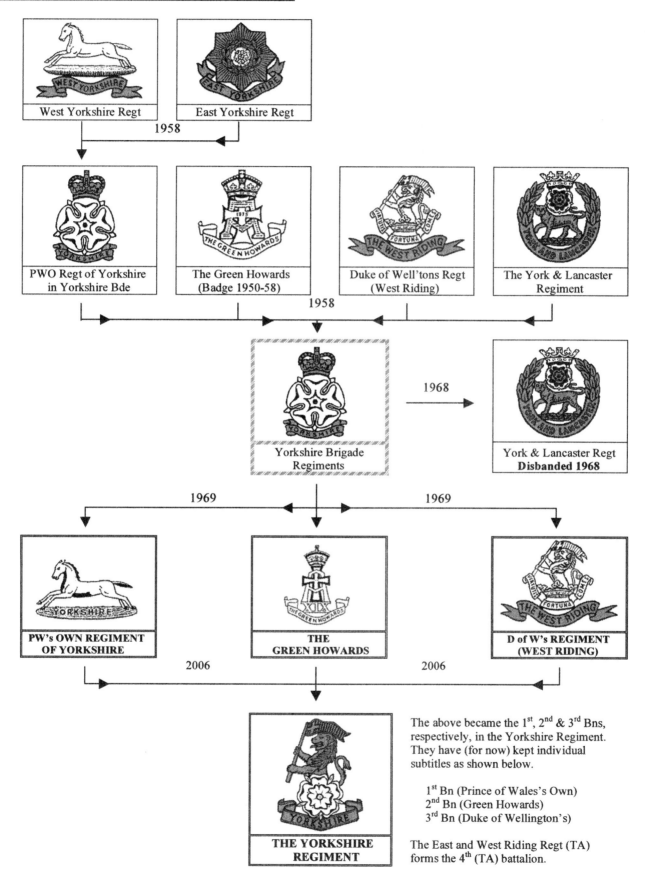

The above became the 1st, 2nd & 3rd Bns, respectively, in the Yorkshire Regiment. They have (for now) kept individual subtitles as shown below.

1st Bn (Prince of Wales's Own)
2nd Bn (Green Howards)
3rd Bn (Duke of Wellington's)

The East and West Riding Regt (TA) forms the 4th (TA) battalion.

2. WEST YORKSHIRE AND EAST YORKSHIRE REGIMENTS

2.1 Pre-1881 Ancestry

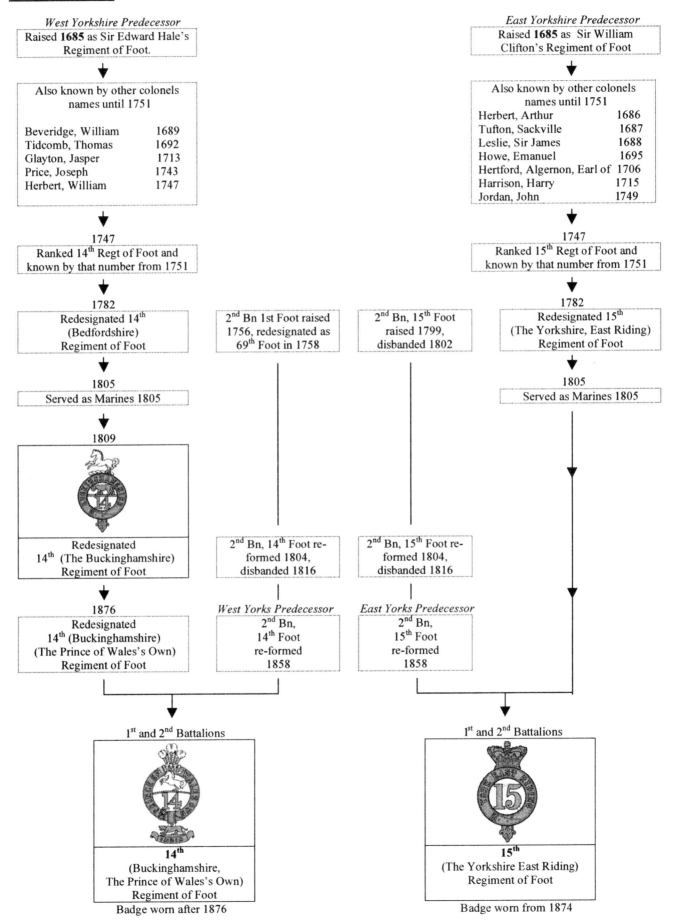

West Yorkshire Predecessor

Raised **1685** as Sir Edward Hale's Regiment of Foot.

↓

Also known by other colonels names until 1751

Beveridge, William	1689
Tidcomb, Thomas	1692
Glayton, Jasper	1713
Price, Joseph	1743
Herbert, William	1747

↓

1747
Ranked 14th Regt of Foot and known by that number from 1751

↓

1782
Redesignated 14th (Bedfordshire) Regiment of Foot

↓

1805
Served as Marines 1805

↓

1809
Redesignated 14th (The Buckinghamshire) Regiment of Foot

↓

1876
Redesignated 14th (Buckinghamshire) (The Prince of Wales's Own) Regiment of Foot

2nd Bn 1st Foot raised 1756, redesignated as 69th Foot in 1758

2nd Bn, 14th Foot re-formed 1804, disbanded 1816

West Yorks Predecessor
2nd Bn, 14th Foot re-formed 1858

2nd Bn, 15th Foot raised 1799, disbanded 1802

2nd Bn, 15th Foot re-formed 1804, disbanded 1816

East Yorks Predecessor
2nd Bn, 15th Foot re-formed 1858

East Yorkshire Predecessor

Raised **1685** as Sir William Clifton's Regiment of Foot

↓

Also known by other colonels names until 1751

Herbert, Arthur	1686
Tufton, Sackville	1687
Leslie, Sir James	1688
Howe, Emanuel	1695
Hertford, Algernon, Earl of	1706
Harrison, Harry	1715
Jordan, John	1749

↓

1747
Ranked 15th Regt of Foot and known by that number from 1751

↓

1782
Redesignated 15th (The Yorkshire, East Riding) Regiment of Foot

↓

1805
Served as Marines 1805

1st and 2nd Battalions

14th
(Buckinghamshire,
The Prince of Wales's Own)
Regiment of Foot
Badge worn after 1876

1st and 2nd Battalions

15th
(The Yorkshire East Riding)
Regiment of Foot
Badge worn from 1874

82

Regular Infantry Regiments   Yorkshire Regiment   West York & East York Components

2.2 1881 – 1958 Ancestry

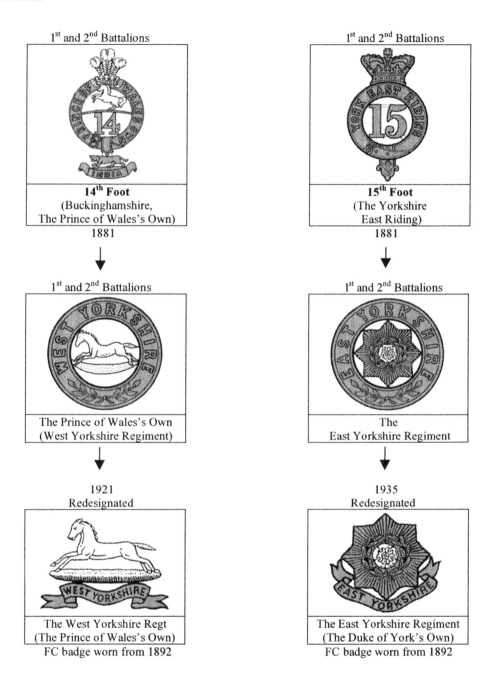

Notes on Regular Battalions

The West Yorkshire Regiment (The Prince of Wales's Own)

The 1st and 2nd battalions were merged in 1948 to form a composite 1st battalion.

The East Yorkshire Regiment (The Duke of York's Own)

The 1st and 2nd battalions were merged in 1948 to form a composite 1st battalion.

The Prince of Wales's Own Regiment of Yorkshire

The 1st battalions of the West and East Yorkshires amalgamated in 1958 (as shown in Part 1) to form the Prince of Wales's Own Regiment of Yorkshire.

83

3. THE GREEN HOWARDS AND THE DUKE OF WELLINGTON'S REGIMENT

3.1 Pre -1881 Ancestry

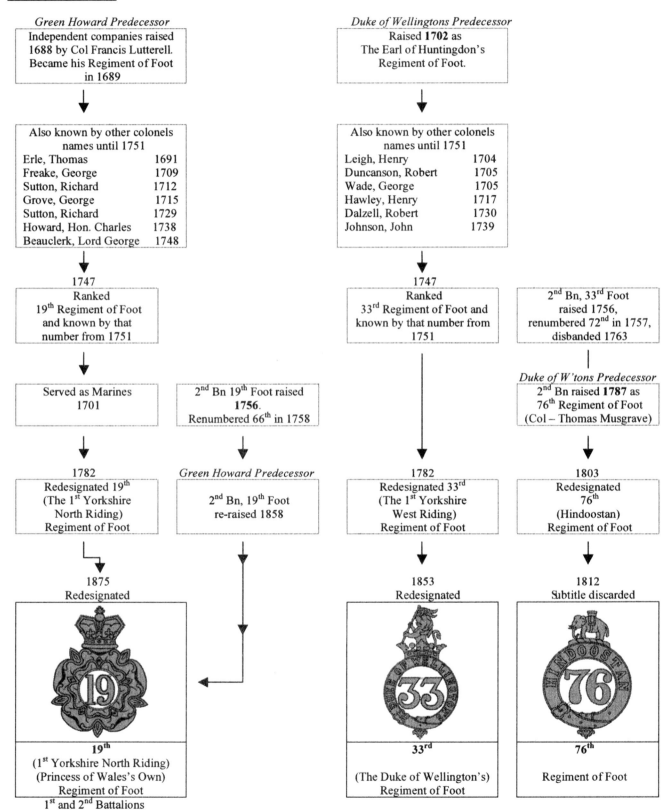

Green Howard Predecessor

Independent companies raised 1688 by Col Francis Lutterell. Became his Regiment of Foot in 1689

Duke of Wellingtons Predecessor

Raised **1702** as The Earl of Huntingdon's Regiment of Foot.

Also known by other colonels names until 1751
Erle, Thomas	1691
Freake, George	1709
Sutton, Richard	1712
Grove, George	1715
Sutton, Richard	1729
Howard, Hon. Charles	1738
Beauclerk, Lord George	1748

Also known by other colonels names until 1751
Leigh, Henry	1704
Duncanson, Robert	1705
Wade, George	1705
Hawley, Henry	1717
Dalzell, Robert	1730
Johnson, John	1739

1747
Ranked 19th Regiment of Foot and known by that number from 1751

1747
Ranked 33rd Regiment of Foot and known by that number from 1751

2nd Bn, 33rd Foot raised 1756, renumbered 72nd in 1757, disbanded 1763

Served as Marines 1701

2nd Bn 19th Foot raised **1756**. Renumbered 66th in 1758

Duke of W'tons Predecessor
2nd Bn raised **1787** as 76th Regiment of Foot (Col – Thomas Musgrave)

1782
Redesignated 19th (The 1st Yorkshire North Riding) Regiment of Foot

Green Howard Predecessor
2nd Bn, 19th Foot re-raised 1858

1782
Redesignated 33rd (The 1st Yorkshire West Riding) Regiment of Foot

1803
Redesignated 76th (Hindoostan) Regiment of Foot

1875
Redesignated

1853
Redesignated

1812
Subtitle discarded

19th
(1st Yorkshire North Riding) (Princess of Wales's Own) Regiment of Foot
1st and 2nd Battalions

33rd
(The Duke of Wellington's) Regiment of Foot

76th
Regiment of Foot

3.2   1881 – 1958 Ancestry

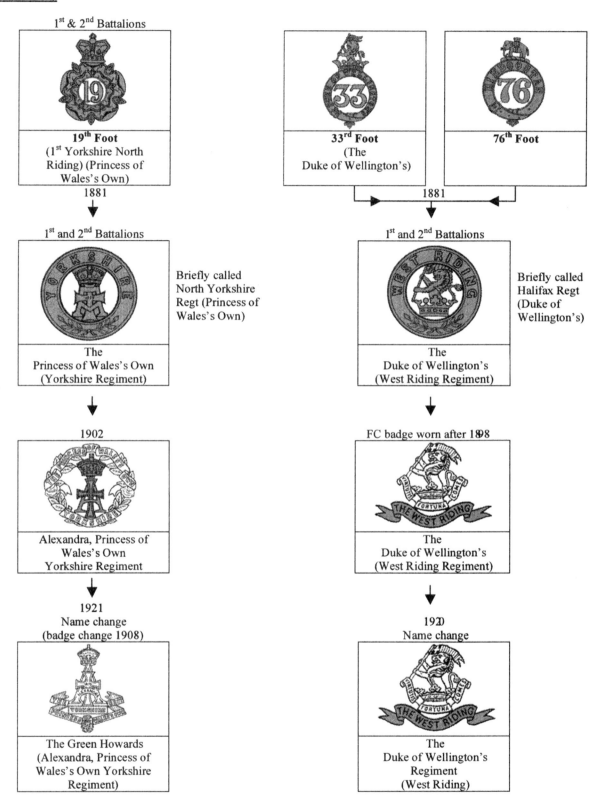

1st & 2nd Battalions

19th Foot
(1st Yorkshire North Riding) (Princess of Wales's Own)

1881

1st and 2nd Battalions

Briefly called North Yorkshire Regt (Princess of Wales's Own)

The Princess of Wales's Own (Yorkshire Regiment)

1902

Alexandra, Princess of Wales's Own Yorkshire Regiment

1921
Name change
(badge change 1908)

The Green Howards (Alexandra, Princess of Wales's Own Yorkshire Regiment)

33rd Foot
(The Duke of Wellington's)

76th Foot

1881

1st and 2nd Battalions

Briefly called Halifax Regt (Duke of Wellington's)

The Duke of Wellington's (West Riding Regiment)

FC badge worn after 1898

The Duke of Wellington's (West Riding Regiment)

1920
Name change

The Duke of Wellington's Regiment (West Riding)

Notes on Regular Battalions

Green Howards

The 2nd battalion was disbanded in 1949. Briefly reformed 1952 but put in suspended animation in 1956.

Duke of Wellington's Regiment

The 1st and 2nd battalions were merged in 1948 to form a composite 1st battalion.

4. YORK AND LANCASTER REGIMENT

4.1 Pre -1881 Ancestry

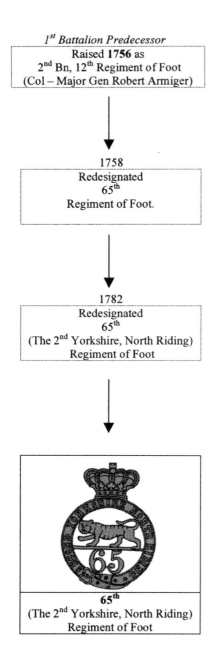

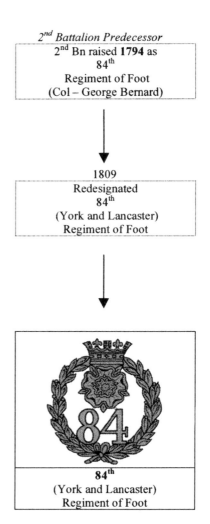

4.2   1881 – 1958 Ancestry

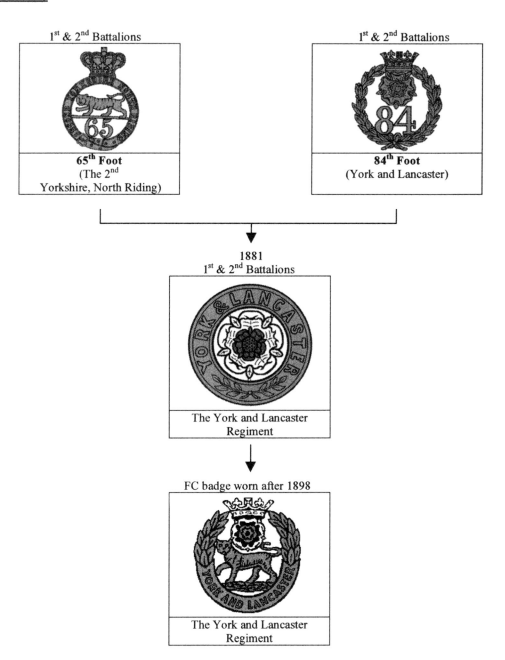

Notes on Regular Battalions

The 1st and 2nd battalions were merged in 1948 to form a composite 1st battalion.

The 2nd battalion was re-formed in 1952 then disbanded in 1955.

The **York and Lancaster Regiment**, itself, was **disbanded in 1968** as shown in subsection 1.

5. OTHER INFORMATION

		UNIFORM COAT COLOURS		
		(Used to differentiate Regiments of Foot in this section in 1768)		
	Foot No.	Post 1881 Identity	Facing Colour	Lace Colour
FACINGS	14	West Yorkshires (1st & 2nd Bns)	Buff	White with a blue stripe, red worm and buff stripe
	15	East Yorkshires (1st & 2nd Bns)	Yellow	White with a yellow and black worm and red stripe
	19	Ps of Wales's Own (Yorkshire) Regt (Green Howards) (1st & 2nd Bns)	Green	White with two stripes, red and green
LACE	33	Duke of Wellington's Regt (1st Bn)	Red	White with red stripe in middle
	65	York & Lancasters (1st Bn)	White	White with a red and black worm and a black stripe
	76*	Duke of Wellington's Regt (2nd Bn)	Red	-
REST OF COAT IS RED	84*	York & Lancasters (2nd Bn)	Yellow	-
		* colours not mentioned in 1768 Warrant?		

18th Century coat example indicates colour placings. Be aware, however, that tailoring differences exist between regiments.
After 1881, facing colours were standardised but some regts were allowed to re-introduce historic colours. The standardised colours were WHITE for English and Welsh regts, YELLOW for Scottish, GREEN for Irish and BLUE for 'Royal' regts.

THE MERCIAN REGIMENT

1. FORMATION (and Mercian Brigade Lineage)

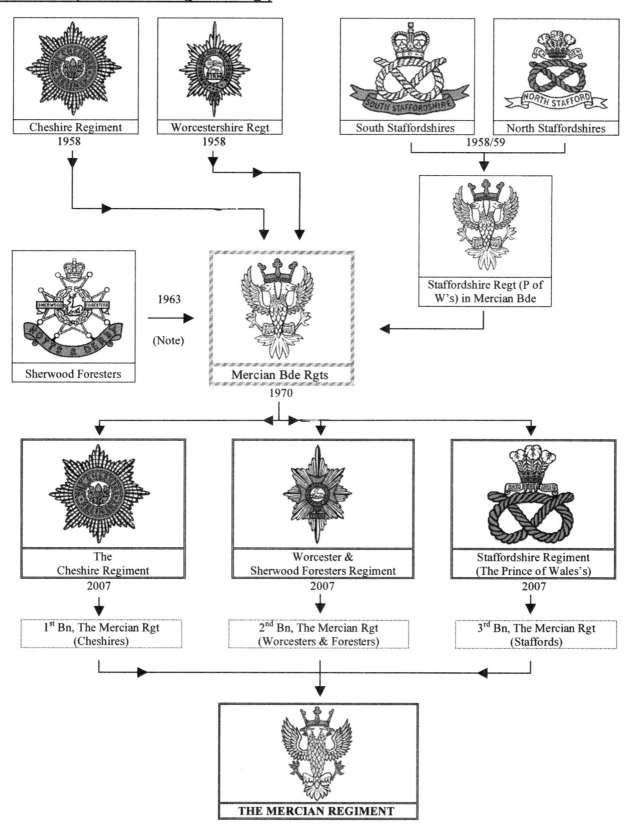

Note: The Sherwood Foresters joined the Mercian Brigade in 1963 (after the dissolution of the Foresters Brigade). In 1970 they merged with the Worcesters to form the Worcester and Sherwood Foresters Regt.

The 4th Mercian TA Bn was formed from the West Midlands Regt, plus elements from the King's and Cheshire Regt and the East of England Regt.

2. CHESHIRE REGIMENT

2.1 Pre-1881 Ancestry

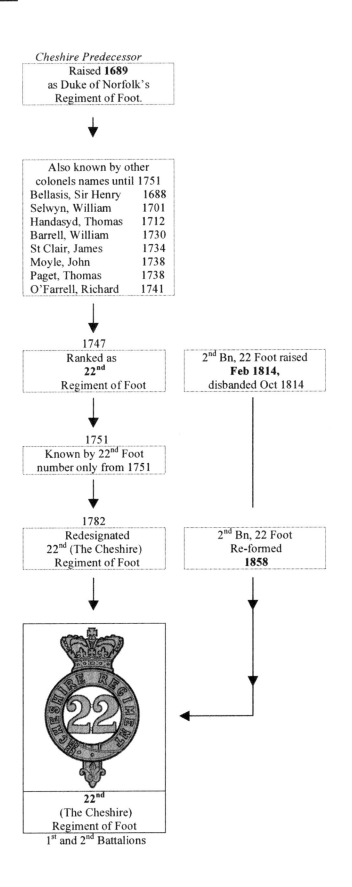

Cheshire Predecessor
Raised **1689**
as Duke of Norfolk's
Regiment of Foot.

Also known by other
colonels names until 1751
Bellasis, Sir Henry	1688
Selwyn, William	1701
Handasyd, Thomas	1712
Barrell, William	1730
St Clair, James	1734
Moyle, John	1738
Paget, Thomas	1738
O'Farrell, Richard	1741

1747
Ranked as
22nd
Regiment of Foot

2nd Bn, 22 Foot raised
Feb 1814,
disbanded Oct 1814

1751
Known by 22nd Foot
number only from 1751

1782
Redesignated
22nd (The Cheshire)
Regiment of Foot

2nd Bn, 22 Foot
Re-formed
1858

22nd
(The Cheshire)
Regiment of Foot
1st and 2nd Battalions

2.2   1881 – 1958 Ancestry

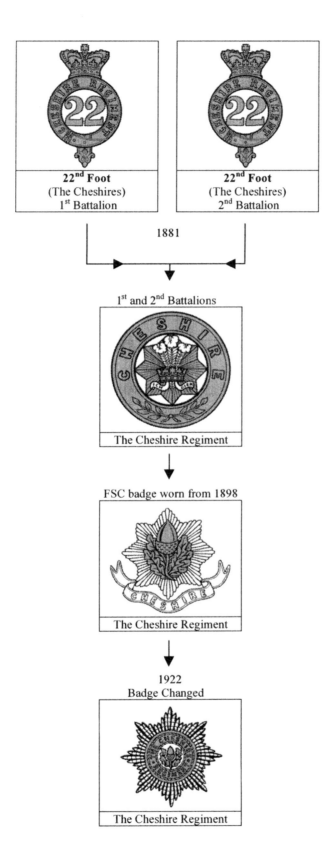

22nd Foot
(The Cheshires)
1st Battalion

22nd Foot
(The Cheshires)
2nd Battalion

1881

1st and 2nd Battalions

The Cheshire Regiment

FSC badge worn from 1898

The Cheshire Regiment

1922
Badge Changed

The Cheshire Regiment

Notes on Regular Battalions

The Cheshire Regiment

The 1st and 2nd battalions were merged in 1948 to form a composite 1st battalion.

3. WORCESTERSHIRE REGIMENT AND SHERWOOD FORESTERS (NOTTS & DERBY REGIMENT)

3.1 Pre-1881 Ancestry

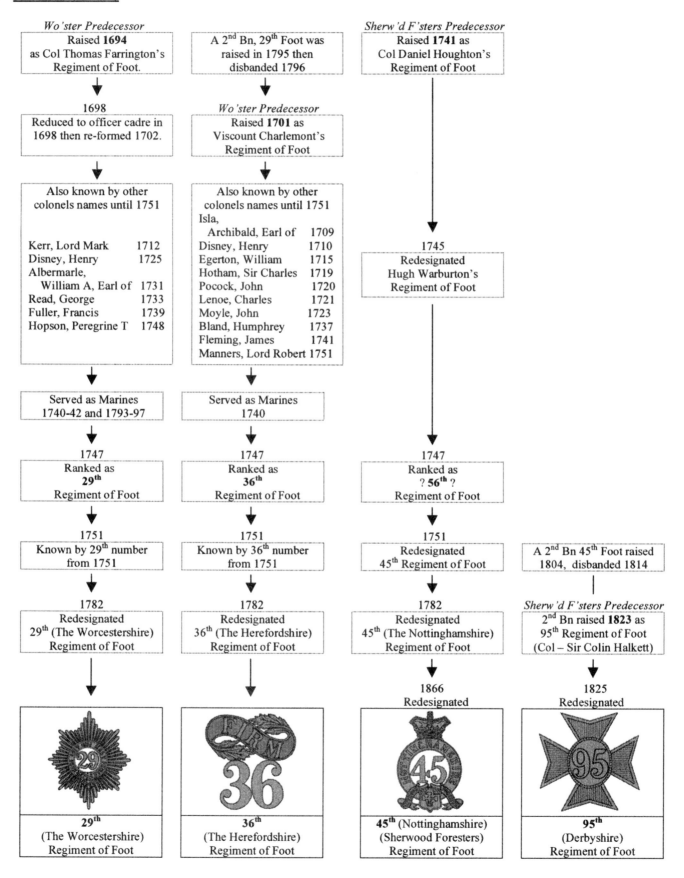

3.2 1881 – 1958 Ancestry

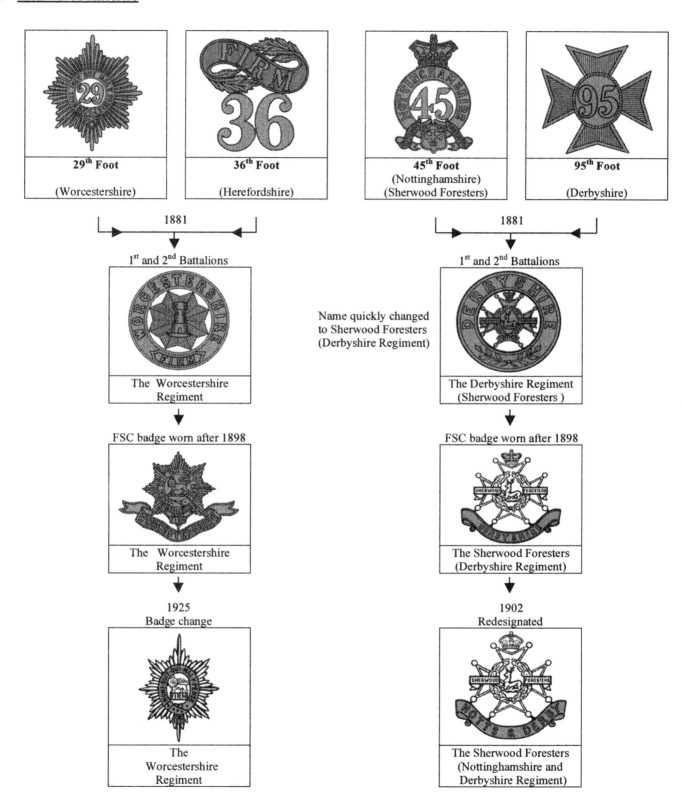

Notes on Regular Battalions

The Worcestershire Regiment

The 1st and 2nd battalions were merged in 1948 to form a composite 1st battalion.

The Sherwood Foresters (Nottinghamshire and Derbyshire Regiment)

The 1st and 2nd battalions were merged in 1948 to form a composite 1st battalion.

4. SOUTH STAFFORDSHIRE AND NORTH STAFFORDSHIRE REGIMENTS

4.1 Pre-1881 Ancestry

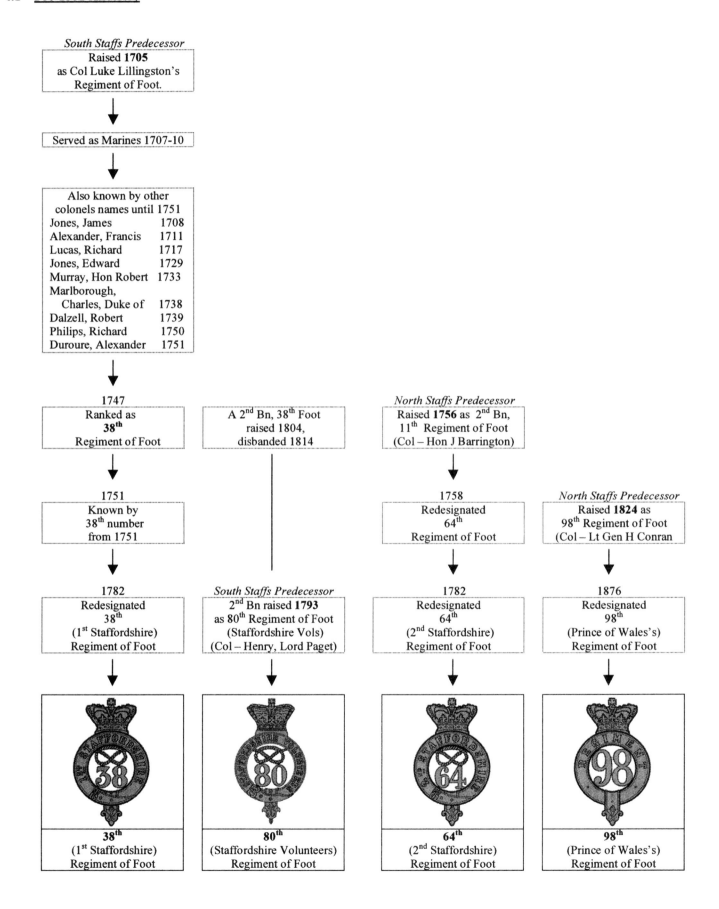

South Staffs Predecessor
Raised **1705**
as Col Luke Lillingston's
Regiment of Foot.

↓

Served as Marines 1707-10

↓

Also known by other
colonels names until 1751
Jones, James   1708
Alexander, Francis   1711
Lucas, Richard   1717
Jones, Edward   1729
Murray, Hon Robert   1733
Marlborough,
    Charles, Duke of   1738
Dalzell, Robert   1739
Philips, Richard   1750
Duroure, Alexander   1751

↓

1747
Ranked as
38th
Regiment of Foot

A 2nd Bn, 38th Foot
raised 1804,
disbanded 1814

North Staffs Predecessor
Raised **1756** as 2nd Bn,
11th Regiment of Foot
(Col – Hon J Barrington)

↓   ↓

1751
Known by
38th number
from 1751

1758
Redesignated
64th
Regiment of Foot

North Staffs Predecessor
Raised **1824** as
98th Regiment of Foot
(Col – Lt Gen H Conran

↓   ↓   ↓

1782
Redesignated
38th
(1st Staffordshire)
Regiment of Foot

South Staffs Predecessor
2nd Bn raised **1793**
as 80th Regiment of Foot
(Staffordshire Vols)
(Col – Henry, Lord Paget)

1782
Redesignated
64th
(2nd Staffordshire)
Regiment of Foot

1876
Redesignated
98th
(Prince of Wales's)
Regiment of Foot

↓   ↓   ↓   ↓

38th
(1st Staffordshire)
Regiment of Foot

80th
(Staffordshire Volunteers)
Regiment of Foot

64th
(2nd Staffordshire)
Regiment of Foot

98th
(Prince of Wales's)
Regiment of Foot

4.2   1881 – 1958 Ancestry

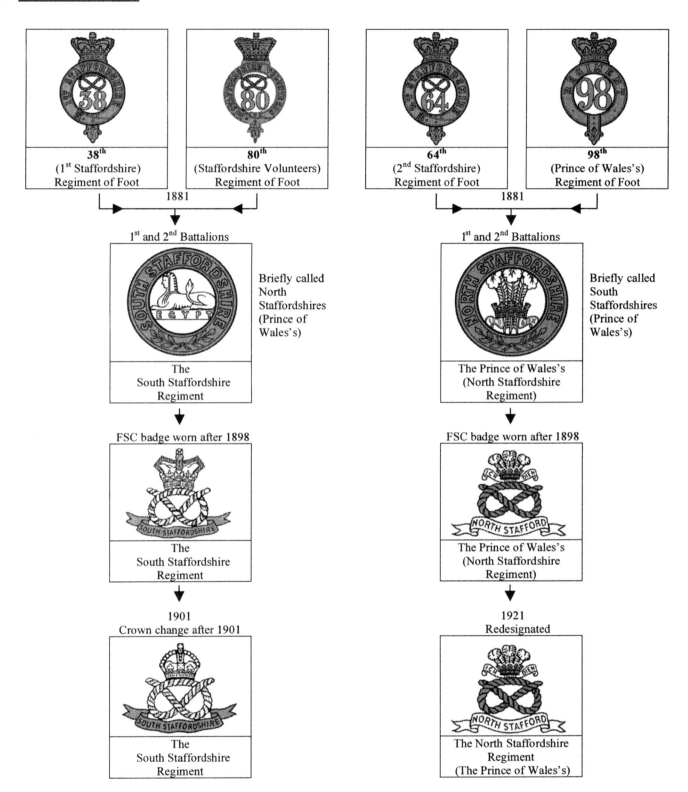

38th
(1st Staffordshire)
Regiment of Foot

80th
(Staffordshire Volunteers)
Regiment of Foot

64th
(2nd Staffordshire)
Regiment of Foot

98th
(Prince of Wales's)
Regiment of Foot

1881

1881

1st and 2nd Battalions

1st and 2nd Battalions

Briefly called
North
Staffordshires
(Prince of
Wales's)

Briefly called
South
Staffordshires
(Prince of
Wales's)

The
South Staffordshire
Regiment

The Prince of Wales's
(North Staffordshire
Regiment)

FSC badge worn after 1898

FSC badge worn after 1898

The
South Staffordshire
Regiment

The Prince of Wales's
(North Staffordshire
Regiment)

1901
Crown change after 1901

1921
Redesignated

The
South Staffordshire
Regiment

The North Staffordshire
Regiment
(The Prince of Wales's)

Notes on Regular Battalions

The South Staffordshire Regiment

The 1st and 2nd battalions were merged in 1948 to form a composite 1st battalion.

The North Staffordshire Regiment

The 1st and 2nd battalions were merged in 1949 to form a composite 1st battalion.

5. OTHER INFORMATION

<table>
<tr><td colspan="5">UNIFORM COAT COLOURS
(Used to differentiate Regiments of Foot in this section in 1768)</td></tr>
<tr><td rowspan="11">FACINGS

LACE

REST OF COAT IS RED</td><td>Foot
No.</td><td>Post 1881
Identity</td><td>Facing
Colour</td><td>Lace
Colour</td></tr>
<tr><td>22</td><td>Cheshire Regt (1st & 2nd Bns)</td><td>Buff</td><td>White with one blue and one red stripe</td></tr>
<tr><td>29</td><td>Worcestershires (1st Bn)</td><td>Yellow</td><td>White with two blue and one yellow stripe</td></tr>
<tr><td>36</td><td>Worcestershires (2nd Bn)</td><td>Green</td><td>White with one red and one green stripe</td></tr>
<tr><td>38</td><td>South Staffords (1st Bn)</td><td>Yellow</td><td>White with two red and one yellow stripe</td></tr>
<tr><td>45</td><td>Sherwood Foresters (1st Bn)</td><td>Green</td><td>White with a green stripe</td></tr>
<tr><td>64</td><td>North Staffords (1st Bn)</td><td>Black</td><td>White with a red and a black stripe</td></tr>
<tr><td>80*</td><td>South Staffords (2nd Bn)</td><td>Yellow</td><td>-</td></tr>
<tr><td>95*</td><td>Sherwood Foresters (2nd Bn)</td><td>Yellow</td><td>-</td></tr>
<tr><td>98*</td><td>North Staffords (2nd Bn)</td><td>White</td><td>-</td></tr>
<tr><td></td><td>*   colours not mentioned in 1768 Warrant?</td><td></td><td></td></tr>
<tr><td colspan="5">18th Century coat example indicates colour placings. Be aware, however, that tailoring differences exist between regiments.
After 1881, facing colours were standardised but some regts were allowed to re-introduce historic colours. The standardised colours were WHITE for English and Welsh regts, YELLOW for Scottish, GREEN for Irish and BLUE for 'Royal' regts.</td></tr>
</table>

THE ROYAL WELSH

1. FORMATION (and Welsh Brigade Lineage)

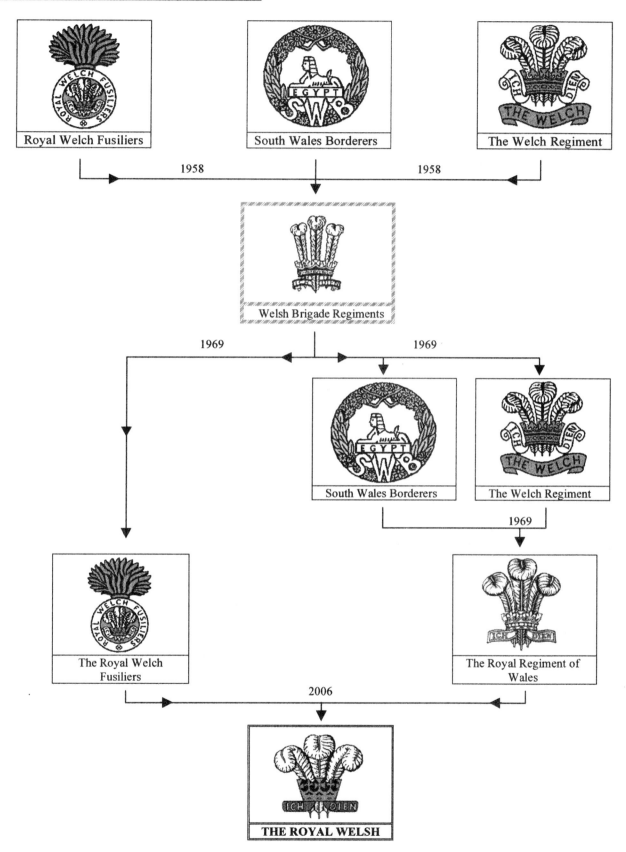

The two original regiments become two battalions in the Royal Welsh. The Royal Welsh *Regiment* (TA) became the 3rd (TA) Bn, Royal Welsh. The Royal Welsh *Regiment* (TA) was previously formed in 1999 by the amalgamation of Volunteer Bns of the Royal Welsh Fusiliers and the Royal Regiment of Wales.

2. ROYAL WELCH FUSILIERS AND SOUTH WALES BORDERERS

2.1 Pre-1881 Ancestry

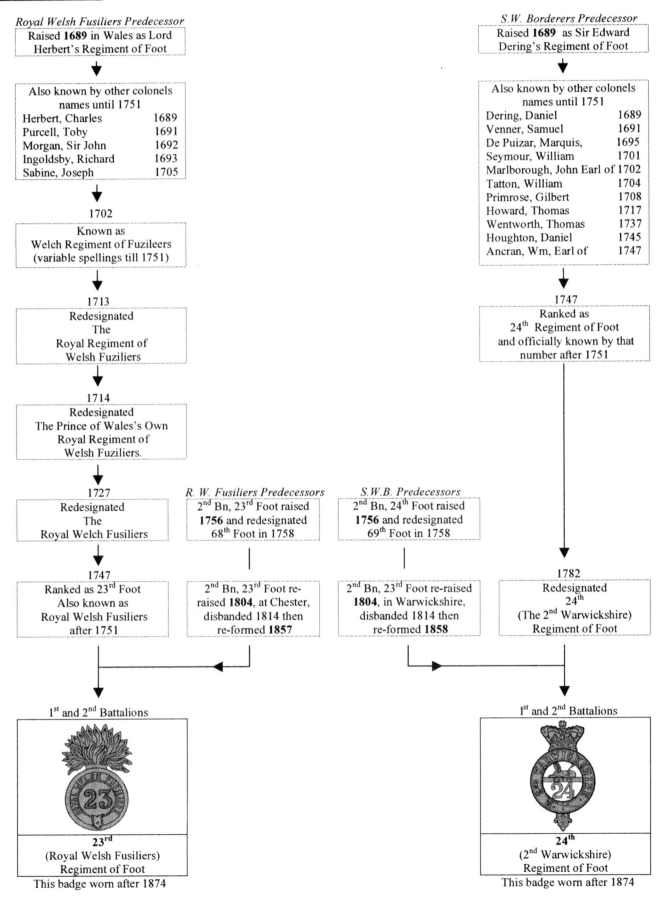

Royal Welsh Fusiliers Predecessor

Raised **1689** in Wales as Lord Herbert's Regiment of Foot

Also known by other colonels names until 1751
Herbert, Charles — 1689
Purcell, Toby — 1691
Morgan, Sir John — 1692
Ingoldsby, Richard — 1693
Sabine, Joseph — 1705

1702
Known as
Welch Regiment of Fuzileers
(variable spellings till 1751)

1713
Redesignated
The
Royal Regiment of
Welsh Fuziliers

1714
Redesignated
The Prince of Wales's Own
Royal Regiment of
Welsh Fuziliers.

1727
Redesignated
The
Royal Welch Fusiliers

1747
Ranked as 23rd Foot
Also known as
Royal Welsh Fusiliers
after 1751

S.W. Borderers Predecessor

Raised **1689** as Sir Edward Dering's Regiment of Foot

Also known by other colonels names until 1751
Dering, Daniel — 1689
Venner, Samuel — 1691
De Puizar, Marquis, — 1695
Seymour, William — 1701
Marlborough, John Earl of — 1702
Tatton, William — 1704
Primrose, Gilbert — 1708
Howard, Thomas — 1717
Wentworth, Thomas — 1737
Houghton, Daniel — 1745
Ancran, Wm, Earl of — 1747

1747
Ranked as
24th Regiment of Foot
and officially known by that
number after 1751

R. W. Fusiliers Predecessors

2nd Bn, 23rd Foot raised
1756 and redesignated
68th Foot in 1758

2nd Bn, 23rd Foot re-raised
1804, at Chester,
disbanded 1814 then
re-formed **1857**

S.W.B. Predecessors

2nd Bn, 24th Foot raised
1756 and redesignated
69th Foot in 1758

2nd Bn, 23rd Foot re-raised
1804, in Warwickshire,
disbanded 1814 then
re-formed **1858**

1782
Redesignated
24th
(The 2nd Warwickshire)
Regiment of Foot

1st and 2nd Battalions

23rd
(Royal Welsh Fusiliers)
Regiment of Foot
This badge worn after 1874

1st and 2nd Battalions

24th
(2nd Warwickshire)
Regiment of Foot
This badge worn after 1874

2.2 1881 – 1958 Ancestry

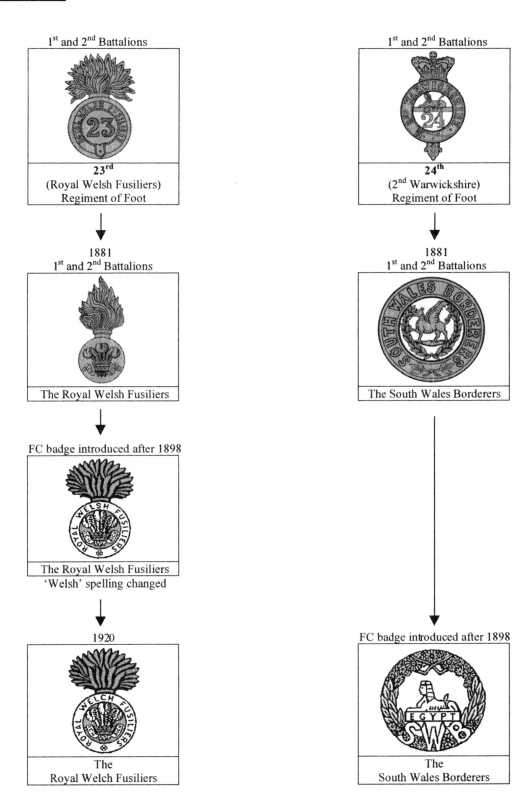

1st and 2nd Battalions

23rd
(Royal Welsh Fusiliers)
Regiment of Foot

1881
1st and 2nd Battalions

The Royal Welsh Fusiliers

FC badge introduced after 1898

The Royal Welsh Fusiliers
'Welsh' spelling changed

1920

The
Royal Welch Fusiliers

1st and 2nd Battalions

24th
(2nd Warwickshire)
Regiment of Foot

1881
1st and 2nd Battalions

The South Wales Borderers

FC badge introduced after 1898

The
South Wales Borderers

Notes on Regular Battalions

The Royal Welch Fusiliers : The 2nd battalion was disbanded in 1948.

The South Wales Borderers : The 2nd battalion was disbanded in 1948.

3.   THE WELCH REGIMENT

3.1   Pre -1881 Ancestry

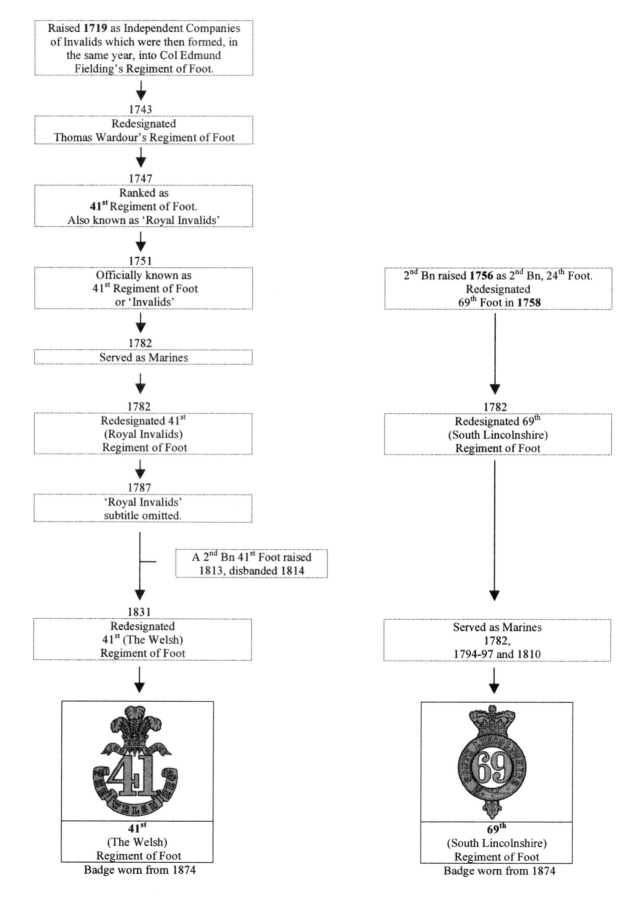

Raised **1719** as Independent Companies of Invalids which were then formed, in the same year, into Col Edmund Fielding's Regiment of Foot.

1743
Redesignated
Thomas Wardour's Regiment of Foot

1747
Ranked as
41st Regiment of Foot.
Also known as 'Royal Invalids'

1751
Officially known as
41st Regiment of Foot
or 'Invalids'

2nd Bn raised **1756** as 2nd Bn, 24th Foot.
Redesignated
69th Foot in **1758**

1782
Served as Marines

1782
Redesignated 41st
(Royal Invalids)
Regiment of Foot

1782
Redesignated 69th
(South Lincolnshire)
Regiment of Foot

1787
'Royal Invalids'
subtitle omitted.

A 2nd Bn 41st Foot raised
1813, disbanded 1814

1831
Redesignated
41st (The Welsh)
Regiment of Foot

Served as Marines
1782,
1794-97 and 1810

41st
(The Welsh)
Regiment of Foot
Badge worn from 1874

69th
(South Lincolnshire)
Regiment of Foot
Badge worn from 1874

3.2   1881 – 1958 Ancestry

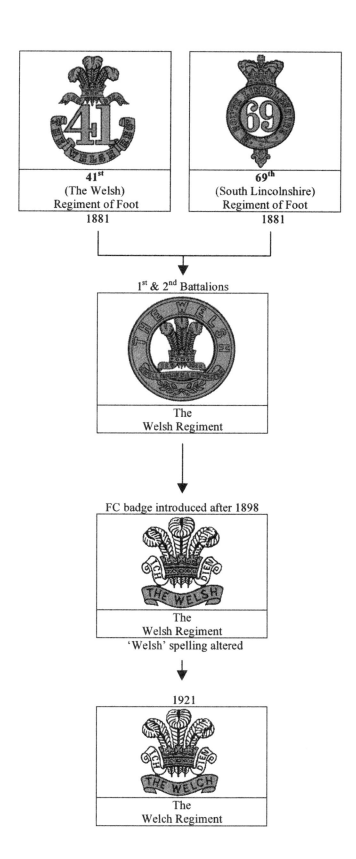

Notes on Regular Battalions

The 1st and 2nd battalions were merged in 1948 to form a composite 1st battalion.

4. OTHER INFORMATION

UNIFORM COAT COLOURS (Used to differentiate Regiments of Foot in this section in 1768)				
	Foot No.	Post 1881 Identity	Facing Colour	Lace Colour
	23	Royal Welsh Fusiliers (1st & 2nd Bs)	Blue	White with red, blue and yellow Stripes
	24	South Wales Borderers (1st & 2nd Bs)	Green	White with one red and one green Stripe
	41	Welsh Regiment (1st Bn) *	Blue*	Plain button holes
	69	Welsh Regiment (2nd Bn)	Green	White with one red and two green stripes
FACINGS LACE REST OF COAT IS RED		* Facing colour changed to red in 1789		

18th Century coat example indicates colour placings. Be aware, however, that tailoring differences exist between regiments. **After 1881, facing colours were standardised but some regts were allowed to re-introduce historic colours. The standardised colours were WHITE for English and Welsh regts, YELLOW for Scottish, GREEN for Irish and BLUE for 'Royal' regts.**

THE ROYAL IRISH REGIMENT

1. FORMATION (and North Irish Brigade Lineage)

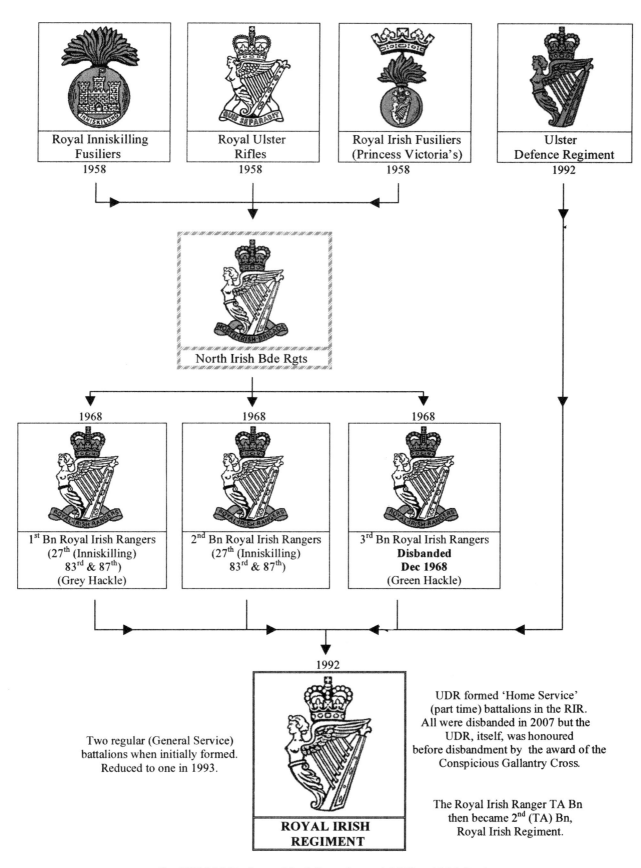

See 'Old Irish Regiments' for information on 'old' Royal Irish Regiment.

2. ROYAL INNISKILLING FUSILIERS AND ROYAL ULSTER RIFLES

2.1 Pre-1881 Ancestry

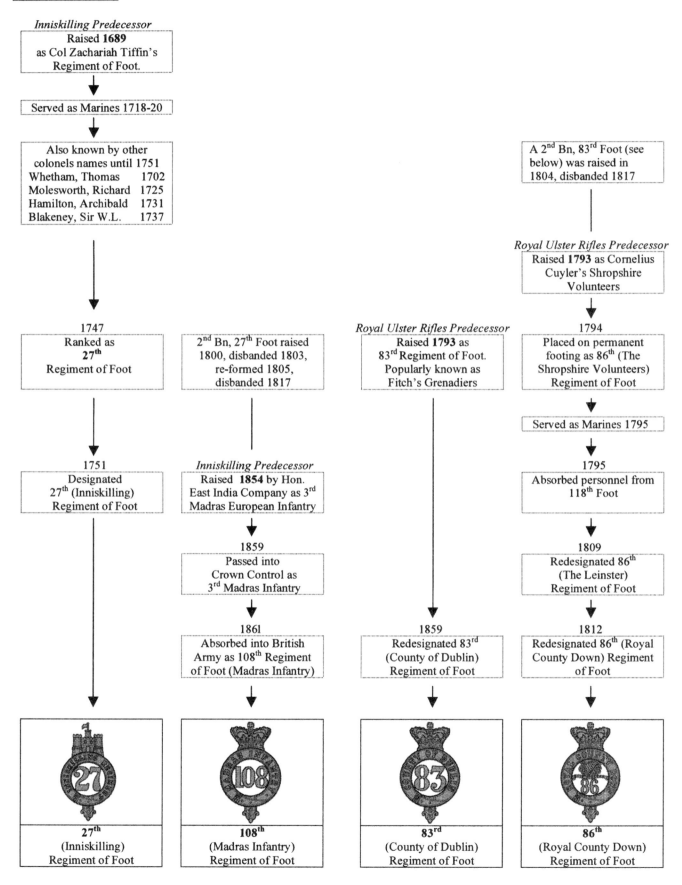

Inniskilling Predecessor
Raised **1689**
as Col Zachariah Tiffin's
Regiment of Foot.

Served as Marines 1718-20

Also known by other
colonels names until 1751
Whetham, Thomas   1702
Molesworth, Richard   1725
Hamilton, Archibald   1731
Blakeney, Sir W.L.   1737

A 2nd Bn, 83rd Foot (see
below) was raised in
1804, disbanded 1817

Royal Ulster Rifles Predecessor
Raised **1793** as Cornelius
Cuyler's Shropshire
Volunteers

1747
Ranked as
27th
Regiment of Foot

2nd Bn, 27th Foot raised
1800, disbanded 1803,
re-formed 1805,
disbanded 1817

Royal Ulster Rifles Predecessor
Raised **1793** as
83rd Regiment of Foot.
Popularly known as
Fitch's Grenadiers

1794
Placed on permanent
footing as 86th (The
Shropshire Volunteers)
Regiment of Foot

Served as Marines 1795

1751
Designated
27th (Inniskilling)
Regiment of Foot

Inniskilling Predecessor
Raised **1854** by Hon.
East India Company as 3rd
Madras European Infantry

1795
Absorbed personnel from
118th Foot

1859
Passed into
Crown Control as
3rd Madras Infantry

1809
Redesignated 86th
(The Leinster)
Regiment of Foot

1861
Absorbed into British
Army as 108th Regiment
of Foot (Madras Infantry)

1859
Redesignated 83rd
(County of Dublin)
Regiment of Foot

1812
Redesignated 86th (Royal
County Down) Regiment
of Foot

27th
(Inniskilling)
Regiment of Foot

108th
(Madras Infantry)
Regiment of Foot

83rd
(County of Dublin)
Regiment of Foot

86th
(Royal County Down)
Regiment of Foot

2.2   1881 – 1958 Ancestry

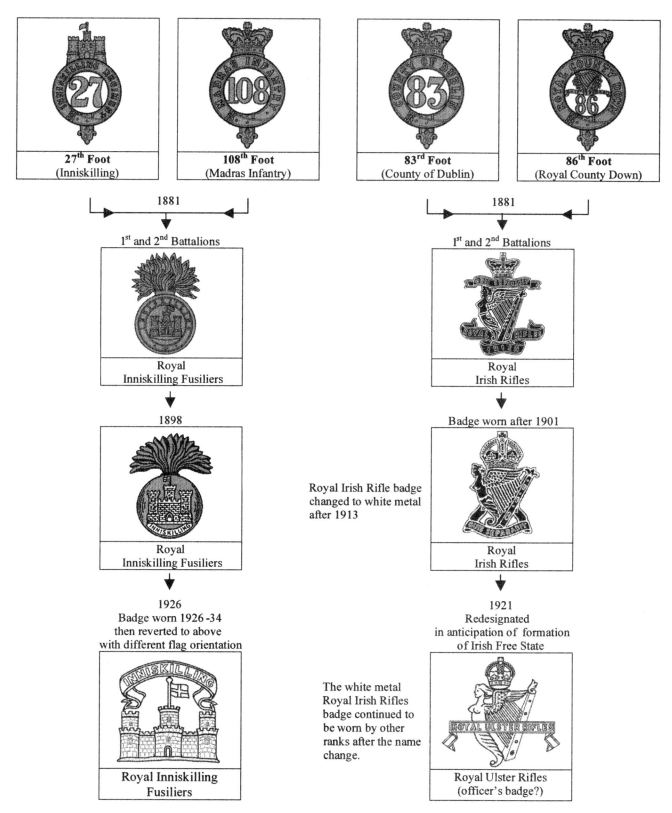

Notes on Regular Battalions

Royal Inniskilling Fusiliers

The 2nd Bn was disbanded in 1922 then re-formed in 1937. Disbanded again in 1948, re-formed in 1952 then effectively disbanded in 1956.

Royal Ulster Rifles

The 1st and 2nd battalions were merged in 1948 to form a composite 1st battalion.

3. ROYAL IRISH FUSILIERS AND ULSTER DEFENCE REGIMENT

3.1 Pre-1881 Ancestry

The Ulster Defence Regiment was formed in 1970 to replace Ulster Special Constabulary units (B Specials). Consequently, as an army unit, it does not have any pre-1881 ancestry and does not feature in this subsection.

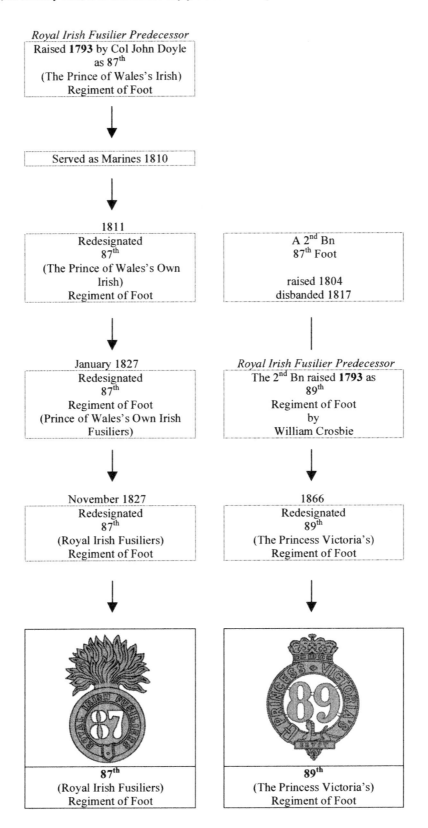

3.2   1881 – 1958 Ancestry (UDR from 1970)

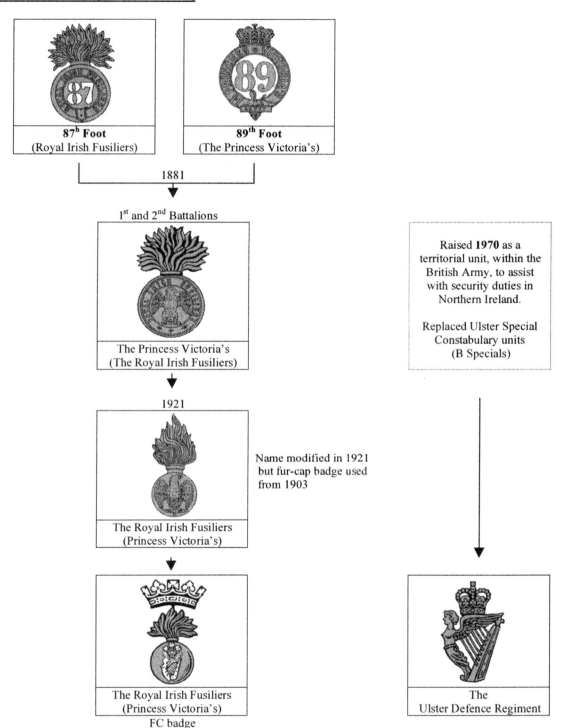

87^h Foot
(Royal Irish Fusiliers)

89th Foot
(The Princess Victoria's)

1881

1st and 2nd Battalions

The Princess Victoria's
(The Royal Irish Fusiliers)

1921

The Royal Irish Fusiliers
(Princess Victoria's)

Name modified in 1921
but fur-cap badge used
from 1903

The Royal Irish Fusiliers
(Princess Victoria's)
FC badge

Raised **1970** as a
territorial unit, within the
British Army, to assist
with security duties in
Northern Ireland.

Replaced Ulster Special
Constabulary units
(B Specials)

The
Ulster Defence Regiment

Notes on Regular Battalions

The Royal Irish Fusiliers (Princess Victoria's)

The 1st and 2nd battalions were merged in 1948 to form a composite 1st battalion.

The Ulster Defence Regiment

This was, in it's time, the largest regiment in the army. It was originally formed with seven battalions with others added later. It wasn't a regular army unit so, strictly speaking, it should not be in this volume. However, it eventually merged with a regular army unit (The Royal Irish Rangers) to form the new 'Royal Irish Regiment'. It provided so-called 'Home Battalions' within that regiment until the 'Home Battalions' were disbanded in 2007 (See Part 1 of this Section).

4. OTHER INFORMATION

UNIFORM COAT COLOURS				
(Used to differentiate Regiments of Foot in this section in 1768)				
	Foot No.	Post 1881 Identity	Facing Colour	Lace Colour
	27	Royal Inniskilling Fusiliers (1st Bn)	Buff	White with one blue and one red Stripe
	83*	Royal Irish Rifles (1st Bn)	Yellow	-
	86*	Royal Irish Rifles (2nd Bn)	Blue	-
	87*	Royal Irish Fusiliers (1st Bn)	Blue	-
	89*	Royal Irish Fusiliers (2nd Bn)	Black	-
	108*	Royal Inniskilling Fusiliers (2nd Bn)	Yellow	-
FACINGS / LACE / REST OF COAT IS RED		* colours not mentioned in 1768 Warrant?		

18th Century coat example indicates colour placings. Be aware, however, that tailoring differences exist between regiments.
After 1881, facing colours were standardised but some regts were allowed to re-introduce historic colours. The standardised colours were WHITE for English and Welsh regts, YELLOW for Scottish, GREEN for Irish and BLUE for 'Royal' regts.

THE ROYAL GURKHA RIFLES

1. FORMATION

At the start of the 20th century there were ten numbered regiments of Gurkha Rifles in the Indian Army (with an 11th briefly in existence between 1919 and 1920). With the advent of Indian independence in 1947, four were transferred to the British Army, in January 1948, and the rest remained with the (new) Indian Army. The following ancestry guide refers to the transferred four.

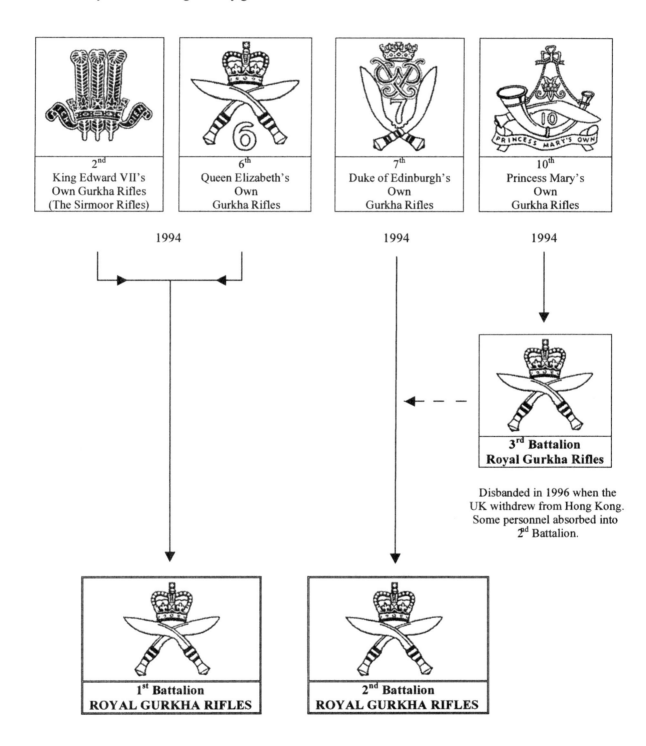

2nd	6th	7th	10th
King Edward VII's Own Gurkha Rifles (The Sirmoor Rifles)	Queen Elizabeth's Own Gurkha Rifles	Duke of Edinburgh's Own Gurkha Rifles	Princess Mary's Own Gurkha Rifles

1994   1994   1994

3rd Battalion Royal Gurkha Rifles

Disbanded in 1996 when the UK withdrew from Hong Kong. Some personnel absorbed into 2[d] Battalion.

1st Battalion ROYAL GURKHA RIFLES

2nd Battalion ROYAL GURKHA RIFLES

2. Ancestry

2.1 Pre-1904 Ancestry

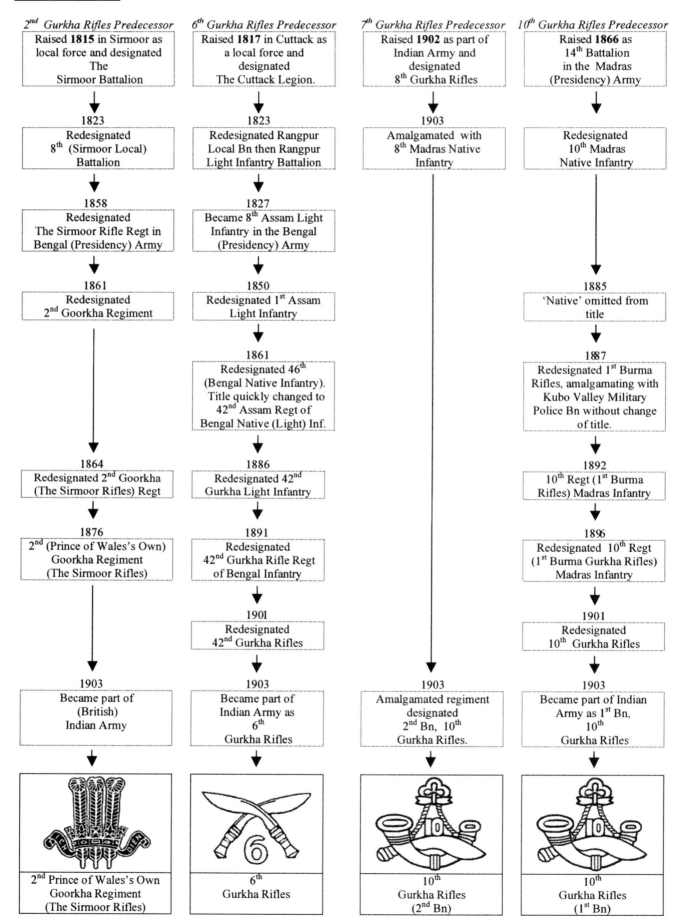

2.2 Post-1904 Ancestry

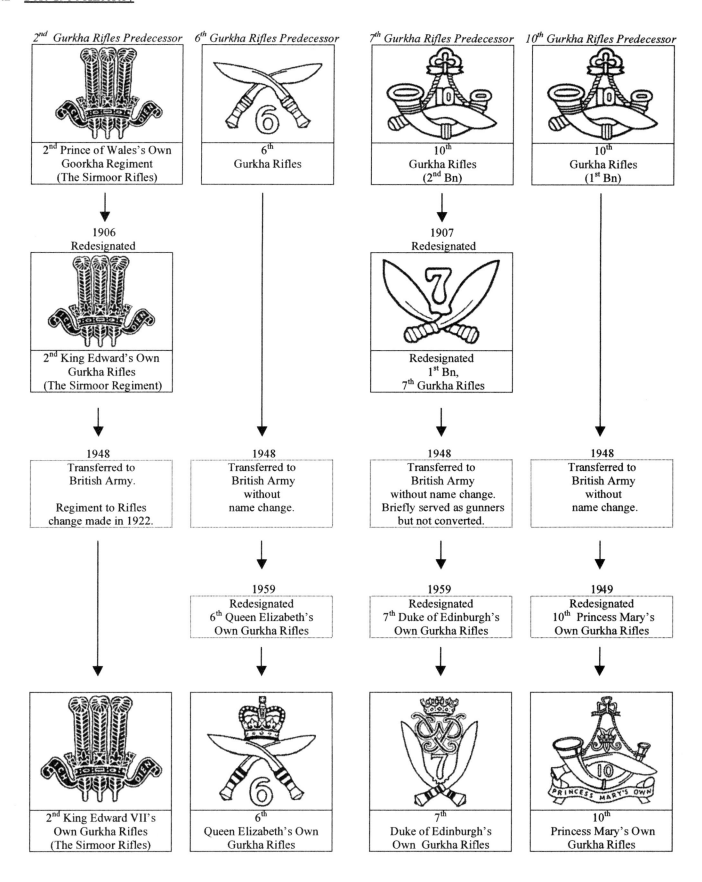

3. OTHER INFORMATION

The Gurkha Rifles were grouped into a brigade with their own support services.   As the latter were specifically Gurkha in character, they have been outlined here instead of in the part addressing Arms and Services. Representative badges and names are given below.

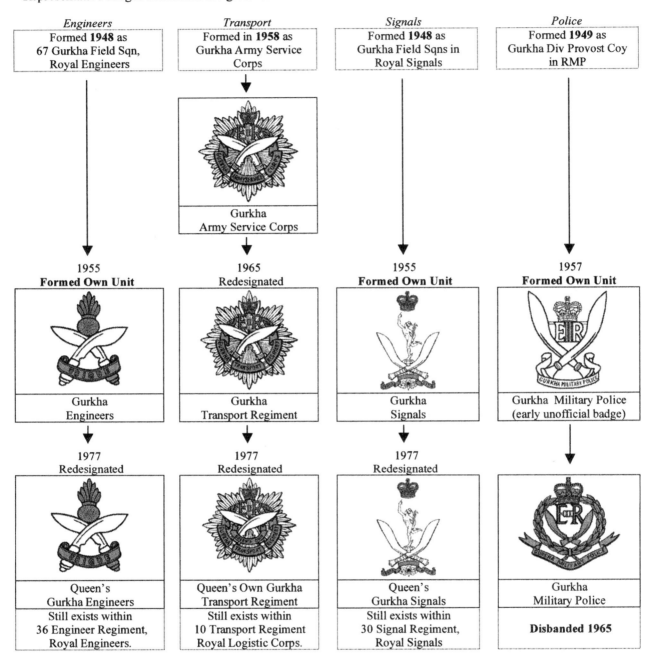

Engineers	*Transport*	*Signals*	*Police*
Formed **1948** as 67 Gurkha Field Sqn, Royal Engineers	Formed in **1958** as Gurkha Army Service Corps	Formed **1948** as Gurkha Field Sqns in Royal Signals	Formed **1949** as Gurkha Div Provost Coy in RMP

Gurkha Army Service Corps

1955 **Formed Own Unit**	1965 Redesignated	1955 **Formed Own Unit**	1957 **Formed Own Unit**
Gurkha Engineers	Gurkha Transport Regiment	Gurkha Signals	Gurkha Military Police (early unofficial badge)

1977 Redesignated	1977 Redesignated	1977 Redesignated	
Queen's Gurkha Engineers	Queen's Own Gurkha Transport Regiment	Queen's Gurkha Signals	Gurkha Military Police
Still exists within 36 Engineer Regiment, Royal Engineers.	Still exists within 10 Transport Regiment Royal Logistic Corps.	Still exists within 30 Signal Regiment, Royal Signals	**Disbanded 1965**

Other units were also formed – as shown below

Gurkha Staff Band

Gurkha Parachute Company
Formed 1961
Disbanded 1970

Gurkha Boys Company

THE RIFLES

1. FORMATION

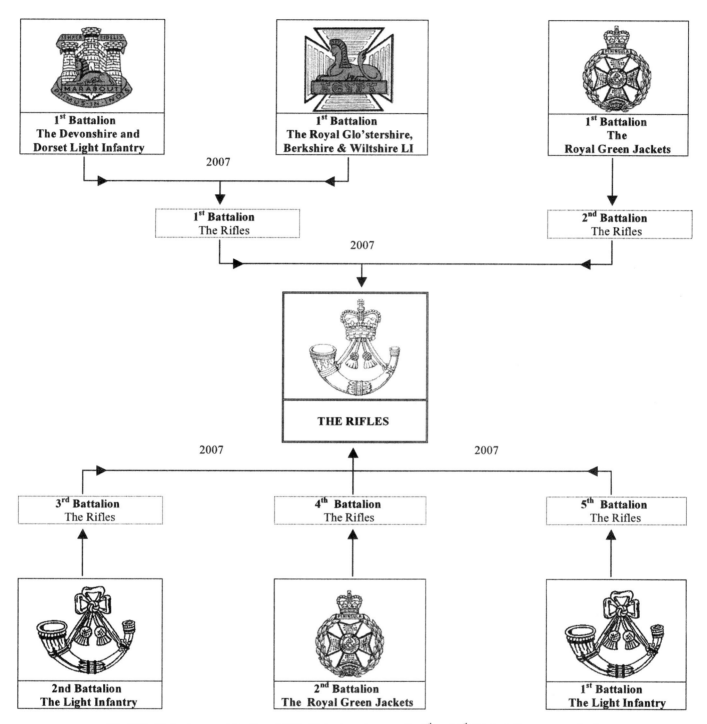

The Rifle Volunteers and the Royal Rifle Volunteers became the 6th and 7th TA battalions, respectively.

The above are descendents of (almost all) the constituents of three '1958' Brigades:- Wessex, Green Jackets and Light Infantry. As such, they are the concentrated essence of 21 Regiments of Foot plus the (un-numbered) Rifle Brigade. Because of the numbers involved, ancestral details in the rest of the section have been subdivided as follows:-

Devon & Dorsets LI,   Royal Gloster, Berks & Wilts LI,   All Royal Green Jacket Components,   All Light Infantry Components

In addition, each subdivision starts with lineage details of the associated '1958' Brigade.

2. DEVONSHIRE AND DORSET LIGHT INFANTRY COMPONENTS

2.1 Wessex Brigade and Post - 1957 Lineage

The Glos'ter, Berks, Wilts and Hants regiments have been included to show the Wessex Brigade inter-relationships.

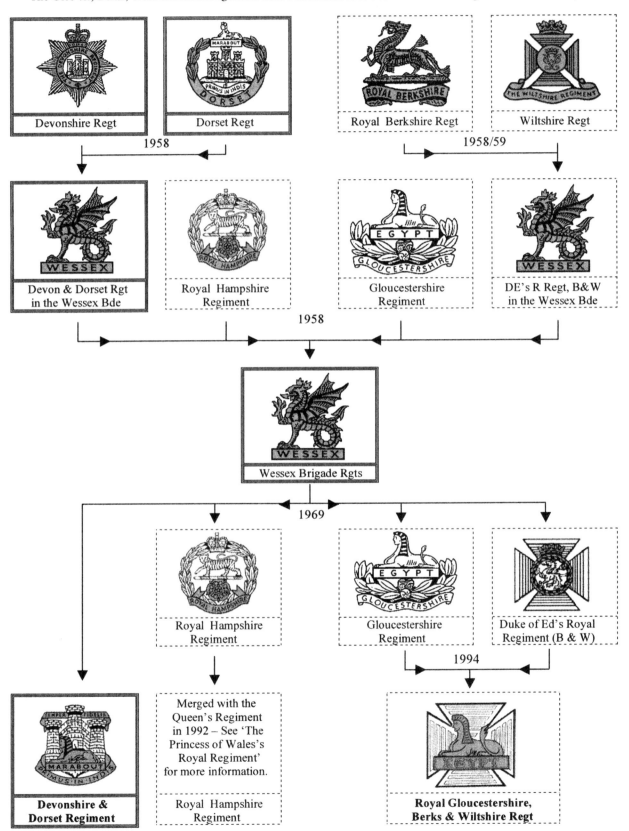

The Devon and Dorset Regt and the Royal Gloster, Berks and Wilts Regt were converted to Light Infantry in 2005.

2.2 Pre- 1881 ancestry

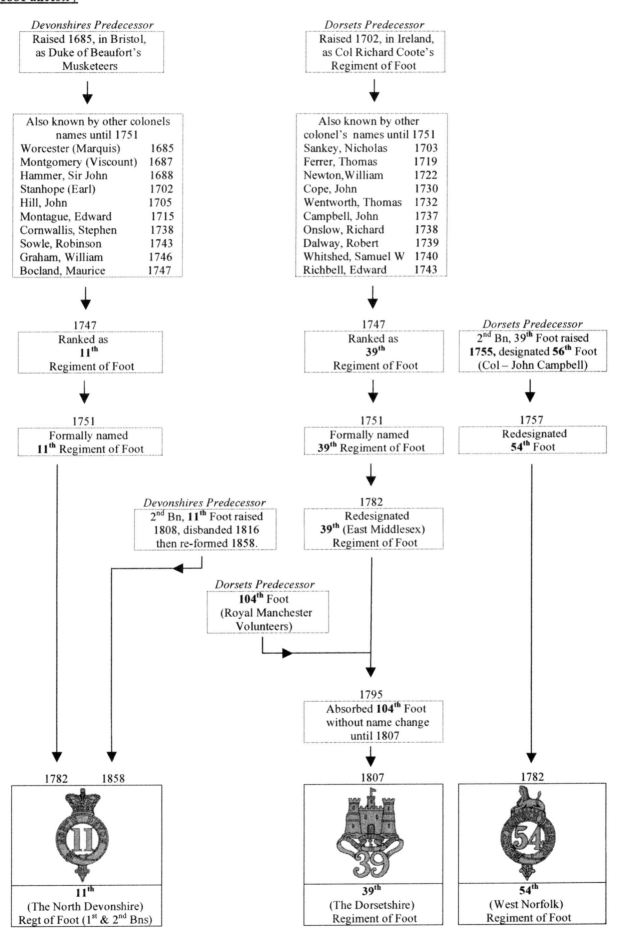

Devonshires Predecessor
Raised 1685, in Bristol,
as Duke of Beaufort's
Musketeers

Dorsets Predecessor
Raised 1702, in Ireland,
as Col Richard Coote's
Regiment of Foot

Also known by other colonels
names until 1751
Worcester (Marquis)   1685
Montgomery (Viscount) 1687
Hammer, Sir John   1688
Stanhope (Earl)   1702
Hill, John   1705
Montague, Edward   1715
Cornwallis, Stephen   1738
Sowle, Robinson   1743
Graham, William   1746
Bocland, Maurice   1747

Also known by other
colonel's names until 1751
Sankey, Nicholas   1703
Ferrer, Thomas   1719
Newton, William   1722
Cope, John   1730
Wentworth, Thomas   1732
Campbell, John   1737
Onslow, Richard   1738
Dalway, Robert   1739
Whitshed, Samuel W   1740
Richbell, Edward   1743

1747
Ranked as
11th
Regiment of Foot

1747
Ranked as
39th
Regiment of Foot

Dorsets Predecessor
2nd Bn, 39th Foot raised
1755, designated 56th Foot
(Col – John Campbell)

1751
Formally named
11th Regiment of Foot

1751
Formally named
39th Regiment of Foot

1757
Redesignated
54th Foot

Devonshires Predecessor
2nd Bn, 11th Foot raised
1808, disbanded 1816
then re-formed 1858.

1782
Redesignated
39th (East Middlesex)
Regiment of Foot

Dorsets Predecessor
104th Foot
(Royal Manchester
Volunteers)

1795
Absorbed 104th Foot
without name change
until 1807

1782   1858

11th
(The North Devonshire)
Regt of Foot (1st & 2nd Bns)

1807

39th
(The Dorsetshire)
Regiment of Foot

1782

54th
(West Norfolk)
Regiment of Foot

2.3   1881 – 1957   Ancestry

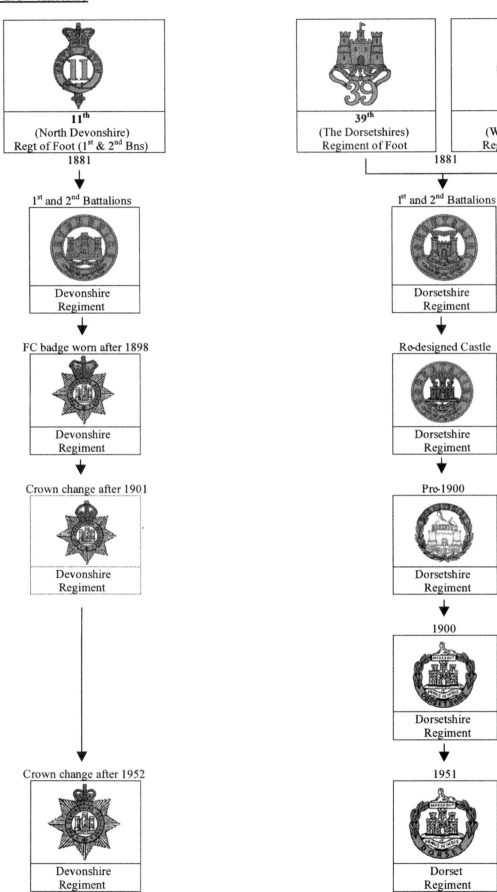

11th
(North Devonshire)
Regt of Foot (1st & 2nd Bns)
1881

1st and 2nd Battalions

Devonshire
Regiment

FC badge worn after 1898

Devonshire
Regiment

Crown change after 1901

Devonshire
Regiment

Crown change after 1952

Devonshire
Regiment

39th
(The Dorsetshires)
Regiment of Foot

54th
(West Norfolk)
Regiment of Foot

1881

1st and 2nd Battalions

Dorsetshire
Regiment

Re-designed Castle

Dorsetshire
Regiment

Pre-1900

Dorsetshire
Regiment

1900

Dorsetshire
Regiment

1951

Dorset
Regiment

Notes on Regular Battalions

Devonshire Regiment
2nd battalion disbanded in 1948.

Dorset Regiment
1st and 2nd Battalions amalgamated in 1948 to form 1st Bn.

3. ROYAL GLOUCESTERSHIRE, BERKSHIRE AND WILTSHIRE COMPONENTS

3.1 Wessex Brigade and Post - 1957 Lineage

The Devon, Dorset and Hants regiments have been included to show the Wessex Brigade inter-relationships.

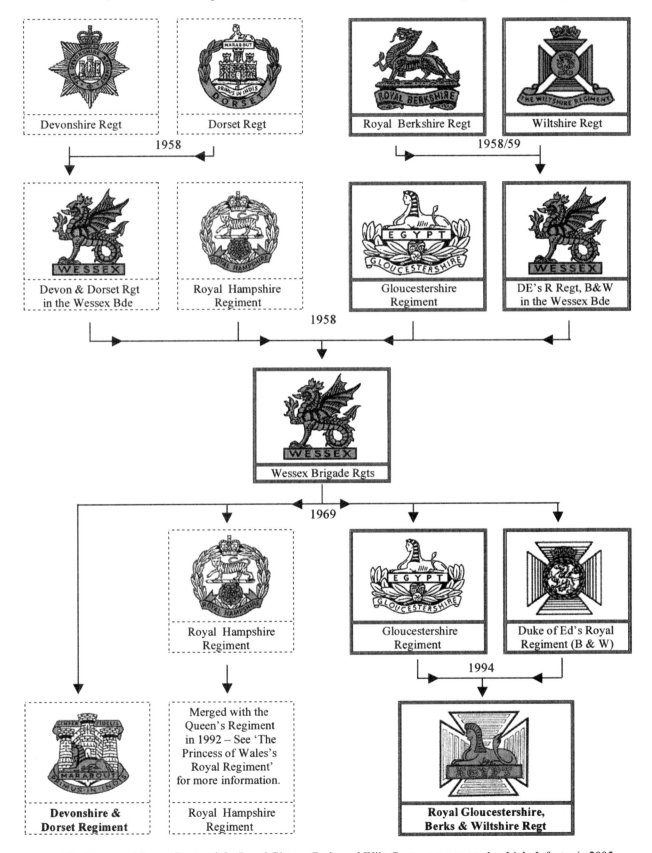

The Devon and Dorset Regt and the Royal Gloster, Berks and Wilts Regt were converted to Light Infantry in 2005.

3.2 Pre- 1881 Ancestry

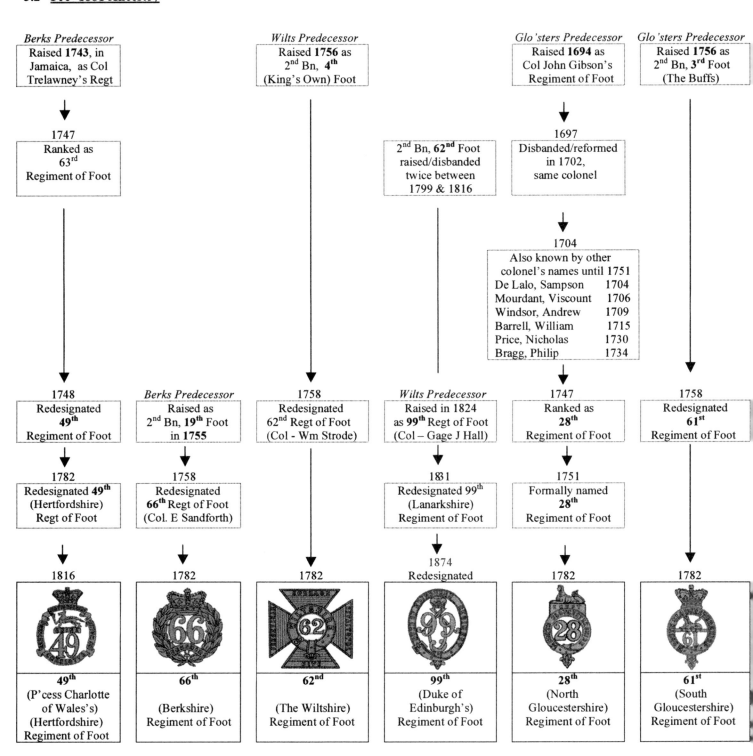

Berks Predecessor
Raised **1743**, in Jamaica, as Col Trelawney's Regt

1747
Ranked as **63rd** Regiment of Foot

Wilts Predecessor
Raised **1756** as 2nd Bn, **4th** (King's Own) Foot

Glo'sters Predecessor
Raised **1694** as Col John Gibson's Regiment of Foot

Glo'sters Predecessor
Raised **1756** as 2nd Bn, **3rd** Foot (The Buffs)

2nd Bn, **62nd** Foot raised/disbanded twice between 1799 & 1816

1697
Disbanded/reformed in 1702, same colonel

1704
Also known by other colonel's names until 1751
De Lalo, Sampson 1704
Mourdant, Viscount 1706
Windsor, Andrew 1709
Barrell, William 1715
Price, Nicholas 1730
Bragg, Philip 1734

1748
Redesignated **49th** Regiment of Foot

Berks Predecessor
Raised as 2nd Bn, **19th** Foot in **1755**

1758
Redesignated **62nd** Regt of Foot (Col - Wm Strode)

Wilts Predecessor
Raised in 1824 as **99th** Regt of Foot (Col – Gage J Hall)

1747
Ranked as **28th** Regiment of Foot

1758
Redesignated **61st** Regiment of Foot

1782
Redesignated **49th** (Hertfordshire) Regt of Foot

1758
Redesignated **66th** Regt of Foot (Col. E Sandforth)

1831
Redesignated 99th (Lanarkshire) Regiment of Foot

1751
Formally named **28th** Regiment of Foot

1816
49th (P'cess Charlotte of Wales's) (Hertfordshire) Regiment of Foot

1782
66th (Berkshire) Regiment of Foot

1782
62nd (The Wiltshire) Regiment of Foot

1874
Redesignated

99th (Duke of Edinburgh's) Regiment of Foot

1782
28th (North Gloucestershire) Regiment of Foot

1782
61st (South Gloucestershire) Regiment of Foot

3.3 1881 – 1957 Ancestry

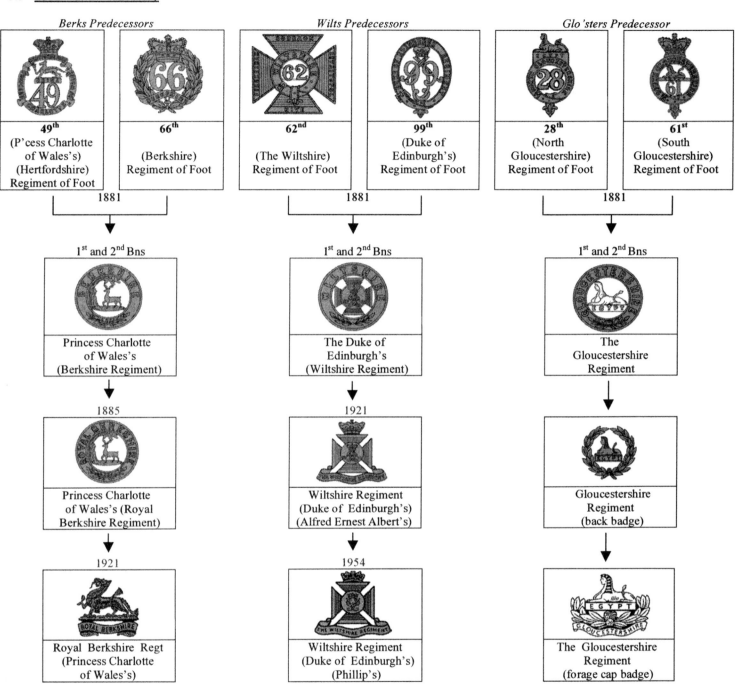

Notes on Regular Battalions

Royal Berkshire Regiment

1st and 2nd Battalions amalgamated in 1949 to form 1st Bn.

Wiltshire Regiment

1st and 2nd Battalions amalgamated in 1948 to form 1st Bn.
The penultimate badge, shown above, features the coronet and entwined 'AEA' letters of Queen Victoria's second son, Alfred Ernest Albert. The final badge features the coronet and entwined 'P's of Phillip, the current Duke of Edinburgh.

Gloucestershire Regiment

1st and 2nd Battalions amalgamated in 1948 to form 1st Bn.

4. ROYAL GREEN JACKETS COMPONENTS

4.1 Green Jacket Brigade and Post- 1957 Lineage

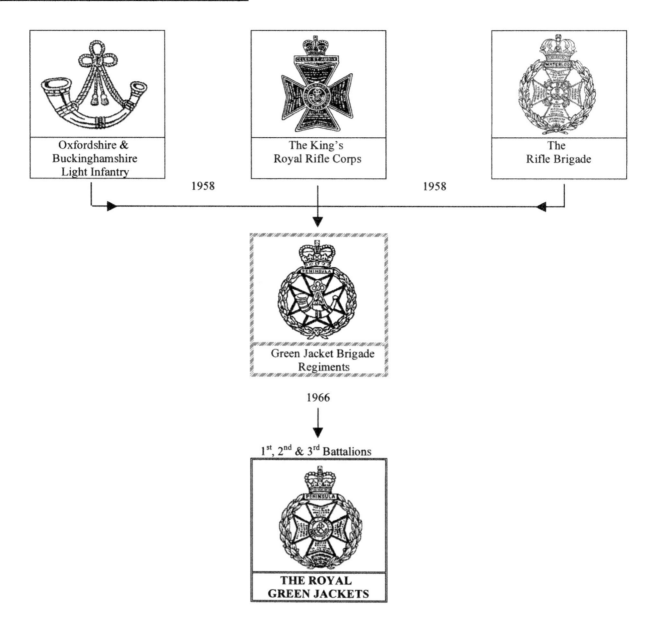

Notes on Regular Battalions of the Royal Green Jackets

1st Battalion

Known as 1st Battalion, The Royal Green Jackets (43rd and 52nd) until 1968. The 43rd / 52nd reference was then removed.

2nd Battalion

Known as 2nd Battalion, The Royal Green Jackets (The King's Royal Rifle Corps) until 1968. The KRRC reference was then removed.

3rd Battalion

Known as 3rd Battalion, The Royal Green Jackets (The Rifle Brigade) until 1968. The RB reference was then removed.

4.2 Pre - 1881 Ancestry

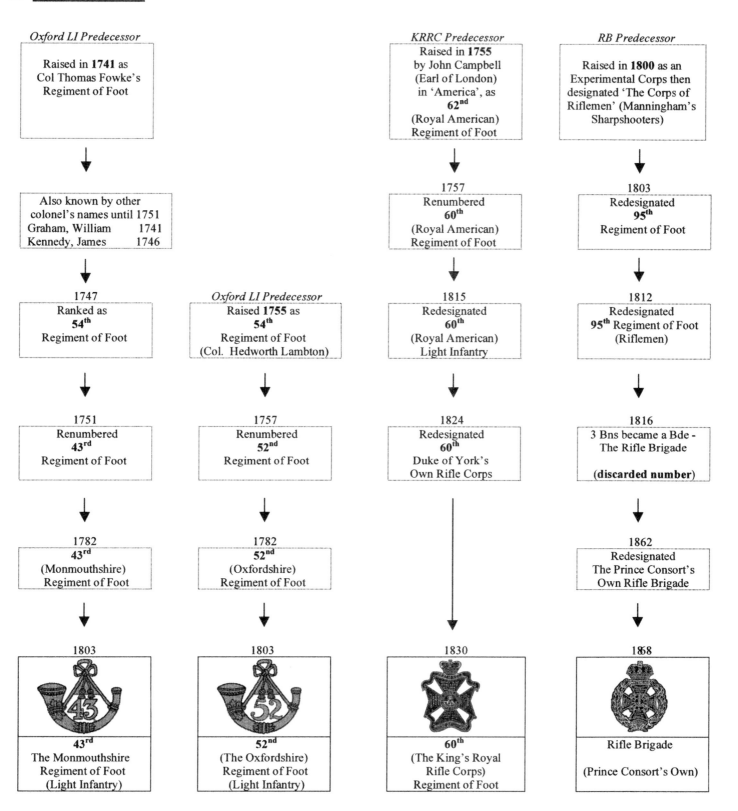

Oxford LI Predecessor

Raised in **1741** as
Col Thomas Fowke's
Regiment of Foot

↓

Also known by other
colonel's names until 1751
Graham, William   1741
Kennedy, James   1746

↓

1747
Ranked as
54th
Regiment of Foot

↓

1751
Renumbered
43rd
Regiment of Foot

↓

1782
43rd
(Monmouthshire)
Regiment of Foot

↓

1803

43rd
The Monmouthshire
Regiment of Foot
(Light Infantry)

Oxford LI Predecessor

Raised **1755** as
54th
Regiment of Foot
(Col. Hedworth Lambton)

↓

1757
Renumbered
52nd
Regiment of Foot

↓

1782
52nd
(Oxfordshire)
Regiment of Foot

↓

1803

52nd
(The Oxfordshire)
Regiment of Foot
(Light Infantry)

KRRC Predecessor

Raised in **1755**
by John Campbell
(Earl of London)
in 'America', as
62nd
(Royal American)
Regiment of Foot

↓

1757
Renumbered
60th
(Royal American)
Regiment of Foot

↓

1815
Redesignated
60th
(Royal American)
Light Infantry

↓

1824
Redesignated
60th
Duke of York's
Own Rifle Corps

↓

1830

60th
(The King's Royal
Rifle Corps)
Regiment of Foot

RB Predecessor

Raised in **1800** as an
Experimental Corps then
designated 'The Corps of
Riflemen' (Manningham's
Sharpshooters)

↓

1803
Redesignated
95th
Regiment of Foot

↓

1812
Redesignated
95th Regiment of Foot
(Riflemen)

↓

1816
3 Bns became a Bde -
The Rifle Brigade

(discarded number)

↓

1862
Redesignated
The Prince Consort's
Own Rifle Brigade

↓

1868

Rifle Brigade

(Prince Consort's Own)

4.3   1881 – 1957   Ancestry

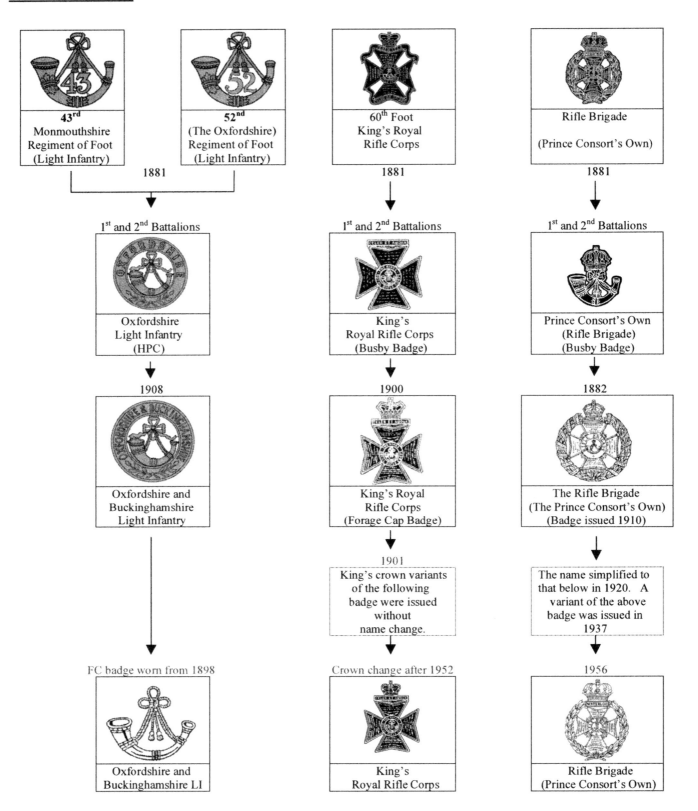

Notes on Regular Battalions

Oxfordshire and Buckinghamshire Light Infantry
1st and 2nd Battalions amalgamated in 1948 to form 1st Bn.

Rifle Brigade
2nd Battalion disbanded in 1948. R-formed in 1950 then disbanded in 1957.

King's Royal Rifle Corps
2nd Battalion disbanded in 1948. Re-formed in 1950 then effectively disbanded in 1957.

5. LIGHT INFANTRY COMPONENTS

5.1 Light Infantry Brigade and Post - 1957 Lineage

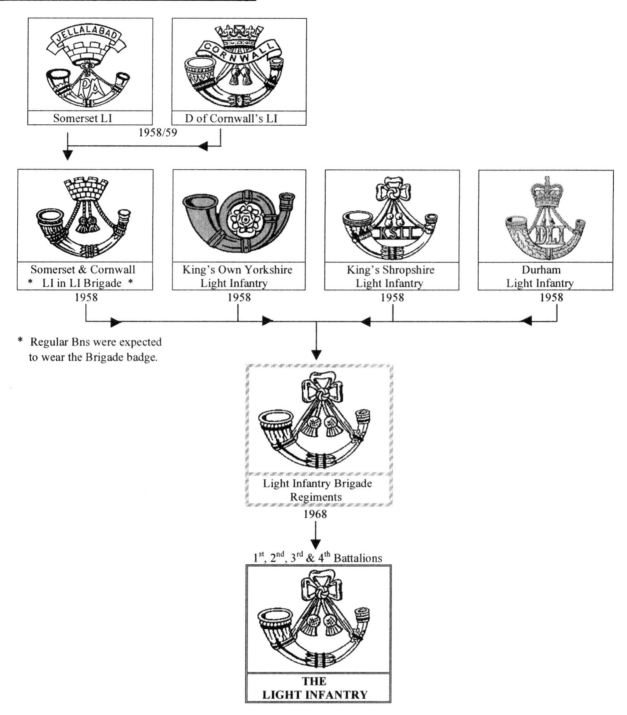

* Regular Bns were expected
  to wear the Brigade badge.

Notes on Regular Battalions of The Light Infantry

The 1st Battalion, previously The Somerset and Cornwall Light Infantry, was disbanded in 1993.

The 2nd Battalion, previously The King's Own Yorkshire Light Infantry, was renumbered 1st Battalion in 1993.

The 3rd Battalion, previously The King's Shropshire Light Infantry, was renumbered 2nd Battalion in 1993.

The 4th Battalion, previously The Durham Light Infantry, was disbanded in 1969.

5.2   Somerset Light Infantry, Cornwall Light Infantry and King's Own Yorkshire Light Infantry

5.2.1   Pre-1881 Ancestry

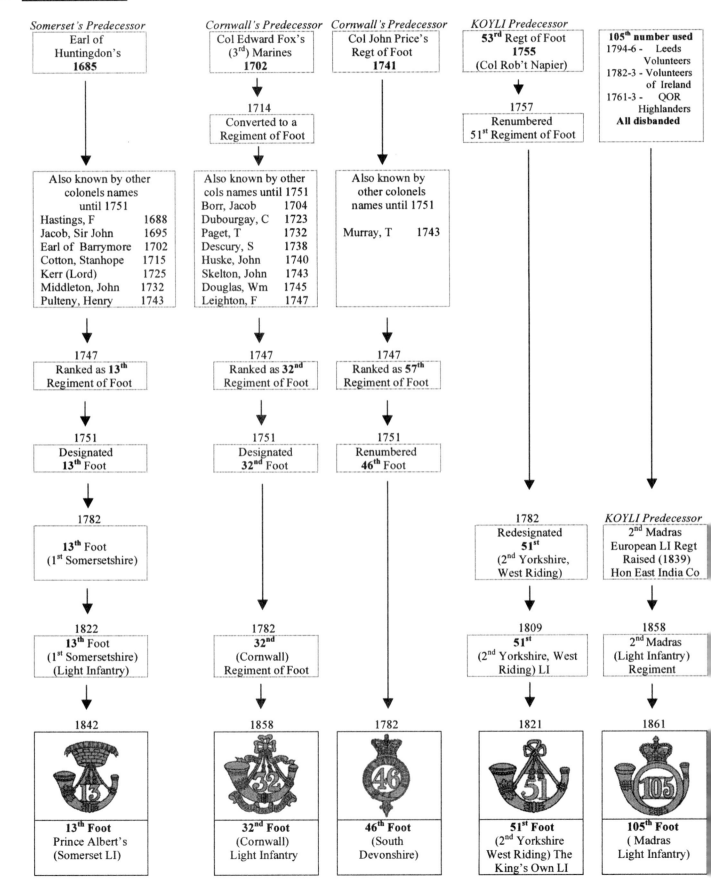

5.2.2   1881-1957 Ancestry

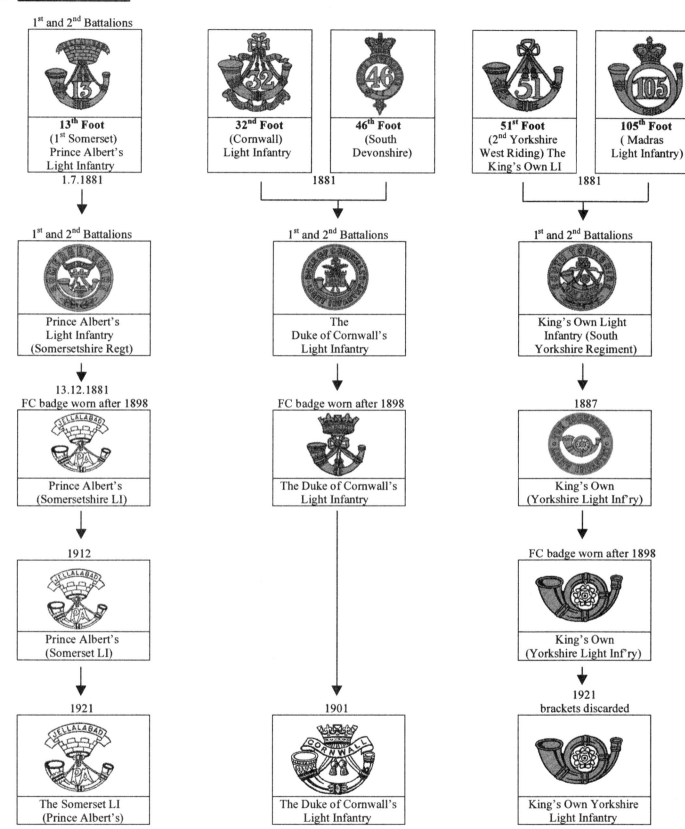

Notes on Regular Battalions

1st and 2nd Battalions of all three regiments were amalgamated in 1948 to form individual 1st Battalions.

5.3   King's Shropshire Light Infantry and Durham Light Infantry

5.3.1 Pre- 1881 Ancestry

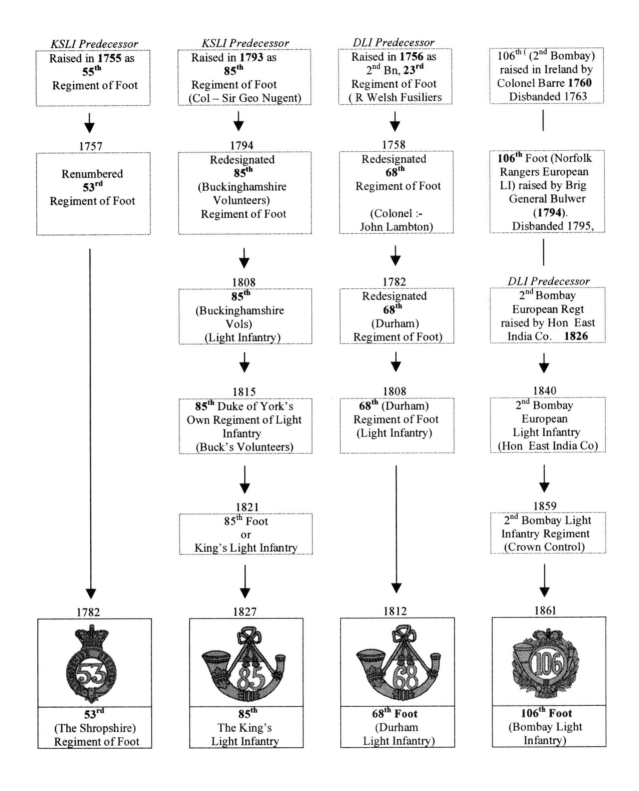

KSLI Predecessor
Raised in **1755** as
55th
Regiment of Foot

KSLI Predecessor
Raised in **1793** as
85th
Regiment of Foot
(Col – Sir Geo Nugent)

DLI Predecessor
Raised in **1756** as
2nd Bn, **23rd**
Regiment of Foot
(R Welsh Fusiliers

106th ((2nd Bombay)
raised in Ireland by
Colonel Barre **1760**
Disbanded 1763

1757

Renumbered
53rd
Regiment of Foot

1794
Redesignated
85th
(Buckinghamshire
Volunteers)
Regiment of Foot

1758
Redesignated
68th
Regiment of Foot

(Colonel :-
John Lambton)

106th Foot (Norfolk
Rangers European
LI) raised by Brig
General Bulwer
(**1794**).
Disbanded 1795,

1808
85th
(Buckinghamshire
Vols)
(Light Infantry)

1782
Redesignated
68th
(Durham)
Regiment of Foot)

DLI Predecessor
2nd Bombay
European Regt
raised by Hon East
India Co.   **1826**

1815
85th Duke of York's
Own Regiment of Light
Infantry
(Buck's Volunteers)

1808
68th (Durham)
Regiment of Foot
(Light Infantry)

1840
2nd Bombay
European
Light Infantry
(Hon East India Co)

1821
85th Foot
or
King's Light Infantry

1859
2nd Bombay Light
Infantry Regiment
(Crown Control)

1782

53rd
(The Shropshire)
Regiment of Foot

1827

85th
The King's
Light Infantry

1812

68th Foot
(Durham
Light Infantry)

1861

106th Foot
(Bombay Light
Infantry)

126

5.3.2 **1881-1957 Ancestry**

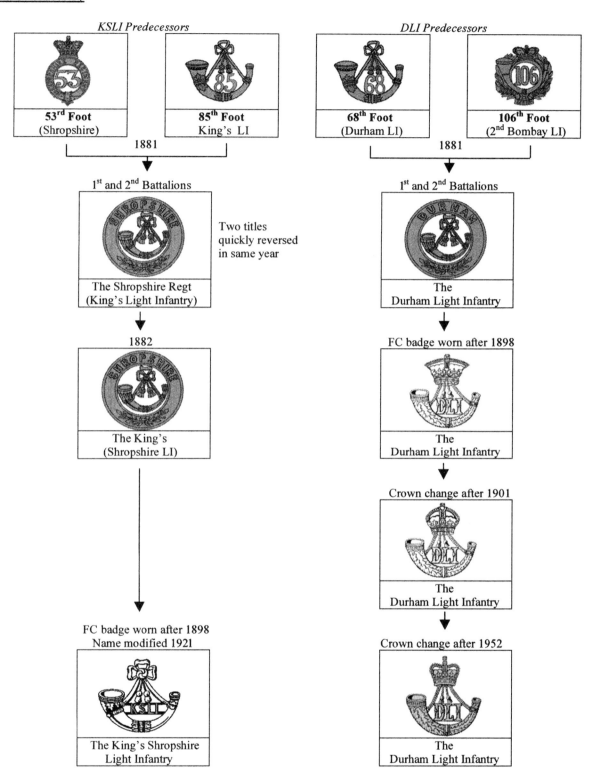

KSLI Predecessors

53rd Foot
(Shropshire)

85th Foot
King's LI

1881

1st and 2nd Battalions

Two titles
quickly reversed
in same year

The Shropshire Regt
(King's Light Infantry)

1882

The King's
(Shropshire LI)

FC badge worn after 1898
Name modified 1921

The King's Shropshire
Light Infantry

DLI Predecessors

68th Foot
(Durham LI)

106th Foot
(2nd Bombay LI)

1881

1st and 2nd Battalions

The
Durham Light Infantry

FC badge worn after 1898

The
Durham Light Infantry

Crown change after 1901

The
Durham Light Infantry

Crown change after 1952

The
Durham Light Infantry

Notes on Regular Battalions

The King's Shropshire Light Infantry

1st and 2nd Battalions amalgamated in 1948 to form 1st Bn.

The Durham Light Infantry

1st and 2nd Battalions amalgamated in 1948 to form 1st Bn.
New 2nd Battalion formed in 1952 but absorbed into 1st Battalion in 1955.

6. OTHER INFORMATION

<table>
<tr><th colspan="5">UNIFORM COAT COLOURS
(Used to differentiate Regiments of Foot in this section in 1768)</th></tr>
<tr><th></th><th>Foot
No.</th><th>Post 1881
Identity</th><th>Facing
Colour</th><th>Lace
Colour</th></tr>
<tr><td rowspan="24">
FACINGS

LACE

REST OF COAT IS RED</td><td>11</td><td>Devonshires (1st & 2nd Bns)</td><td>Green</td><td>White with two red and two green stripes</td></tr>
<tr><td>13</td><td>Somerset LI (1st & 2nd Bns)</td><td>Yellow</td><td>White with a yellow stripe</td></tr>
<tr><td>28</td><td>Gloucestershires (1st Bn)</td><td>Yellow</td><td>White with one yellow and two black stripes</td></tr>
<tr><td>32</td><td>D of Cornwall's LI (1st Bn)</td><td>White</td><td>White with a black worm and a black stripe</td></tr>
<tr><td>39</td><td>Dorsetshires (1st Bn)</td><td>Green</td><td>White with one red and one green stripe</td></tr>
<tr><td>43</td><td>Oxfordshire LI (1st Bn)</td><td>White</td><td>White with a red and a black stripe</td></tr>
<tr><td>46</td><td>D of Cornwall's LI (2nd Bn)</td><td>Yellow</td><td>White with red and purple worms</td></tr>
<tr><td>49</td><td>Berkshires (1st Bn)</td><td>Green</td><td>White with two red and one green stripe</td></tr>
<tr><td>51</td><td>KO LI (South Yorks) (1st Bn)</td><td>Green^</td><td>White with green worm stripe</td></tr>
<tr><td>52</td><td>Oxfordshire LI (2nd Bn)</td><td>Buff</td><td>White with red worm and one orange stripe</td></tr>
<tr><td>53</td><td>K's LI (Shropshire) (1st Bn)</td><td>Red</td><td>White with a red stripe</td></tr>
<tr><td>54</td><td>Dorsetshires (2nd Bn)</td><td>Green</td><td>White with a green stripe</td></tr>
<tr><td>60</td><td>KR Rifle Corps (1st & 2nd Bns)</td><td>Blue</td><td>White with two blue stripes</td></tr>
<tr><td>61</td><td>Gloucestershires (2nd Bn)</td><td>Buff</td><td>White with a blue stripe</td></tr>
<tr><td>62</td><td>Wiltshires (1st Bn)</td><td>Buff</td><td>White with two blue and one straw-coloured stripe</td></tr>
<tr><td>66</td><td>Berkshires (2nd Bn)</td><td>Green</td><td>White with one crimson and green and one green stripe</td></tr>
<tr><td>68</td><td>Durham LI (1st Bn)</td><td>Green</td><td>White with yellow and black stripes</td></tr>
<tr><td>85*</td><td>K's LI (Shropshire) (1st Bn)</td><td>Yellow^</td><td>-</td></tr>
<tr><td>99*</td><td>Wiltshires (2nd Bn)</td><td>Yellow</td><td>-</td></tr>
<tr><td>105*</td><td>KO LI (South Yorks) (2nd Bn)</td><td>Buff</td><td>-</td></tr>
<tr><td>106*</td><td>Durham LI (2nd Bn)</td><td>Buff^^</td><td>-</td></tr>
<tr><td></td><td>* colours not mentioned in 1768 Warrant?</td><td>^ blue after 1821</td><td></td></tr>
<tr><td></td><td></td><td>^^white after 1842</td><td></td></tr>
</table>

18th Century coat example indicates colour placings. Be aware, however, that tailoring differences exist between regiments.
After 1881, facing colours were standardised but some regts were allowed to re-introduce historic colours. The standardised colours were WHITE for English and Welsh regts, YELLOW for Scottish, GREEN for Irish and BLUE for 'Royal' regts.

THE ROYAL GIBRALTAR REGIMENT

1. FORMATION (and ancestry)

Gibraltar units were generally volunteer/reserves until 1991. From that date the Gibraltar Regiment (as it was then) was formally placed on the British Army's regular establishment even though some of it's constituent companies were still manned by volunteers. It's ancestry is thus addressed here along with our other regular regiments.

Local civilians provided guard and other services from as early as **1720**

↓

1915
Volunteer Corps formed to help defend the Rock during WW1. Officially recognised 1915, disbanded 1920

Gibraltar Volunteer Corps

↓

1939
Territorial Defence Force formed from volunteers to help man the guns on the Rock during WW2.
Reduced to a permanent cadre/reserve at the closing stages of the war.

Gibraltar Defence Force

↓

1958
Permanent cadre and reserve of above force formed into the Gibraltar Regiment, with dual infantry and artillery roles.

Gibraltar Regiment

↓

1991
Re-organised into an all-infantry unit and place on British Army regular establishment. 'Royal' prefix **awarded** in 1999.

Royal Gibraltar Regiment

129

THE FORESTERS BRIGADE
(Formerly the 'Midland' Brigade)

1. FORMATION

This is obviously not a regiment. However, formation of the brigade represented an important event in the evolution of the regiments involved and is briefly referred to in the details associated with those regiments. The identity of the regimental sections containing those details can be easily deduced from the information given at the end of this section.

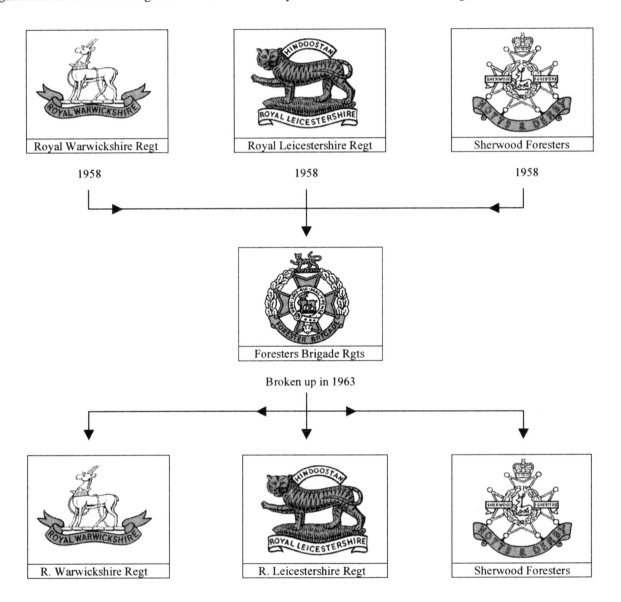

The Midland Brigade changed it's name to the Foresters Brigade shortly after it was formed. The Foresters did not last. The brigade was broken up in 1963 and it's constituents transferred to other brigades.

The **Warwicks** went to the Fusilier Brigade (being reclassified 'Fusiliers' in the process) and eventually became part of the **Royal Regiment of Fusiliers**.

The **Leicesters** went to the East Anglian Brigade and eventually into the **Royal Anglians**.

The **Sherwood Foresters** went to the Mercian Brigade and eventually (via a merger with the Worcestershire Regiment) into the **Mercian Regiment**.

OLD IRISH REGIMENTS

1. INTRODUCTION

The formation of the Irish Free State in 1922 (from which Northern Ireland quickly opted out) led to the disbandment of the five Irish regiments (within the British Army) that had recruited in the south. The regiments are illustrated below.

As the five regiments had been part of the British Army for some considerable time, their ancestral and amalgamation details have been provided in the following pages.

The
Royal Irish Regiment

Prince of Wales's Leinster Regt
(Royal Canadians)

The
Connaught Rangers

The
Royal Munster Fusiliers

The
Royal Dublin Fusiliers

The Northern Ireland region rejoined the United Kingdom in 1922 almost immediately after the Irish Free State was formed and those infantry regiments which were considered 'Northern Irish' remained within the British Army. One of the regiments – 'The Royal Irish Rifles' – anticipated the change and modified it's name to 'The Royal Ulster Rifles' in 1921.

The standard Northern Irish infantry regiments eventually merged into one large Irish regiment in 1992. The 'Royal Irish Regiment' name which had disappeared with the advent of the Irish Free State, seventy years earlier, was resurrected as the name of that large regiment. Details can be found in the Royal Irish Regiment section.

2. ROYAL IRISH REGIMENT AND PRINCE OF WALES'S LEINSTER REGIMENT (ROYAL CANADIANS)

2.1 Pre -1881 Ancestry

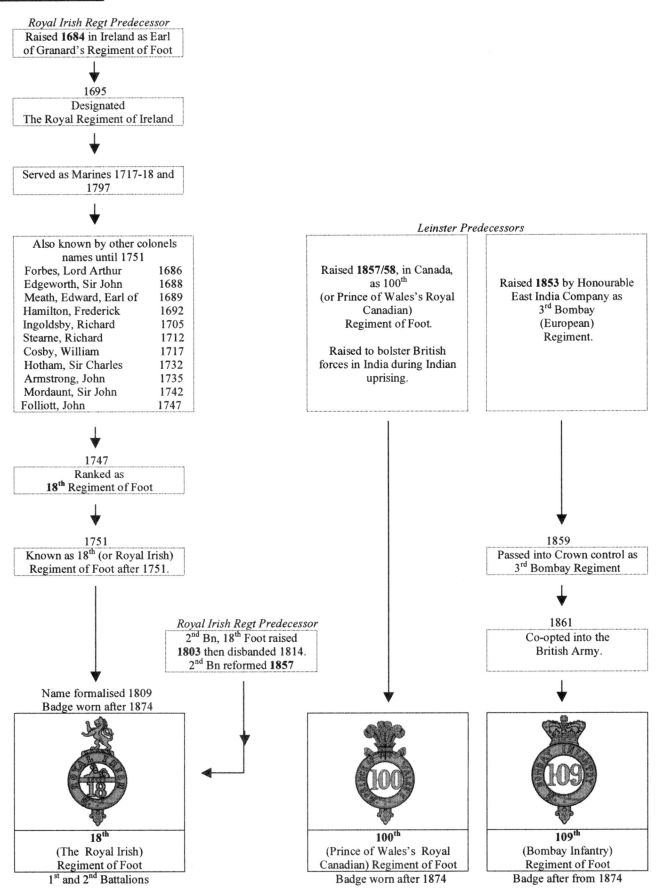

Royal Irish Regt Predecessor
Raised **1684** in Ireland as Earl of Granard's Regiment of Foot

1695
Designated
The Royal Regiment of Ireland

Served as Marines 1717-18 and 1797

Leinster Predecessors

Also known by other colonels names until 1751	
Forbes, Lord Arthur	1686
Edgeworth, Sir John	1688
Meath, Edward, Earl of	1689
Hamilton, Frederick	1692
Ingoldsby, Richard	1705
Stearne, Richard	1712
Cosby, William	1717
Hotham, Sir Charles	1732
Armstrong, John	1735
Mordaunt, Sir John	1742
Folliott, John	1747

Raised **1857/58**, in Canada, as 100th (or Prince of Wales's Royal Canadian) Regiment of Foot.

Raised to bolster British forces in India during Indian uprising.

Raised **1853** by Honourable East India Company as 3rd Bombay (European) Regiment.

1747
Ranked as
18th Regiment of Foot

1751
Known as 18th (or Royal Irish) Regiment of Foot after 1751.

1859
Passed into Crown control as 3rd Bombay Regiment

Royal Irish Regt Predecessor
2nd Bn, 18th Foot raised **1803** then disbanded 1814. 2nd Bn reformed **1857**

1861
Co-opted into the British Army.

Name formalised 1809
Badge worn after 1874

18th
(The Royal Irish)
Regiment of Foot
1st and 2nd Battalions

100th
(Prince of Wales's Royal Canadian) Regiment of Foot
Badge worn after 1874

109th
(Bombay Infantry)
Regiment of Foot
Badge after from 1874

2.2 1881 – 1922 Ancestry

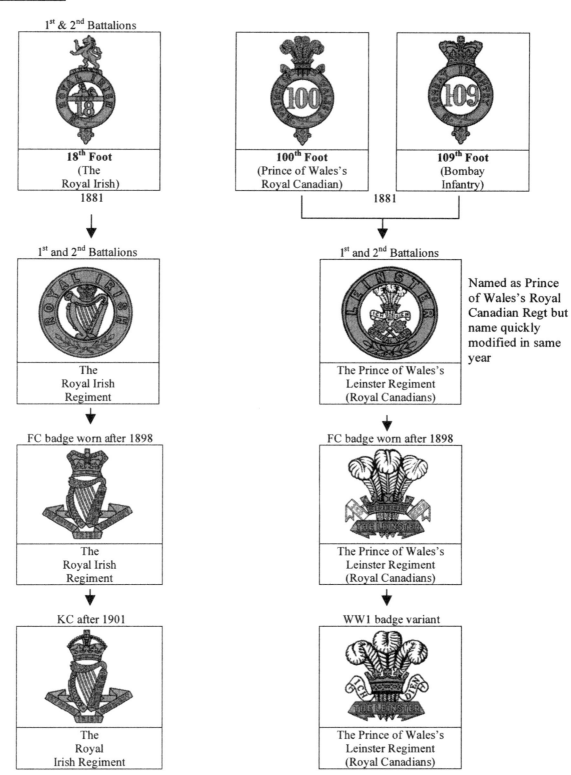

Notes on Regular Battalions

Royal Irish Regiment

The 1st and 2nd battalions were both disbanded in 1922. A new Royal Irish Regiment was formed in 1992. See section of that name.

Prince of Wales's Leinster Regiment (Royal Canadians)

The 1st and 2nd battalions were both disbanded in 1922.

3. CONNAUGHT RANGERS AND ROYAL MUNSTER FUSILIERS

3.1 Pre -1881 Ancestry

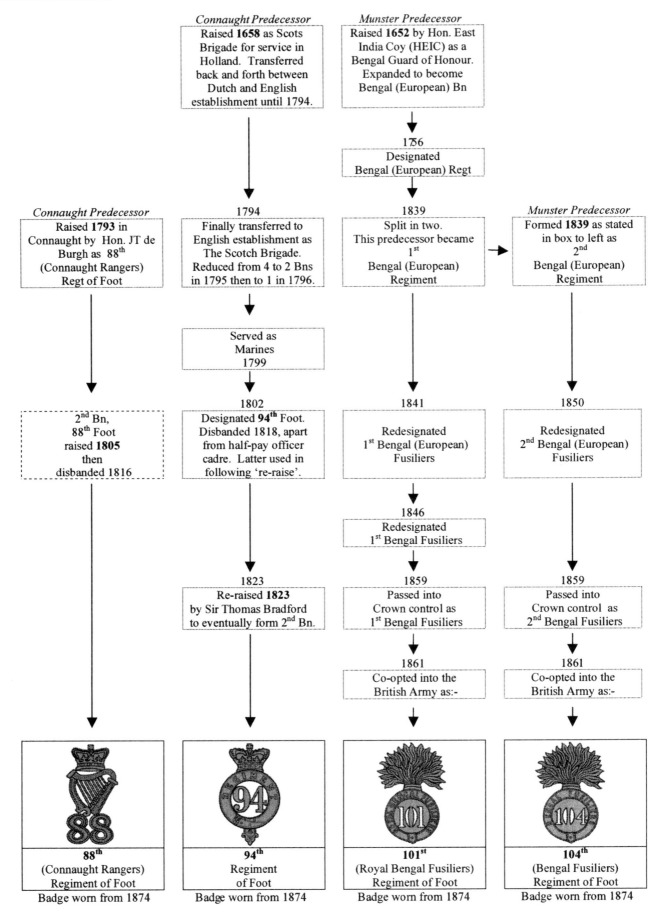

Connaught Predecessor

Raised 1658 as Scots Brigade for service in Holland. Transferred back and forth between Dutch and English establishment until 1794.

Munster Predecessor

Raised 1652 by Hon. East India Coy (HEIC) as a Bengal Guard of Honour. Expanded to become Bengal (European) Bn

1756
Designated
Bengal (European) Regt

Connaught Predecessor

Raised 1793 in Connaught by Hon. JT de Burgh as 88th (Connaught Rangers) Regt of Foot

1794
Finally transferred to English establishment as The Scotch Brigade. Reduced from 4 to 2 Bns in 1795 then to 1 in 1796.

1839
Split in two.
This predecessor became
1st
Bengal (European)
Regiment

Munster Predecessor

Formed **1839** as stated in box to left as
2nd
Bengal (European)
Regiment

Served as
Marines
1799

2nd Bn,
88th Foot
raised **1805**
then
disbanded 1816

1802
Designated **94th** Foot. Disbanded 1818, apart from half-pay officer cadre. Latter used in following 're-raise'.

1841
Redesignated
1st Bengal (European)
Fusiliers

1850
Redesignated
2nd Bengal (European)
Fusiliers

1846
Redesignated
1st Bengal Fusiliers

1823
Re-raised **1823**
by Sir Thomas Bradford
to eventually form 2nd Bn.

1859
Passed into
Crown control as
1st Bengal Fusiliers

1859
Passed into
Crown control as
2nd Bengal Fusiliers

1861
Co-opted into the
British Army as:-

1861
Co-opted into the
British Army as:-

88th
(Connaught Rangers)
Regiment of Foot
Badge worn from 1874

94th
Regiment
of Foot
Badge worn from 1874

101st
(Royal Bengal Fusiliers)
Regiment of Foot
Badge worn from 1874

104th
(Bengal Fusiliers)
Regiment of Foot
Badge worn from 1874

3.2   <u>1881 – 1922 Ancestry</u>

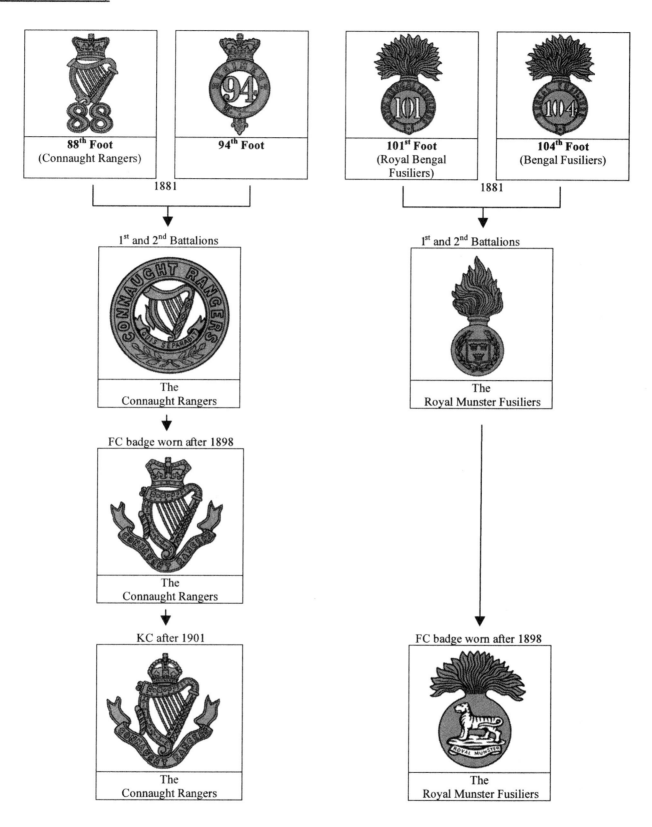

Notes on Regular Battalions

<u>Connaught Rangers</u>

The 1st and 2nd battalions were both disbanded in 1922.

<u>Royal Munster Fusiliers</u>

The 1st and 2nd battalions were both disbanded in 1922.

4. ROYAL DUBLIN FUSILIERS

4.1 Pre -1881 Ancestry

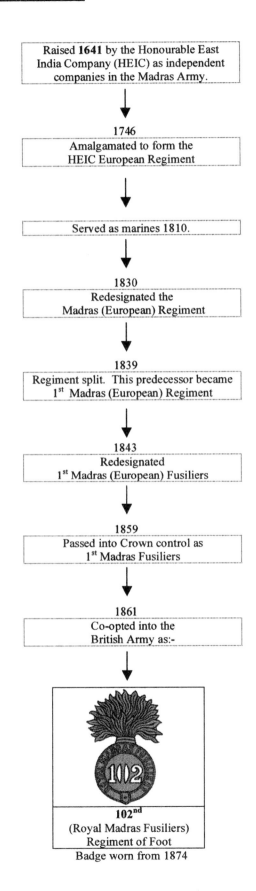

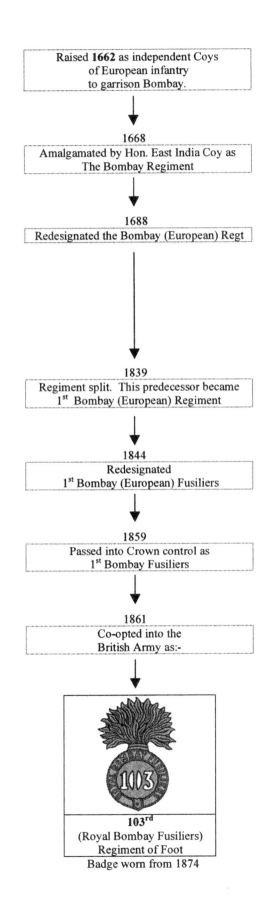

4.2 1881-1922 Ancestry

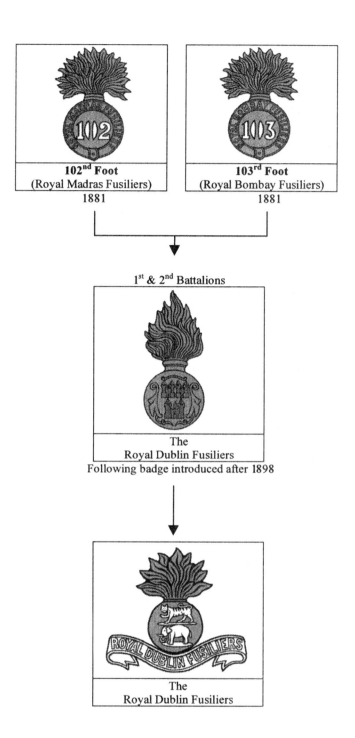

102nd Foot
(Royal Madras Fusiliers)
1881

103rd Foot
(Royal Bombay Fusiliers)
1881

1st & 2nd Battalions

The
Royal Dublin Fusiliers
Following badge introduced after 1898

The
Royal Dublin Fusiliers

Notes on Regular Battalions

The 1st and 2nd battalions were both disbanded in 1922.

5. OTHER INFORMATION

UNIFORM COAT COLOURS
(Used to differentiate Regiments of Foot in this section in 1768)

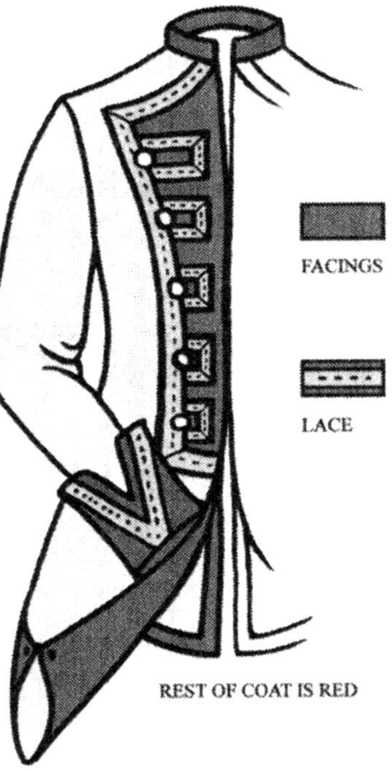

	Foot No.	Post 1881 Identity	Facing Colour	Lace Colour
	18	Royal Irish (1st & 2nd Bns)	Blue	White with blue stripe
	88	Connaught Rangers (1st Bn)	Yellow	White with a red and a yellow stripe
	94	Connaught Rangers (2nd Bn)	-	-
	100	Leinsters (1st Bn)	-	-
	101	Royal Munster Fusiliers (1st Bn)	-	-
	102	Royal Dublin Fusiliers (1st Bn)	-	-
	103	Royal Dublin Fusiliers (2nd Bn)	-	-
	104	Royal Munster Fusiliers (2nd Bn)	-	-
	109	Leinsters (2nd Bn)	-	-

FACINGS

LACE

REST OF COAT IS RED

Note:
Regiments numbered 101 -109 in the above list were Indian Presidency Regts.

Regt 100 was the Royal Canadians.

18th Century coat example indicates colour placings. Be aware, however, that tailoring differences exist between regiments.
After 1881, facing colours were standardised but some regts were allowed to re-introduce historic colours. The standardised colours were WHITE for English and Welsh regts, YELLOW for Scottish, GREEN for Irish and BLUE for 'Royal' regts.

WAR-RAISED INFANTRY

1   SOUTH AFRICA 1899-1902

1.1   Her Majesty's Royal Reserve Regiments

Raised **March 1900** from reservists to provide replacements for first-line infantry sent to South Africa. **Disbanded after the war.**

Royal Rifles
Reserve Regiment

Royal Scottish
Reserve Regiment

Royal Irish
Reserve Regiment

Royal Lancashire
Reserve Regiment

Royal Irish Fusilier
Reserve Regiment

Royal Home Counties
Reserve Regiment

Royal Northern
Reserve Regiment

Royal Southern
Reserve Regiment

Royal Eastern
Reserve Regiment

The Regular Cavalry and the Foot Guards also formed HMRR's. See relevant sections.

2.   WORLD WAR ONE 1914-1919

More and more men were needed during WW1 to fight as infantry. Consequently, the powers-that-be left no stone unturned in their quest for more – even to the extent of using personnel from battalions and services not normally classed as infantry. Two such units are addressed in this subsection. The first is an infantry battalion made up of Household Cavalry reservists and the second is a whole infantry division initially made up of Royal Navy reservists.

2.1   The Household Battalion

Formed in **1916** from Household Cavalry reservists. **Disbanded after the war.**

Household Battalion

2.2   The Royal Naval Division

Royal Naval reservists were formed into a Divisional group of battalions in **1914** and used as infantry. They wore naval type uniforms. Each battalion was named after a famous British naval commander, as shown below, and the Division was called (unsurprisingly) the Royal Naval Division. It fought at Gallipoli where losses were so great that the Benbow and Collingwood battalions were disbanded in 1916.

The Division was then transferred to the Western Front in the same year. Because of Gallipoli and other losses, the 'naval' character of the Division diminished as battalions from non-naval units were added. These included battalions from the Royal Irish Regiment, the Royal Fusiliers, the Bedfordshires, the King's Shropshire Light Infantry, the London Regiment, the Royal Marine Light Infantry and the Honourable Artillery Company. Consequently, the 'Royal Naval' element of the Divisional name was removed and replaced by **63rd**, a number which had become available after the disbandment of the 63rd (2nd Northumbrian) Division.

The following badges and names address original RND components (including supporting troops). All surviving battalions continued on after 1916 but uniforms and caps changed to those worn by the infantry rather than the navy. Metal badges were thus produced to replace the normal sailor's tally bands. These are shown below.

All naval battalions were **disbanded** as infantry units after the war.

1st Royal Naval Brigade			
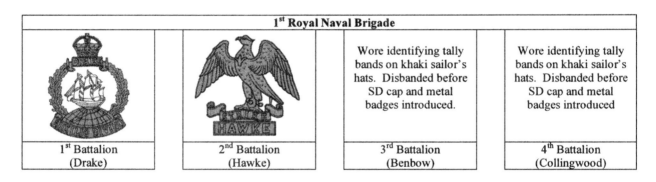		Wore identifying tally bands on khaki sailor's hats. Disbanded before SD cap and metal badges introduced.	Wore identifying tally bands on khaki sailor's hats. Disbanded before SD cap and metal badges introduced
1st Battalion (Drake)	2nd Battalion (Hawke)	3rd Battalion (Benbow)	4th Battalion (Collingwood)

2nd Royal Naval Brigade			
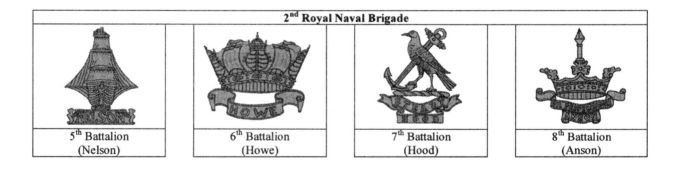			
5th Battalion (Nelson)	6th Battalion (Howe)	7th Battalion (Hood)	8th Battalion (Anson)

3rd Royal Marine Brigade	Machine Gun Support

Royal Marine Light Infantry	Royal Naval Division Machine Gun Battalion

3.   WORLD WAR TWO 1939-45

3.1   Highland and Lowland Regiments

Above were raised (as Corps, within the meaning of the Army Act) as young soldier battalions. The young soldiers were trained until they were old enough (and trained enough) to be transferred to 'standard' Scottish regiments.

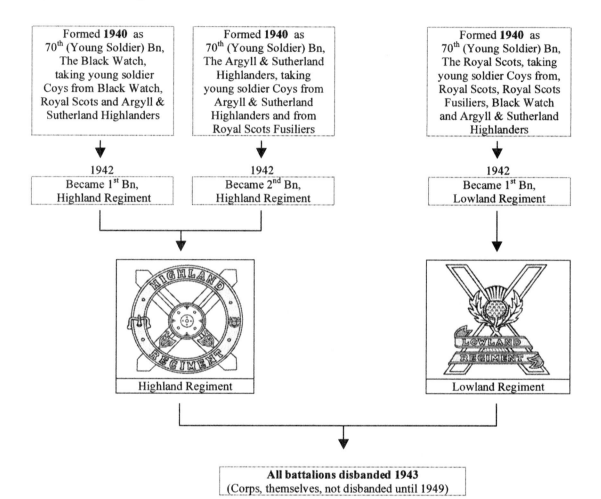

| Formed **1940** as 70th (Young Soldier) Bn, The Black Watch, taking young soldier Coys from Black Watch, Royal Scots and Argyll & Sutherland Highlanders | Formed **1940** as 70th (Young Soldier) Bn, The Argyll & Sutherland Highlanders, taking young soldier Coys from Argyll & Sutherland Highlanders and from Royal Scots Fusiliers | Formed **1940** as 70th (Young Soldier) Bn, The Royal Scots, taking young soldier Coys from, Royal Scots, Royal Scots Fusiliers, Black Watch and Argyll & Sutherland Highlanders |

1942   Became 1st Bn, Highland Regiment

1942   Became 2nd Bn, Highland Regiment

1942   Became 1st Bn, Lowland Regiment

Highland Regiment

Lowland Regiment

All battalions disbanded 1943
(Corps, themselves, not disbanded until 1949)

4. **OTHER INFORMATION**

This section was designed to address new and unusual war-raised infantry units. It was not designed to address the enormous number of extra territorial and 'regular' battalions of **existing** infantry regiments which were formed to swell wartime ranks, especially during WW1.

These 'war-raised' WW1 battalions were raised in such numbers by Lord Kitchener (Secretary of State for War) as to constitute whole new armies.

Most of these so-called service battalions wore the cap badges of their parent regiments but some wore their own, usually in tribute to whoever sponsored their formation. A couple of examples of sponsored battalions are given below.

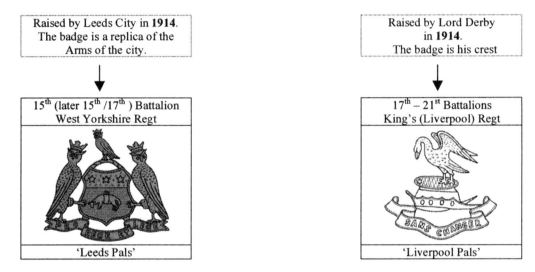

Raised by Leeds City in **1914**. The badge is a replica of the Arms of the city.	Raised by Lord Derby in **1914**. The badge is his crest
15th (later 15th/17th) Battalion West Yorkshire Regt	17th – 21st Battalions King's (Liverpool) Regt
'Leeds Pals'	'Liverpool Pals'

What was left of them were disbanded after the war.

The 'Pals' designation, referred to in the examples, came about because the authorities initially promised you would stay with your pals if you enrolled with them because 'Those who enrol together will serve together'.

AIR, SEA
AND SPECIAL FORCES

AIRBORNE

This section addresses airborne forces under Army command. It covers the Royal Flying Corps, Army Air Corps, Glider Pilot Regiment, Air Observation Post Squadrons (RA), Parachute Regiment and Special Air Service Regiment. A subsection has also been added for the RAF Regiment. Strictly speaking, the latter should not be addressed here but as the RAF is included as an integral evolutionary feature of the RFC and as the RAF Regiment acts primarily as infantry, it is considered reasonable to include it.

1. ROYAL FLYING CORPS

1.1 Formation and Evolution

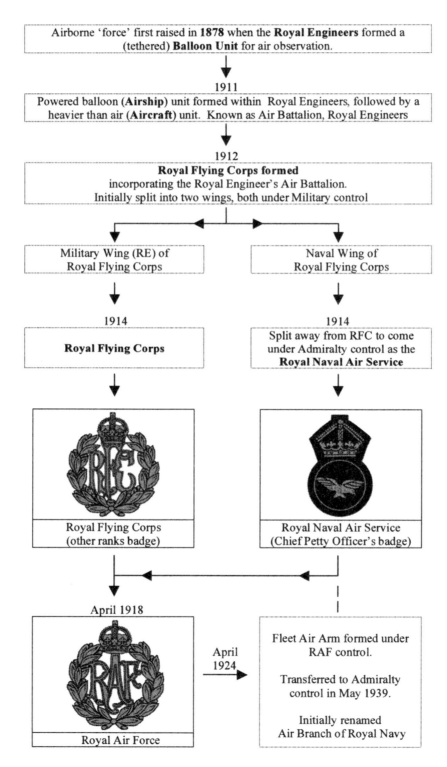

1.2 RAF Regiment

An explanation for the inclusion of the RAF Regiment has been given at the start of this section.

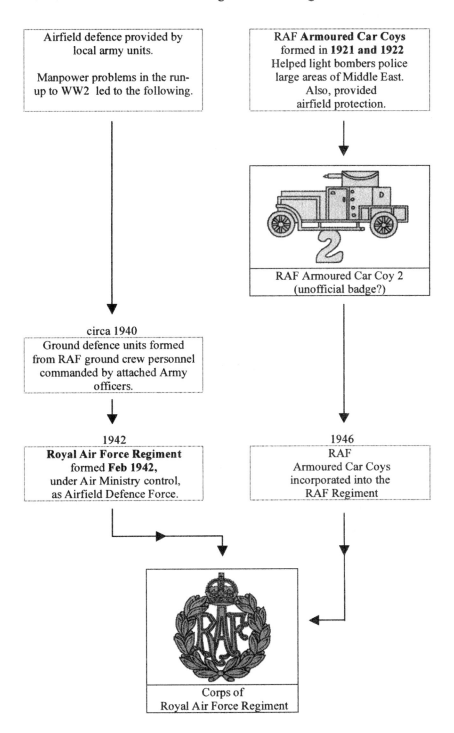

Airfield defence provided by local army units.

Manpower problems in the run-up to WW2 led to the following.

RAF **Armoured Car Coys** formed in **1921 and 1922** Helped light bombers police large areas of Middle East. Also, provided airfield protection.

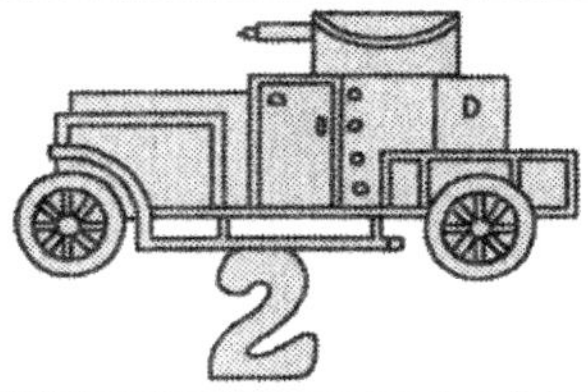

RAF Armoured Car Coy 2 (unofficial badge?)

circa 1940
Ground defence units formed from RAF ground crew personnel commanded by attached Army officers.

1942
Royal Air Force Regiment formed **Feb 1942,** under Air Ministry control, as Airfield Defence Force.

1946
RAF Armoured Car Coys incorporated into the RAF Regiment

Corps of Royal Air Force Regiment

2. ARMY AIR CORPS

2.1 Pre-1949 Ancestry (and Evolution of Associated Regiments)

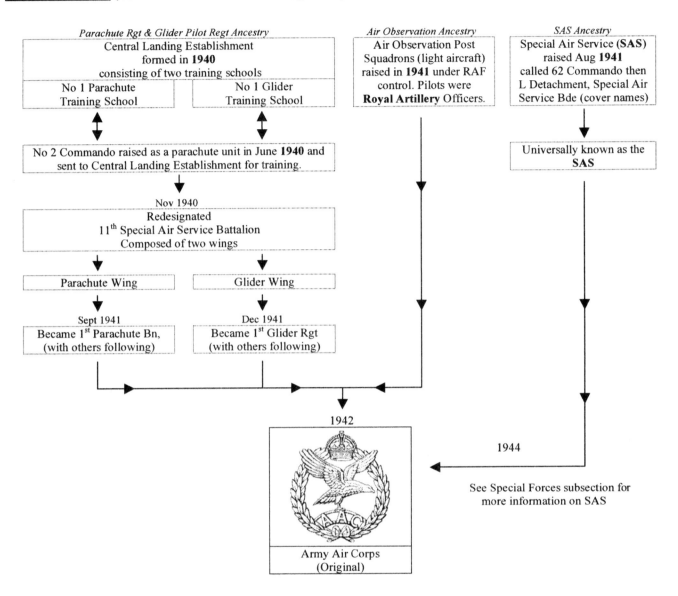

Parachute Rgt & Glider Pilot Regt Ancestry

Central Landing Establishment formed in **1940** consisting of two training schools

| No 1 Parachute Training School | No 1 Glider Training School |

No 2 Commando raised as a parachute unit in June **1940** and sent to Central Landing Establishment for training.

Nov 1940
Redesignated
11th Special Air Service Battalion
Composed of two wings

| Parachute Wing | Glider Wing |

Sept 1941
Became 1st Parachute Bn, (with others following)

Dec 1941
Became 1st Glider Rgt (with others following)

Air Observation Ancestry

Air Observation Post Squadrons (light aircraft) raised in **1941** under RAF control. Pilots were **Royal Artillery** Officers.

SAS Ancestry

Special Air Service (**SAS**) raised Aug **1941** called 62 Commando then L Detachment, Special Air Service Bde (cover names)

Universally known as the **SAS**

1942

Army Air Corps (Original)

1944

See Special Forces subsection for more information on SAS

Changes were made to the three 1941 components as part of the process of forming the Army Air Corps. These are outlined above the following badges. As for the badges - the Parachute Regiment produced their own in May 1943 and wore it from that time onwards. The Glider Pilot Regiment did not produce their own until the demise of the original Army Air Corps. Until that time, they wore the AAC badge. Their own badge is shown in the next subsection. The RA and SAS wore the badges they already had. However, SAS was temporarily disbanded in 1945.

Parachute Regiment **formed Aug 1942**

Parachute Regiment

Glider Pilot Regiment **formed Feb 1942**

The Glider Pilot Regiment

Came under Army control **early 1942**

Air Observation Post Squadrons (RA)

Special Air Service (cloth badge)

2.2 <u>Post 1949 Ancestry</u> **(and Evolution of Associated Regiments)**

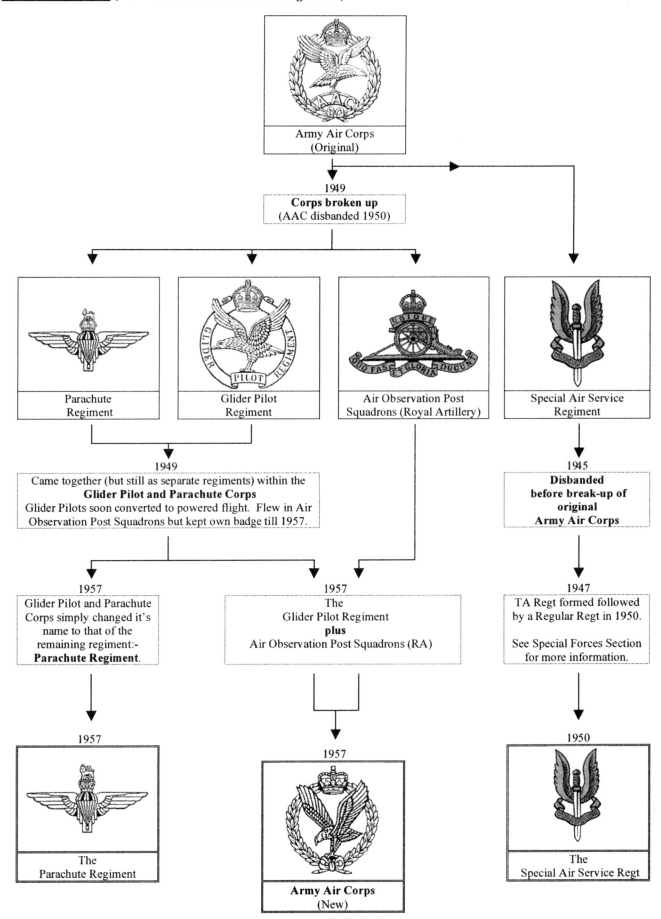

THE CORPS OF ROYAL MARINES

The Royal Marines are not part of the Army. They are part of the Royal Navy. Thus, like the previously mentioned RAF Regiment, they should not be here. However, although they are part of another service, they are the infantry arm of that service so (again like the RAF regiment) an outline ancestry has been provided.

1. FORMATION (and post 1755 Ancestry)

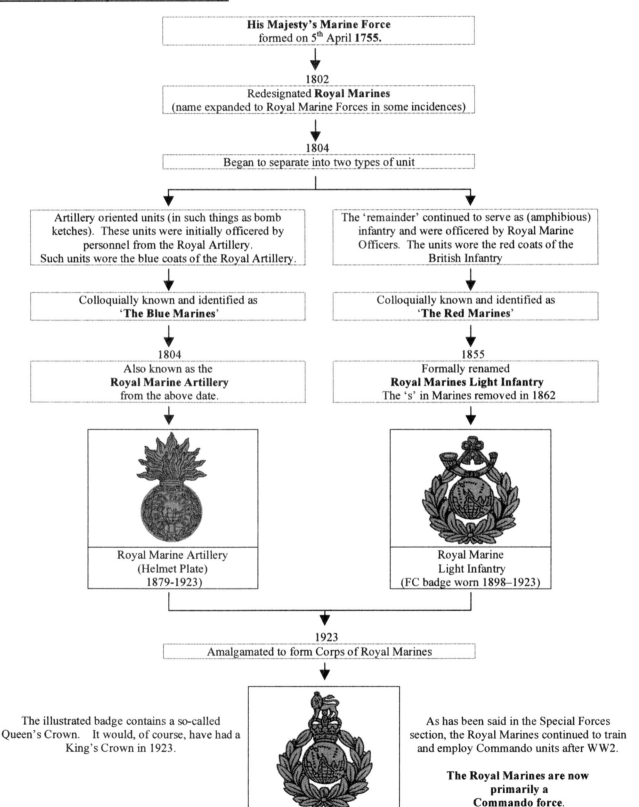

His Majesty's Marine Force
formed on 5th April **1755.**

1802
Redesignated **Royal Marines**
(name expanded to Royal Marine Forces in some incidences)

1804
Began to separate into two types of unit

Artillery oriented units (in such things as bomb ketches). These units were initially officered by personnel from the Royal Artillery.
Such units wore the blue coats of the Royal Artillery.

The 'remainder' continued to serve as (amphibious) infantry and were officered by Royal Marine Officers. The units wore the red coats of the British Infantry

Colloquially known and identified as
'The Blue Marines'

Colloquially known and identified as
'The Red Marines'

1804
Also known as the
Royal Marine Artillery
from the above date.

1855
Formally renamed
Royal Marines Light Infantry
The 's' in Marines removed in 1862

Royal Marine Artillery
(Helmet Plate)
1879-1923)

Royal Marine
Light Infantry
(FC badge worn 1898–1923)

1923
Amalgamated to form Corps of Royal Marines

The illustrated badge contains a so-called Queen's Crown. It would, of course, have had a King's Crown in 1923.

Corps of Royal Marines

As has been said in the Special Forces section, the Royal Marines continued to train and employ Commando units after WW2.

**The Royal Marines are now
primarily a
Commando force.**

2 PRE-1755 ANCESTRY

The direct ancestor of the Royal Marines (His Majesty's Marine Force) did not come being until 1755. Prior to that, ship-based infantry were often provided by seconding detachments of land-based infantry for sea service. Officers, at that time (late 16th century and for some time after) saw nothing unusual in switching backwards and forwards between sea and land service. This was particularly so during various wars when naval manpower had to be increased. Consequently, more than 30 regiments of the line can show they served as marines at some time during their history – although it should be added that some actually started out as marines and later converted to land-based infantry.

This neatly brings us to the next point in Royal Marine ancestry.

A number of regiments were raised specifically as marines. None survived long enough as marines to be considered direct ancestors but, as they started life as marines, they can be highlighted as indirect ancestors. A dated selection is shown below.

1664	The Duke of York and Albany's Maritime Regiment of Foot was raised . It quickly became known as 'The Admiral's Regiment' (the aforementioned Duke being the Lord High Admiral).
1665	The Holland Regiment was raised to serve as marines under Admiralty command. It ceased to be under control of the Navy in 1667 and went on to be the forerunner of the 3rd (East Kent) Foot, otherwise known, from their early uniform facing colour, as 'The Buffs'.
1672	'The Marine Regiment' was raised then disbanded in 1674.
1688	Carmarthen's 1st Marines and Shovell's 2nd Marines raised then disbanded by 1698.
1690	Earl of Pembroke's Regiment and Torrington's (later Lord Berkeley's) Regiment raised as maritime regiments. Disbanded 1696.
1702	Six Marine Regiments raised. In addition, six Regiments of Foot were raised specifically for sea service. All were disbanded in 1713 after the Treaty of Utrecht. Three of the Marine Regiments (Saunderson's, Villiers's and Fox's) were eventually re-raised as line regiments (30th, 31st and 32nd Foot).
1739	Marine Regiments raised during the War of Jenkin's Ear. All were disbanded or ceased to be marines by 1748.
1741	Spotswood Regiment raised in North America. It was later redesignated Gooch's Marines and eventually became a Gloucestershire Regiment forerunner.
1755	Her Majesty's Marine Force raised as what proved to be the direct ancestor of our current Royal Marines.

Royal Marine Band
(Plymouth Division)

The above three-part badge with it's Queen's Crown is obviously not pre-1755. It just fills in a bit of space.

SPECIAL FORCES

1. COMMANDOS (of WW2)

1.1 Formation and Evolution of No 1 to No 12 Commando (WW2)

> Maritime Raiding Force set up in early **1940** on basis of proposals made by Major JFC Holland.
> Authorisation given for formation of 10 Independent Companies of specially-trained volunteers, mainly from
> Territorial Divisions. Some (mis)used in ill-fated Narvick (Norway) operation.

> Lt Col Dudley Clarke received permission, after Dunkirk (mid **1940**) to establish **Commando** raiding units.
> The name stemmed from small, successful Boer raiding forces used in the Boer war.
> Used trained men from above Independent Companies to found first units.
> Others added to form 12 Commando battalions (designated 1 - 12 Commando)
> and 10 independent companies. **All primarily from Army volunteers.**

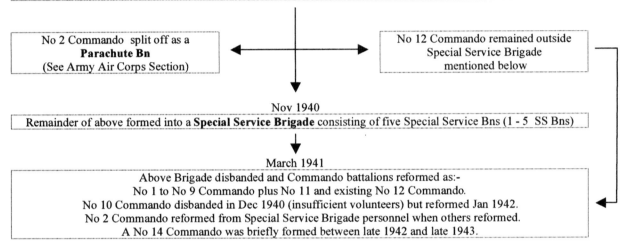

> No 2 Commando split off as a
> **Parachute Bn**
> (See Army Air Corps Section)

> No 12 Commando remained outside
> Special Service Brigade
> mentioned below

Nov 1940
> Remainder of above formed into a **Special Service Brigade** consisting of five Special Service Bns (1 - 5 SS Bns)

March 1941
> Above Brigade disbanded and Commando battalions reformed as:-
> No 1 to No 9 Commando plus No 11 and existing No 12 Commando.
> No 10 Commando disbanded in Dec 1940 (insufficient volunteers) but reformed Jan 1942.
> No 2 Commando reformed from Special Service Brigade personnel when others reformed.
> A No 14 Commando was briefly formed between late 1942 and late 1943.

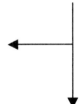

> No 6 Commando included a seaborne
> (101) troop, which went towards
> forming a second Special Boat Section
> – See Special Boat Service subsection
> for further information.

> Battalions began to be disbanded from early 1943.
> **All Army Commando were gone by 1946**

> The above **Army Commando** personnel generally wore the cap badges of their original regiments with **Commando**
> shoulder flashes and other shoulder badges. However, one of them did wear a special cap badge. This was the
> second No 2 Commando (the first having gone off parachuting). Officer and other rank badges are shown below.

No 2 Commando
(officer's badge)

No 2 Commando
(other ranks badge)

1.2 Middle East Commando of WW2

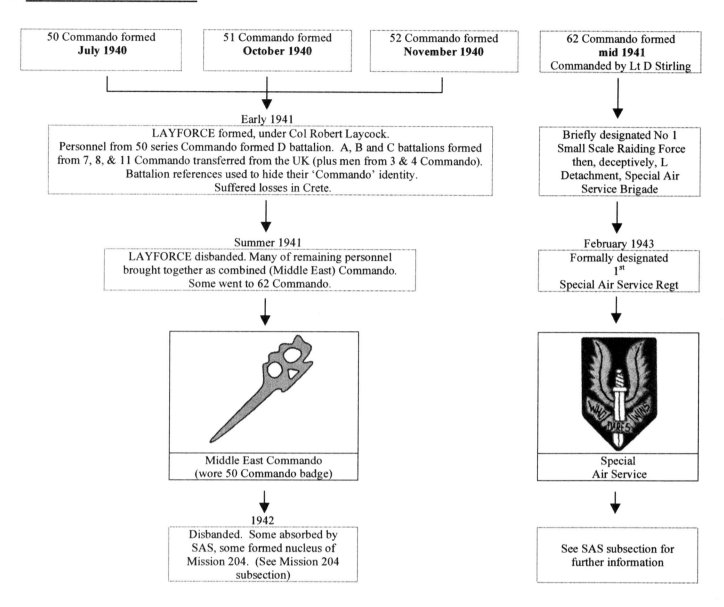

| 50 Commando formed **July 1940** | 51 Commando formed **October 1940** | 52 Commando formed **November 1940** | 62 Commando formed **mid 1941** Commanded by Lt D Stirling |

Early 1941
LAYFORCE formed, under Col Robert Laycock.
Personnel from 50 series Commando formed D battalion. A, B and C battalions formed from 7, 8, & 11 Commando transferred from the UK (plus men from 3 & 4 Commando). Battalion references used to hide their 'Commando' identity.
Suffered losses in Crete.

Briefly designated No 1 Small Scale Raiding Force then, deceptively, L Detachment, Special Air Service Brigade

Summer 1941
LAYFORCE disbanded. Many of remaining personnel brought together as combined (Middle East) Commando. Some went to 62 Commando.

February 1943
Formally designated 1st Special Air Service Regt

Middle East Commando
(wore 50 Commando badge)

Special Air Service

1942
Disbanded. Some absorbed by SAS, some formed nucleus of Mission 204. (See Mission 204 subsection)

See SAS subsection for further information

1.3 Royal Marine Commando of WW2

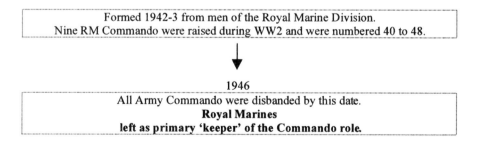

Formed 1942-3 from men of the Royal Marine Division.
Nine RM Commando were raised during WW2 and were numbered 40 to 48.

1946
All Army Commando were disbanded by this date.
Royal Marines
left as primary 'keeper' of the Commando role.

1.4 WW2 Commando – Concluding Comments

WW2 Commando are placed at the beginning of this section because they were the forerunners of several of our Elite and Special Forces. The original 2 Commando led to the Parachute Regiment (and Glider Pilot Regiment); 6 and 8 Commando contributed to the Special Boat Squadron, Middle East Commando contributed to Mission 204; 62 Commando led to the Special Air Service and, finally, Royal Marine Commando kept the Commando name alive.

2.   UNITED KINGDOM SPECIAL FORCES GROUP

2.1   Special Air Service (SAS), Special Boat Service (SBS) and Special Reconnaissance Regiment

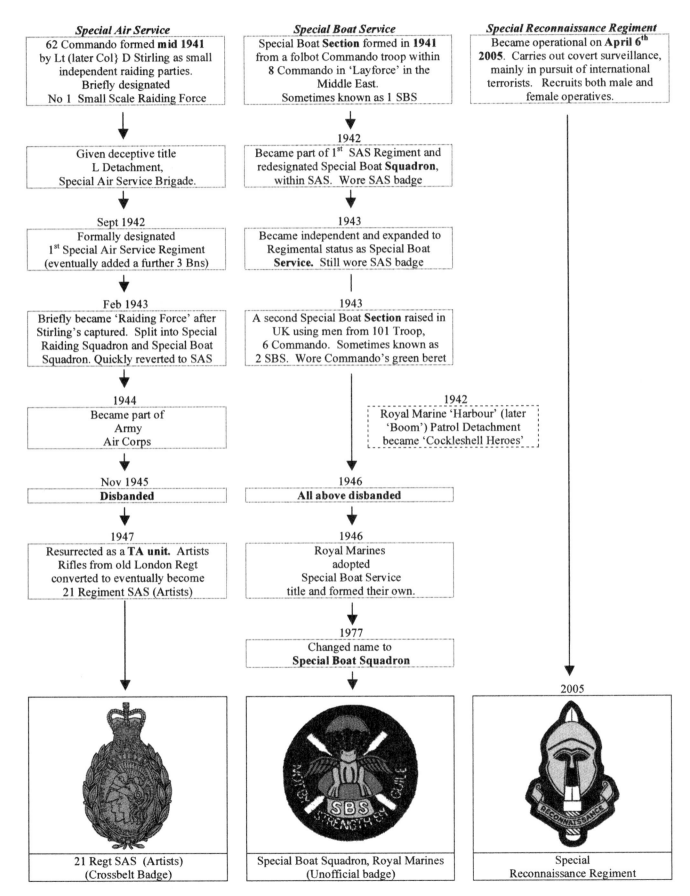

Special Air Service

62 Commando formed **mid 1941** by Lt (later Col} D Stirling as small independent raiding parties. Briefly designated No 1 Small Scale Raiding Force

Given deceptive title L Detachment, Special Air Service Brigade.

Sept 1942
Formally designated 1st Special Air Service Regiment (eventually added a further 3 Bns)

Feb 1943
Briefly became 'Raiding Force' after Stirling's captured. Split into Special Raiding Squadron and Special Boat Squadron. Quickly reverted to SAS

1944
Became part of Army Air Corps

Nov 1945
Disbanded

1947
Resurrected as a **TA unit.** Artists Rifles from old London Regt converted to eventually become 21 Regiment SAS (Artists)

Special Boat Service

Special Boat **Section** formed in **1941** from a folbot Commando troop within 8 Commando in 'Layforce' in the Middle East. Sometimes known as 1 SBS

1942
Became part of 1st SAS Regiment and redesignated Special Boat **Squadron**, within SAS. Wore SAS badge

1943
Became independent and expanded to Regimental status as Special Boat **Service.** Still wore SAS badge

1943
A second Special Boat **Section** raised in UK using men from 101 Troop, 6 Commando. Sometimes known as 2 SBS. Wore Commando's green beret

1942
Royal Marine 'Harbour' (later 'Boom') Patrol Detachment became 'Cockleshell Heroes'

1946
All above disbanded

1946
Royal Marines adopted Special Boat Service title and formed their own.

1977
Changed name to **Special Boat Squadron**

Special Reconnaissance Regiment

Became operational on **April 6th 2005**. Carries out covert surveillance, mainly in pursuit of international terrorists. Recruits both male and female operatives.

2005

21 Regt SAS (Artists) (Crossbelt Badge)

Special Boat Squadron, Royal Marines (Unofficial badge)

Special Reconnaissance Regiment

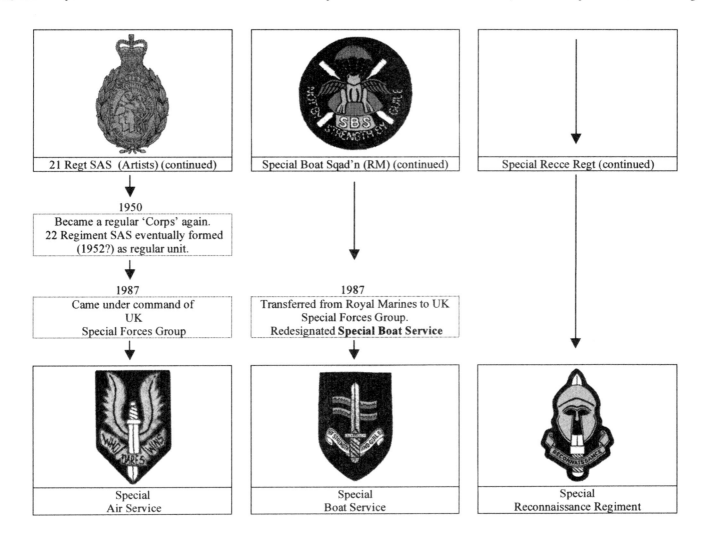

21 Regt SAS (Artists) (continued)	Special Boat Sqad'n (RM) (continued)	Special Recce Regt (continued)
1950 Became a regular 'Corps' again. 22 Regiment SAS eventually formed (1952?) as regular unit.		
1987 Came under command of UK Special Forces Group	**1987** Transferred from Royal Marines to UK Special Forces Group. Redesignated **Special Boat Service**	
Special Air Service	Special Boat Service	Special Reconnaissance Regiment

2.2   Special Forces Support Group (SFSG) and 18 (UK Special Forces) Signals Regiment

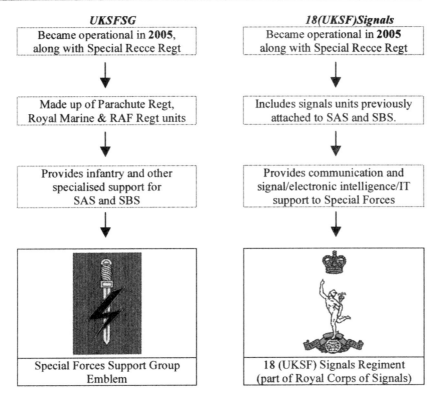

UKSFSG	*18(UKSF)Signals*
Became operational in **2005**, along with Special Recce Regt	Became operational in **2005** along with Special Recce Regt
Made up of Parachute Regt, Royal Marine & RAF Regt units	Includes signals units previously attached to SAS and SBS.
Provides infantry and other specialised support for SAS and SBS	Provides communication and signal/electronic intelligence/IT support to Special Forces
Special Forces Support Group Emblem	18 (UKSF) Signals Regiment (part of Royal Corps of Signals)

3. OTHER DISBANDED RAIDING FORCES

3.1 WW2 – North Africa and Balkans

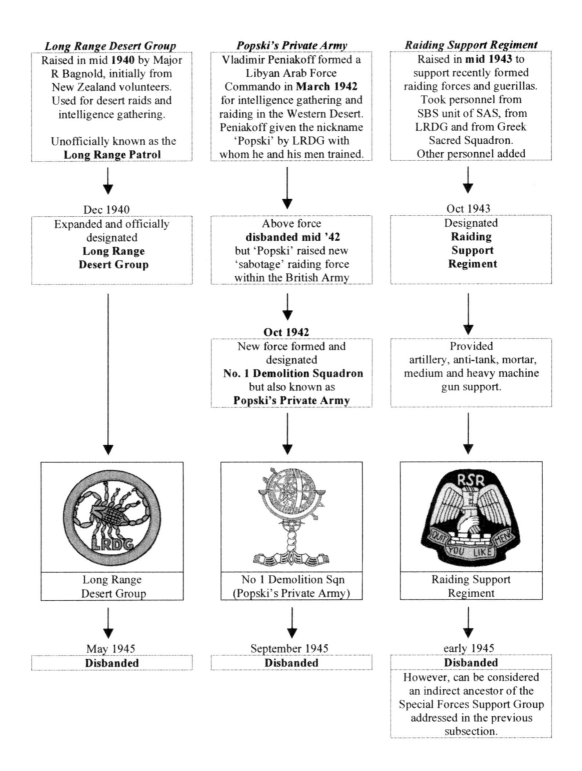

Long Range Desert Group

Raised in mid **1940** by Major R Bagnold, initially from New Zealand volunteers. Used for desert raids and intelligence gathering.

Unofficially known as the **Long Range Patrol**

Dec 1940
Expanded and officially designated **Long Range Desert Group**

Long Range Desert Group

May 1945
Disbanded

Popski's Private Army

Vladimir Peniakoff formed a Libyan Arab Force Commando in **March 1942** for intelligence gathering and raiding in the Western Desert. Peniakoff given the nickname 'Popski' by LRDG with whom he and his men trained.

Above force **disbanded mid '42** but 'Popski' raised new 'sabotage' raiding force within the British Army

Oct 1942
New force formed and designated **No. 1 Demolition Squadron** but also known as **Popski's Private Army**

No 1 Demolition Sqn (Popski's Private Army)

September 1945
Disbanded

Raiding Support Regiment

Raised in **mid 1943** to support recently formed raiding forces and guerillas. Took personnel from SBS unit of SAS, from LRDG and from Greek Sacred Squadron. Other personnel added

Oct 1943
Designated **Raiding Support Regiment**

Provided artillery, anti-tank, mortar, medium and heavy machine gun support.

Raiding Support Regiment

early 1945
Disbanded
However, can be considered an indirect ancestor of the Special Forces Support Group addressed in the previous subsection.

3.2   WW2 – Far East

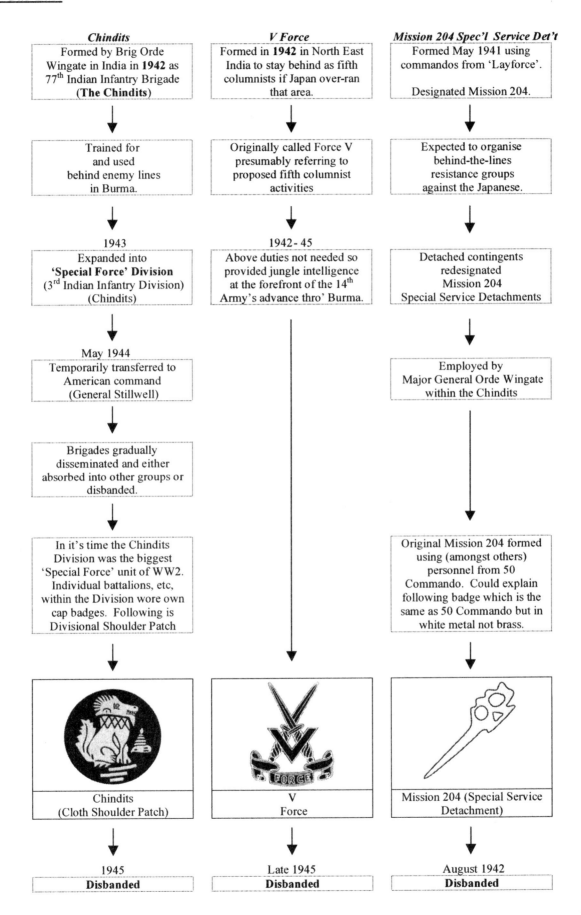

Chindits

Formed by Brig Orde Wingate in India in **1942** as 77th Indian Infantry Brigade **(The Chindits)**

↓

Trained for and used behind enemy lines in Burma.

↓

1943
Expanded into **'Special Force' Division** (3rd Indian Infantry Division) (Chindits)

↓

May 1944
Temporarily transferred to American command (General Stillwell)

↓

Brigades gradually disseminated and either absorbed into other groups or disbanded.

↓

In it's time the Chindits Division was the biggest 'Special Force' unit of WW2. Individual battalions, etc, within the Division wore own cap badges. Following is Divisional Shoulder Patch

↓

Chindits
(Cloth Shoulder Patch)

↓

1945
Disbanded

V Force

Formed in **1942** in North East India to stay behind as fifth columnists if Japan over-ran that area.

↓

Originally called Force V presumably referring to proposed fifth columnist activities

↓

1942 - 45
Above duties not needed so provided jungle intelligence at the forefront of the 14th Army's advance thro' Burma.

↓

V
Force

↓

Late 1945
Disbanded

Mission 204 Spec'l Service Det't

Formed May 1941 using commandos from 'Layforce'.

Designated Mission 204.

↓

Expected to organise behind-the-lines resistance groups against the Japanese.

↓

Detached contingents redesignated Mission 204 Special Service Detachments

↓

Employed by Major General Orde Wingate within the Chindits

↓

Original Mission 204 formed using (amongst others) personnel from 50 Commando. Could explain following badge which is the same as 50 Commando but in white metal not brass.

↓

Mission 204 (Special Service Detachment)

↓

August 1942
Disbanded

<u>WW2-Far East</u> (Continued)

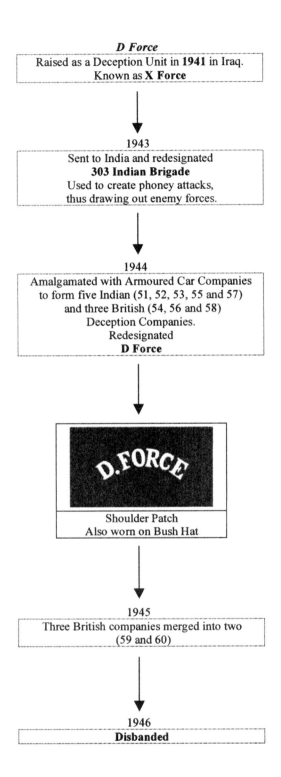

D Force

Raised as a Deception Unit in **1941** in Iraq.
Known as **X Force**

1943

Sent to India and redesignated
303 Indian Brigade
Used to create phoney attacks,
thus drawing out enemy forces.

1944

Amalgamated with Armoured Car Companies
to form five Indian (51, 52, 53, 55 and 57)
and three British (54, 56 and 58)
Deception Companies.
Redesignated
D Force

D.FORCE

Shoulder Patch
Also worn on Bush Hat

1945

Three British companies merged into two
(59 and 60)

1946
Disbanded

ARMS
AND SERVICES

ROYAL REGIMENT OF ARTILLERY
(including Royal Horse Artillery)

Before the 18th Century, 'Artillery Traynes' were raised for a particular campaign then disbanded when the campaign was over. The 'Traynes' were columns of wagons and horses pulling guns and carry equipment for an accompanying (temporarily raised) artillery unit.

1716
Two regular companies of field artillery raised. Title **Royal Artillery** first used a few years later. Artillery under control of **Board of Ordnance** – not the Army

1722
Above expanded and amalgamated with similar units in Gibraltar and Minorca to form
The Royal Regiment of Artillery

Royal Irish Regiment of Artillery formed **1756**	→ 1801 →	Expanding Royal Regiment of Artillery	← 1793 ←	Fully mounted units (**Royal Horse Artillery**) formed in **1793** as part of Royal Regt of Artillery, to provide support for cavalry
Artillery units formed in India, in **1748,** for Bengal, Madras and Bombay Presidencies	→ 1862 →	Expanding Royal Regiment of Artillery	← 1794 ←	Corps of Captains Commissaries and Drivers formed **1794**, renamed Corps of Gunner Drivers then Royal Artillery Drivers

1855
Regiment came under direct War Office Control when Ordnance Board abolished

Royal Regiment of Artillery
Victorian Helmet Plate

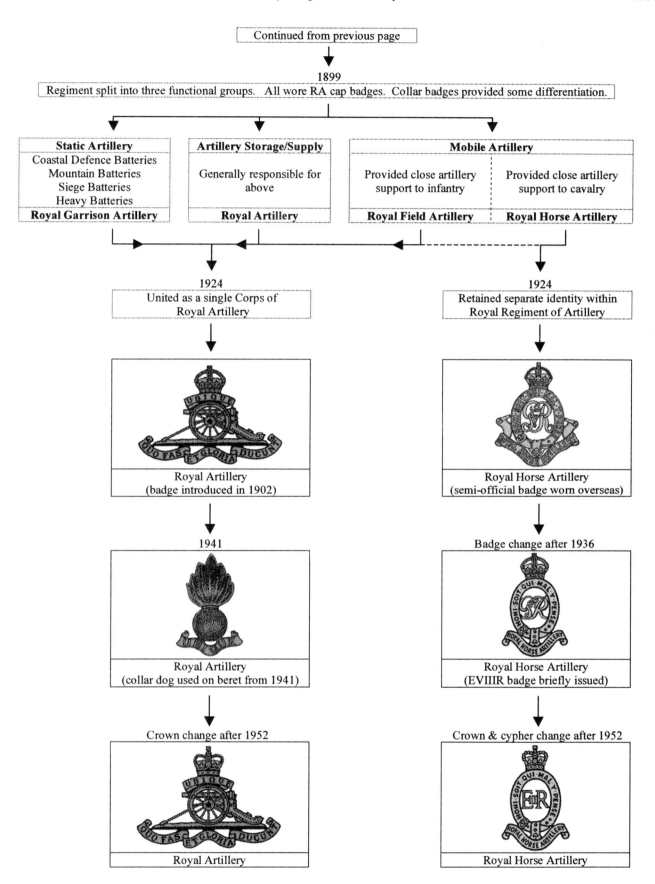

Continued from previous page

1899
Regiment split into three functional groups. All wore RA cap badges. Collar badges provided some differentiation.

Static Artillery
Coastal Defence Batteries
Mountain Batteries
Siege Batteries
Heavy Batteries
Royal Garrison Artillery

Artillery Storage/Supply
Generally responsible for above
Royal Artillery

Mobile Artillery
Provided close artillery support to infantry
Royal Field Artillery
Provided close artillery support to cavalry
Royal Horse Artillery

1924
United as a single Corps of Royal Artillery

1924
Retained separate identity within Royal Regiment of Artillery

Royal Artillery
(badge introduced in 1902)

Royal Horse Artillery
(semi-official badge worn overseas)

1941

Royal Artillery
(collar dog used on beret from 1941)

Badge change after 1936

Royal Horse Artillery
(EVIIIR badge briefly issued)

Crown change after 1952

Royal Artillery

Crown & cypher change after 1952

Royal Horse Artillery

The Royal Regiment of Artillery is large, being made up of many regiments. It is even larger during wartime. For example, the Royal Regiment of Artillery was larger than the Royal Navy at the end of WW2. The Royal Horse Artillery, within the RRofA, currently contains four separate regiments, including a **King's Troop** which carries out ceremonial duties.

CORPS OF ROYAL ENGINEERS
(including Royal Corps of Signals)

Military engineers have been around for a considerable time. William the Conquerer even brought some over when he paid us a permanent visit. Such engineers went on to feature as part of the responsibilities of the **Board of Ordnance** formed in the 16th Century.

1717
Board of Ordnance established a **Corps of Engineers** (officers only)
Actual labour provide by civilian contractors (and later by other rank personnel)

(officers)
Corps of Engineers

(workforce/other ranks)
Civilian Artificer Companies

Corps of Engineers
(officers)

1772
Soldier Artificer Company
formed in Gibraltar

1787
Given 'Royal' title
Corps of Royal Engineers
(officers)

1787
Corps of Royal Military Artificers
formed

Corps of Royal Engineers
(officers)

1797
Gibraltar Company absorbed into
Corps of Royal Military Artificers

Corps of Royal Engineers
(officers)

1812
Redesignated
Corps of Royal Sappers and Miners

1855
Board of Ordnance abolished.
Both Corps came under Army control

1856

Corps of Royal Engineers
Victorian Forage Cap Badge

Engineering Corps from Indian
Presidency Armies absorbed.

1862

1870

A telegraph troop formed
within Royal Engineers

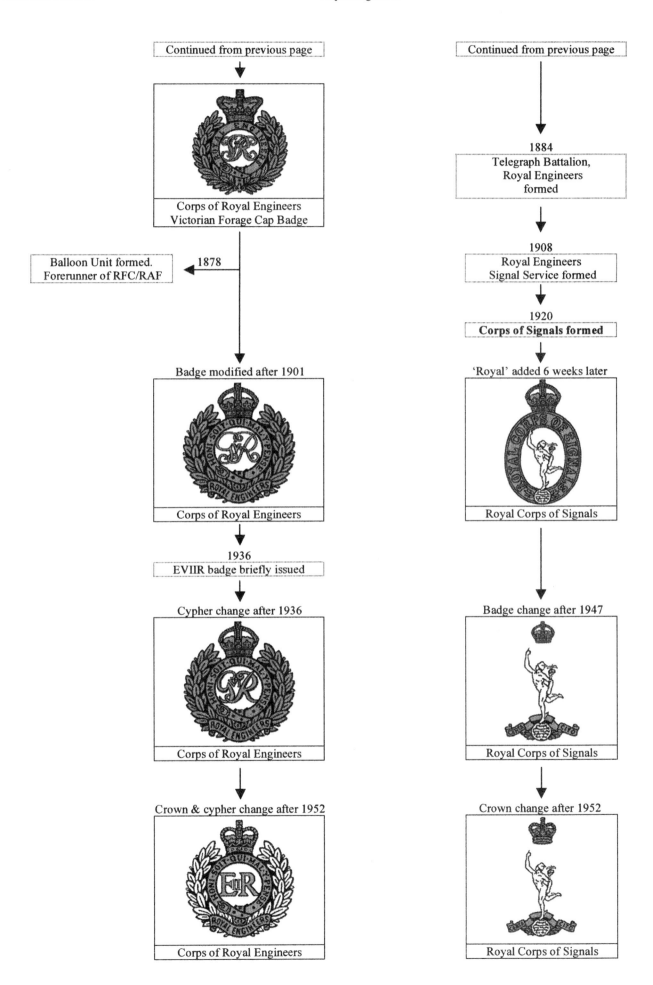

Continued from previous page

Corps of Royal Engineers
Victorian Forage Cap Badge

1878

Balloon Unit formed.
Forerunner of RFC/RAF

Badge modified after 1901

Corps of Royal Engineers

1936
EVIIR badge briefly issued

Cypher change after 1936

Corps of Royal Engineers

Crown & cypher change after 1952

Corps of Royal Engineers

Continued from previous page

1884
Telegraph Battalion,
Royal Engineers
formed

1908
Royal Engineers
Signal Service formed

1920
Corps of Signals formed

'Royal' added 6 weeks later

Royal Corps of Signals

Badge change after 1947

Royal Corps of Signals

Crown change after 1952

Royal Corps of Signals

CORPS OF ROYAL ELECTRICAL AND MECHANICAL ENGINEERS

Responsibility for electrical and mechanical maintenance of army equipment and vehicles was spread between several Corps. The ROAC maintained weapons and armoured vehicles; the RE maintained engineering equipment and their own motor vehicles; The RCS maintained communication equipment and the RASC maintained any remaining vehicles. This wasn't efficient so, in 1942, a separate Corps was set up to centralise the provision and management of the above duties. The new Corps was initially formed around the Engineering Branch of the RAOC, with input from the RE and RASC plus individual transfers from other Corps. Uptake of responsibilities was carried out in two phases, the second phase occurring in 1949.

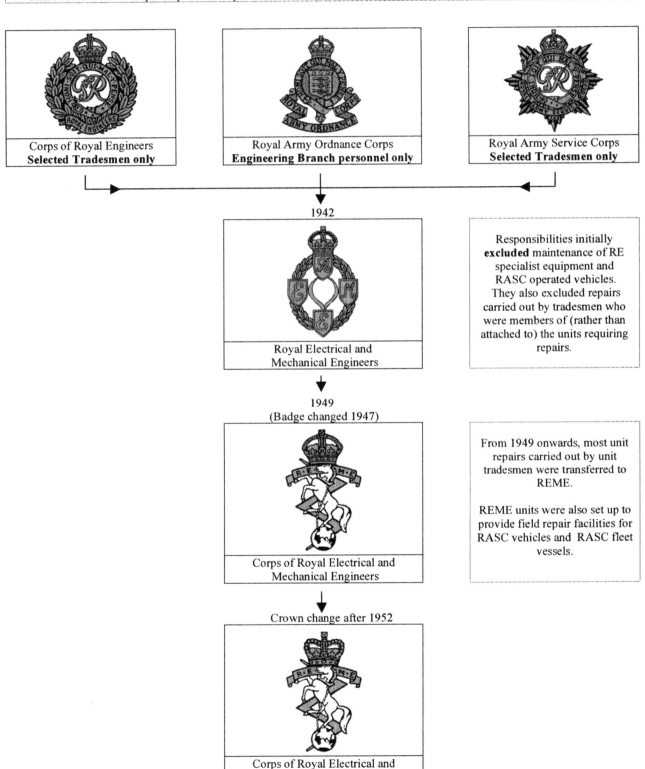

Corps of Royal Engineers
Selected Tradesmen only

Royal Army Ordnance Corps
Engineering Branch personnel only

Royal Army Service Corps
Selected Tradesmen only

1942

Royal Electrical and
Mechanical Engineers

Responsibilities initially **excluded** maintenance of RE specialist equipment and RASC operated vehicles. They also excluded repairs carried out by tradesmen who were members of (rather than attached to) the units requiring repairs.

1949
(Badge changed 1947)

Corps of Royal Electrical and
Mechanical Engineers

From 1949 onwards, most unit repairs carried out by unit tradesmen were transferred to REME.

REME units were also set up to provide field repair facilities for RASC vehicles and RASC fleet vessels.

Crown change after 1952

Corps of Royal Electrical and
Mechanical Engineers

THE ROYAL LOGISTICS CORPS

1. FORMATION

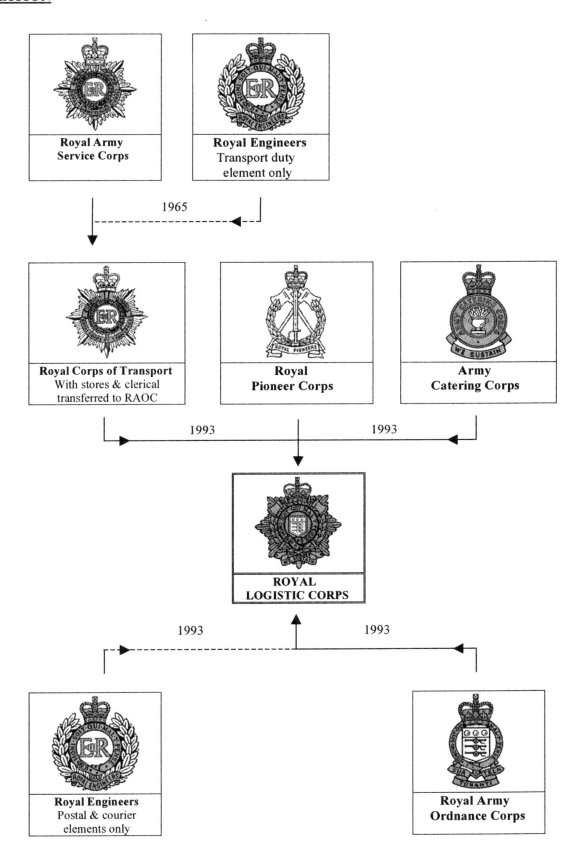

Note: The Royal Engineers remained a separate, albeit slimmer, service and are addressed in their own Section.

2. ROYAL CORPS OF TRANSPORT COMPONENT

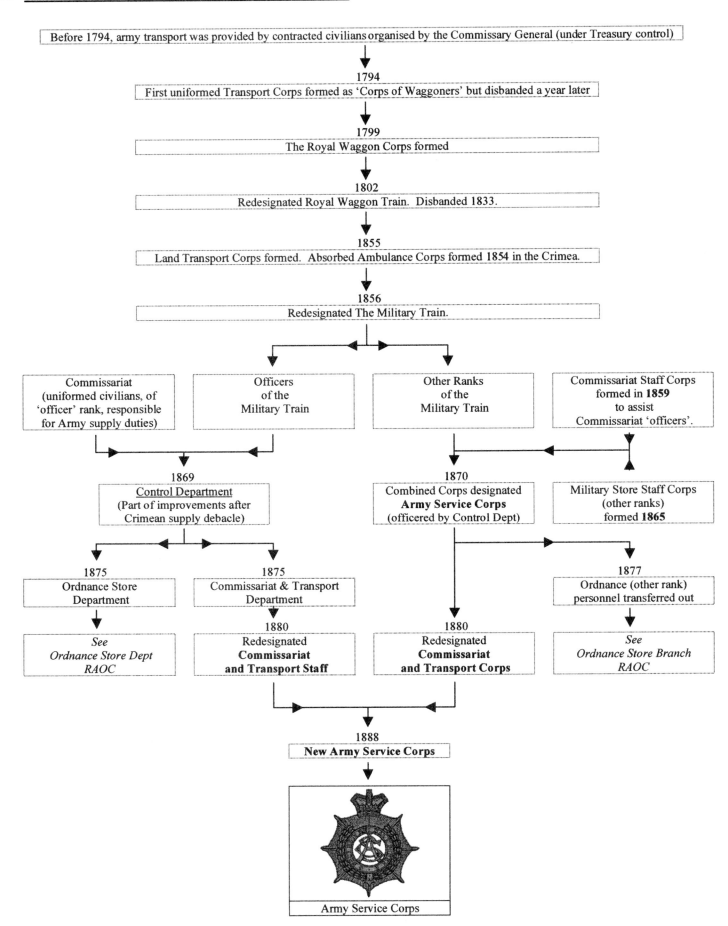

Before 1794, army transport was provided by contracted civilians organised by the Commissary General (under Treasury control)

1794
First uniformed Transport Corps formed as 'Corps of Waggoners' but disbanded a year later

1799
The Royal Waggon Corps formed

1802
Redesignated Royal Waggon Train. Disbanded 1833.

1855
Land Transport Corps formed. Absorbed Ambulance Corps formed 1854 in the Crimea.

1856
Redesignated The Military Train.

Commissariat (uniformed civilians, of 'officer' rank, responsible for Army supply duties)

Officers of the Military Train

Other Ranks of the Military Train

Commissariat Staff Corps formed in **1859** to assist Commissariat 'officers'.

1869
Control Department (Part of improvements after Crimean supply debacle)

1870
Combined Corps designated **Army Service Corps** (officered by Control Dept)

Military Store Staff Corps (other ranks) formed **1865**

1875
Ordnance Store Department

1875
Commissariat & Transport Department

1877
Ordnance (other rank) personnel transferred out

See Ordnance Store Dept RAOC

1880
Redesignated **Commissariat and Transport Staff**

1880
Redesignated **Commissariat and Transport Corps**

See Ordnance Store Branch RAOC

1888
New Army Service Corps

Army Service Corps

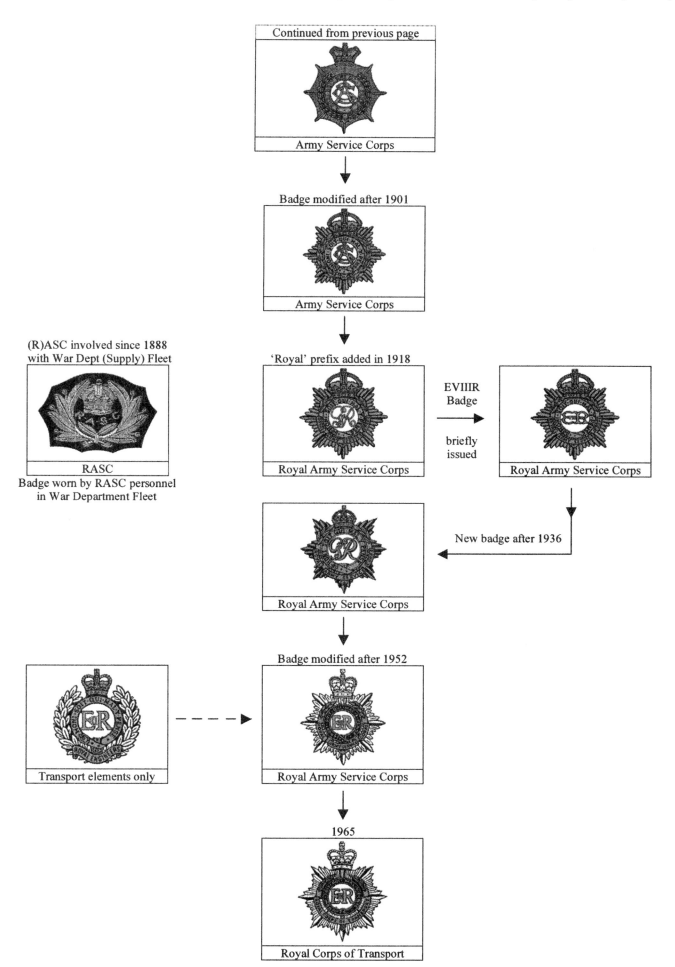

Continued from previous page

Army Service Corps

Badge modified after 1901

Army Service Corps

(R)ASC involved since 1888 with War Dept (Supply) Fleet

RASC

Badge worn by RASC personnel in War Department Fleet

'Royal' prefix added in 1918

Royal Army Service Corps

EVIIIR Badge

briefly issued

Royal Army Service Corps

New badge after 1936

Royal Army Service Corps

Transport elements only

Badge modified after 1952

Royal Army Service Corps

1965

Royal Corps of Transport

3.   ROYAL ARMY ORDNANCE CORPS COMPONENT

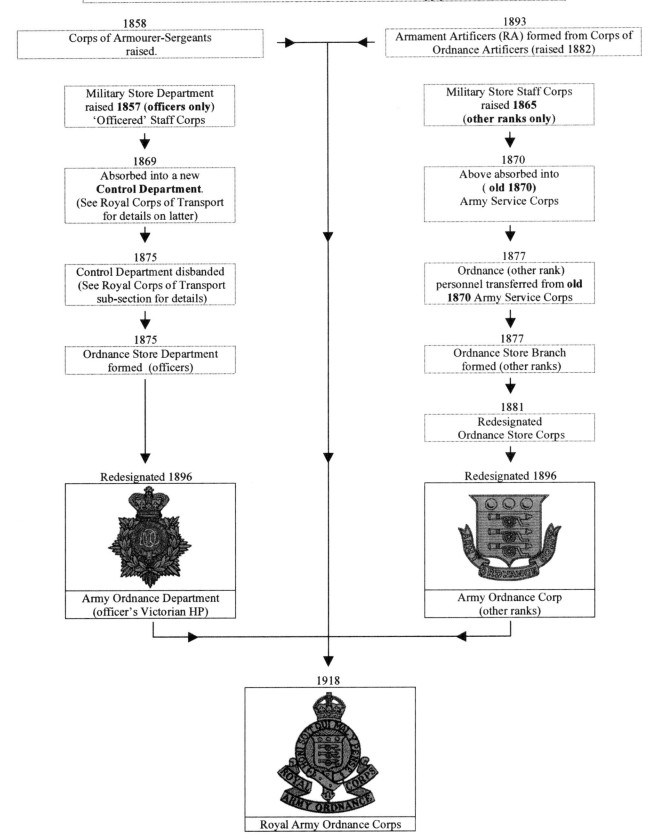

Master of Ordnance appointed in 14th Century to manage weapons, arsenals and castle etc.
Office of Ordnance created in **1544** by Henry VIII, becoming **Board of Ordnance** in 1597.
Duties were to supply guns, ammunition, stores etc to the Navy and the Army.
Board of Ordnance abolished in 1855 after Crimean supply debacle.

1858
Corps of Armourer-Sergeants raised.

1893
Armament Artificers (RA) formed from Corps of Ordnance Artificers (raised 1882)

Military Store Department raised **1857 (officers only)** 'Officered' Staff Corps

Military Store Staff Corps raised **1865 (other ranks only)**

1869
Absorbed into a new **Control Department**.
(See Royal Corps of Transport for details on latter)

1870
Above absorbed into (**old 1870**) Army Service Corps

1875
Control Department disbanded (See Royal Corps of Transport sub-section for details)

1877
Ordnance (other rank) personnel transferred from **old 1870** Army Service Corps

1875
Ordnance Store Department formed (officers)

1877
Ordnance Store Branch formed (other ranks)

1881
Redesignated Ordnance Store Corps

Redesignated 1896
Army Ordnance Department (officer's Victorian HP)

Redesignated 1896
Army Ordnance Corp (other ranks)

1918
Royal Army Ordnance Corps

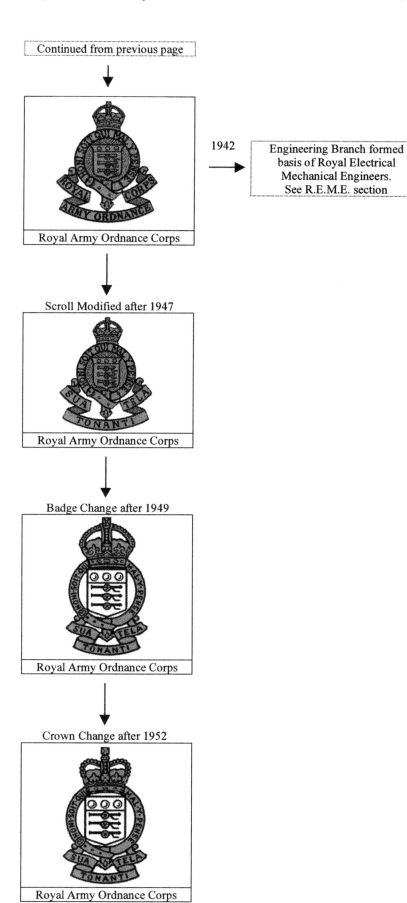

Continued from previous page

Royal Army Ordnance Corps

1942 → Engineering Branch formed basis of Royal Electrical Mechanical Engineers. See R.E.M.E. section

Scroll Modified after 1947

Royal Army Ordnance Corps

Badge Change after 1949

Royal Army Ordnance Corps

Crown Change after 1952

Royal Army Ordnance Corps

4. ROYAL PIONEER CORPS AND ARMY CARERING CORPS COMPONENTS

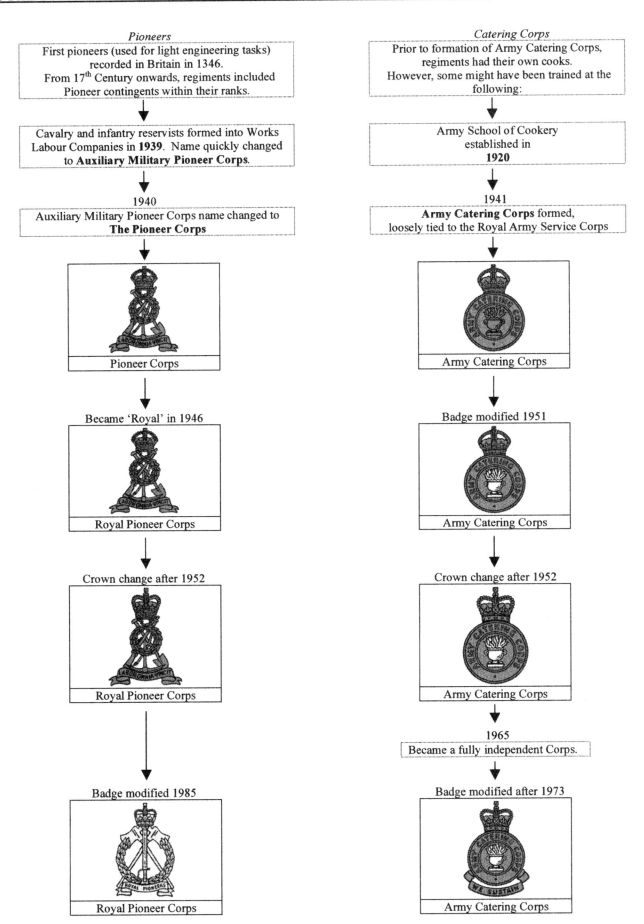

Pioneers

First pioneers (used for light engineering tasks) recorded in Britain in 1346.
From 17th Century onwards, regiments included Pioneer contingents within their ranks.

Cavalry and infantry reservists formed into Works Labour Companies in **1939**. Name quickly changed to **Auxiliary Military Pioneer Corps**.

1940
Auxiliary Military Pioneer Corps name changed to **The Pioneer Corps**

Pioneer Corps

Became 'Royal' in 1946

Royal Pioneer Corps

Crown change after 1952

Royal Pioneer Corps

Badge modified 1985

Royal Pioneer Corps

Catering Corps

Prior to formation of Army Catering Corps, regiments had their own cooks.
However, some might have been trained at the following:

Army School of Cookery established in **1920**

1941
Army Catering Corps formed, loosely tied to the Royal Army Service Corps

Army Catering Corps

Badge modified 1951

Army Catering Corps

Crown change after 1952

Army Catering Corps

1965
Became a fully independent Corps.

Badge modified after 1973

Army Catering Corps

ARMY MEDICAL SERVICES

1. ROYAL ARMY MEDICAL CORPS AND ROYAL ARMY DENTAL CORPS

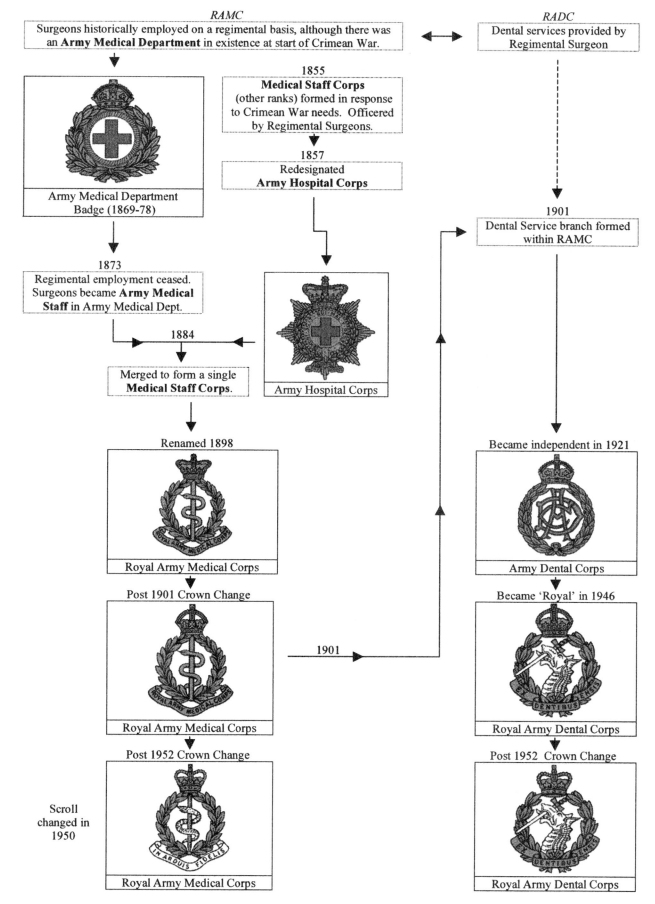

2. ROYAL ARMY VETERINARY CORPS AND QUEEN ALEXANDRA'S ROYAL ARMY NURSING CORPS

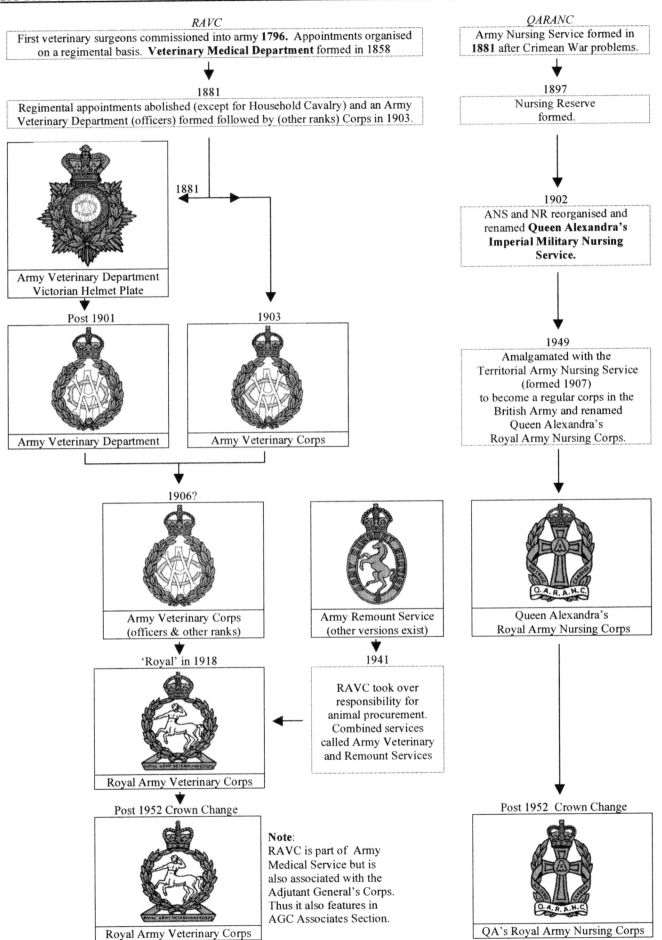

RAVC

First veterinary surgeons commissioned into army **1796.** Appointments organised on a regimental basis. **Veterinary Medical Department** formed in 1858

QARANC

Army Nursing Service formed in **1881** after Crimean War problems.

1881

Regimental appointments abolished (except for Household Cavalry) and an Army Veterinary Department (officers) formed followed by (other ranks) Corps in 1903.

1897

Nursing Reserve formed.

1881

Army Veterinary Department Victorian Helmet Plate

1902

ANS and NR reorganised and renamed **Queen Alexandra's Imperial Military Nursing Service.**

Post 1901

Army Veterinary Department

1903

Army Veterinary Corps

1949

Amalgamated with the Territorial Army Nursing Service (formed 1907) to become a regular corps in the British Army and renamed Queen Alexandra's Royal Army Nursing Corps.

1906?

Army Veterinary Corps (officers & other ranks)

Army Remount Service (other versions exist)

Queen Alexandra's Royal Army Nursing Corps

'Royal' in 1918

Royal Army Veterinary Corps

1941

RAVC took over responsibility for animal procurement. Combined services called Army Veterinary and Remount Services

Post 1952 Crown Change

Royal Army Veterinary Corps

Note:
RAVC is part of Army Medical Service but is also associated with the Adjutant General's Corps. Thus it also features in AGC Associates Section.

Post 1952 Crown Change

QA's Royal Army Nursing Corps

THE ADJUTANT GENERAL'S CORPS

1. FORMATION (plus Post-Formation Information)

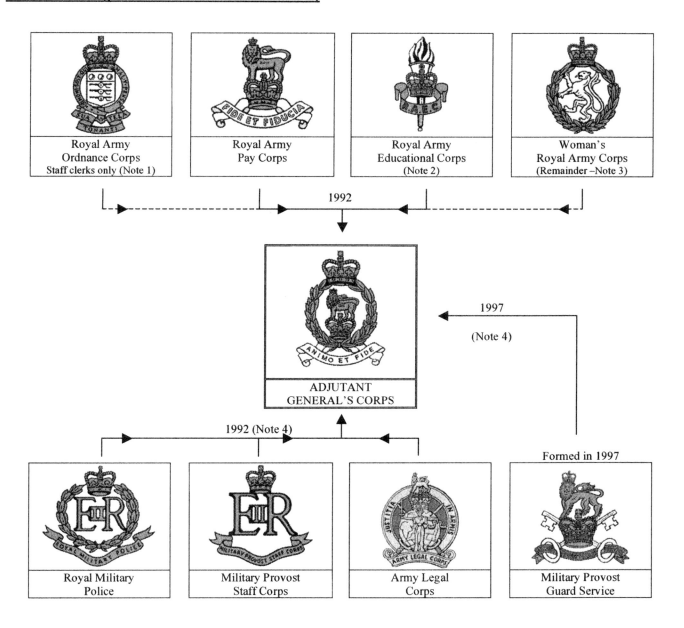

Note 1: The RAOC lost clerks to the AGC but did not become part of the AGC. It merged into the Royal Logistics Corps (RLC) and is addressed in the RLC section.

Note 2: RAEC name changed to Educational & Training Service. In 2007, they started to wear their own badge again. It was the same as the one shown above but with ETS in place of RAEC.

Note 3: The WRAC ceased to exist as a separate unit in 1992. Most WRAC personnel then adopted the badge of the unit in which they were currently serving. The remainder became part of the AGC.

Note 4: Although they became part of the AGC, the RMP, MPSC, ALC and MPGS continued to wear their own cap badges.

The AGC is organised into four branches - Provost, Staff and Personnel Support, Educational & Training Services and Army Legal Service. In addition, the AGC has administrative responsibility for some of the smaller Corps. These are addressed in an AGC Associates Section.

Arms and Services								Adjutant General's Corps								Police and Provost Components

2. <u>CORPS OF ROYAL MILITARY POLICE, MILITARY PROVOST STAFF CORPS AND MILITARY PROVOST GUARD SERVICE COMPONENTS</u>

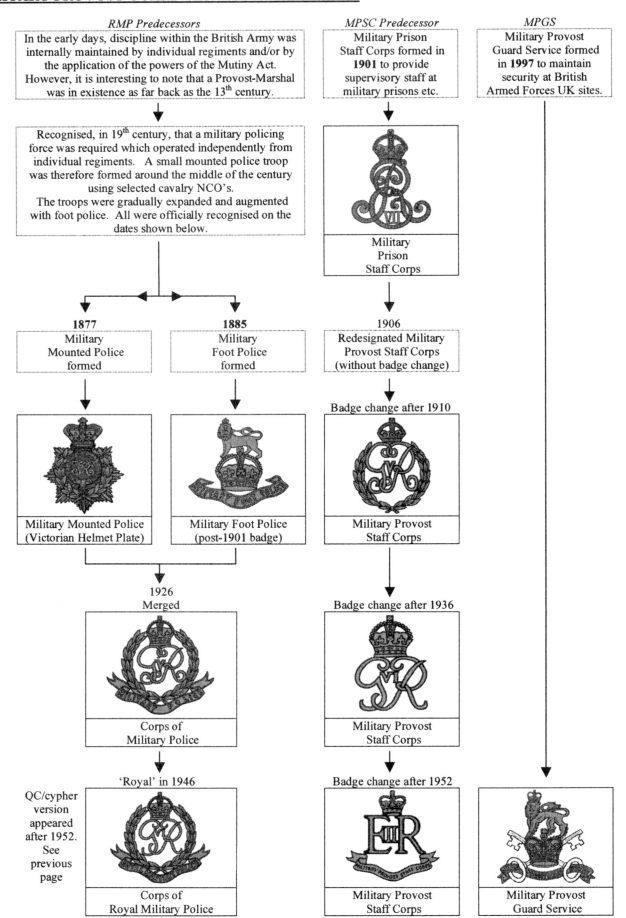

RMP Predecessors

In the early days, discipline within the British Army was internally maintained by individual regiments and/or by the application of the powers of the Mutiny Act. However, it is interesting to note that a Provost-Marshal was in existence as far back as the 13th century.

MPSC Predecessor

Military Prison Staff Corps formed in **1901** to provide supervisory staff at military prisons etc.

MPGS

Military Provost Guard Service formed in **1997** to maintain security at British Armed Forces UK sites.

Recognised, in 19th century, that a military policing force was required which operated independently from individual regiments. A small mounted police troop was therefore formed around the middle of the century using selected cavalry NCO's.
The troops were gradually expanded and augmented with foot police. All were officially recognised on the dates shown below.

Military Prison Staff Corps

1877
Military Mounted Police formed

1885
Military Foot Police formed

1906
Redesignated Military Provost Staff Corps (without badge change)

Badge change after 1910

Military Mounted Police (Victorian Helmet Plate)

Military Foot Police (post-1901 badge)

Military Provost Staff Corps

1926
Merged

Badge change after 1936

Corps of Military Police

Military Provost Staff Corps

'Royal' in 1946

Badge change after 1952

QC/cypher version appeared after 1952. See previous page

Corps of Royal Military Police

Military Provost Staff Corps

Military Provost Guard Service

3. <u>ROYAL ARMY PAY CORPS COMPONENT</u>

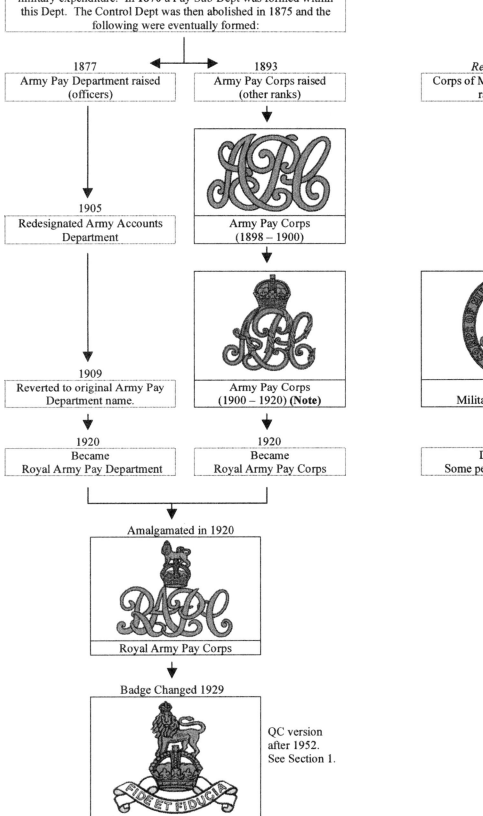

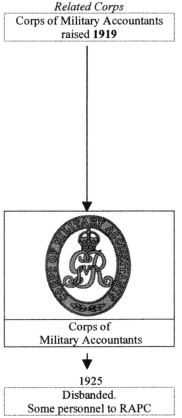

RAPC Predecessors
Prior to 1870, paymasters were employed on a regimental basis. In 1869 a Control Dept was set up to control (amongst other things) military expenditure. In **1870** a Pay Sub-Dept was formed within this Dept. The Control Dept was then abolished in 1875 and the following were eventually formed:

1877
Army Pay Department raised (officers)

1893
Army Pay Corps raised (other ranks)

Related Corps
Corps of Military Accountants raised **1919**

Army Pay Corps
(1898 – 1900)

1905
Redesignated Army Accounts Department

Army Pay Corps
(1900 – 1920) **(Note)**

Corps of
Military Accountants

1909
Reverted to original Army Pay Department name.

1920
Became
Royal Army Pay Department

1920
Became
Royal Army Pay Corps

1925
Disbanded.
Some personnel to RAPC

Amalgamated in 1920

Royal Army Pay Corps

Badge Changed 1929

QC version
after 1952.
See Section 1.

Royal Army Pay Corps

Note : A version was briefly issued featuring a (so-called) Victorian crown.

4. ROYAL ARMY EDUCATIONAL CORPS AND WOMEN'S ROYAL ARMY CORPS COMPONENTS

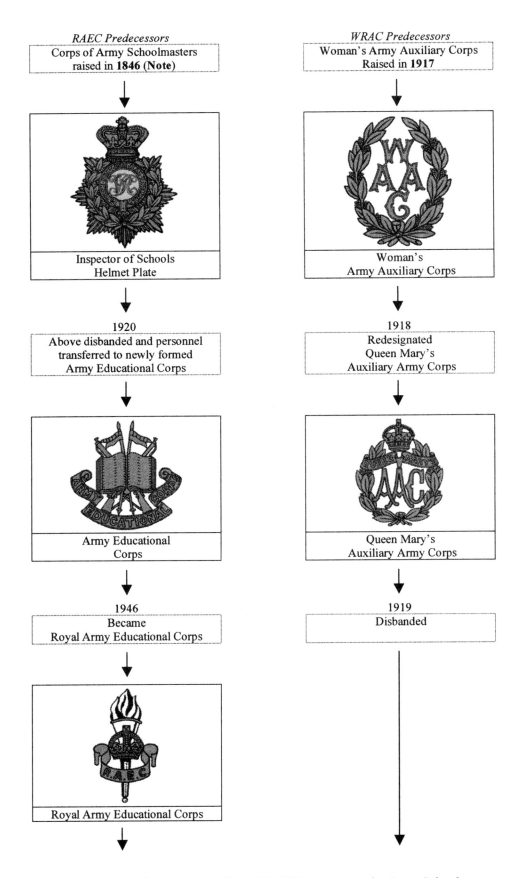

RAEC Predecessors

Corps of Army Schoolmasters
raised in **1846** (Note)

Inspector of Schools
Helmet Plate

1920
Above disbanded and personnel
transferred to newly formed
Army Educational Corps

Army Educational
Corps

1946
Became
Royal Army Educational Corps

Royal Army Educational Corps

WRAC Predecessors

Woman's Army Auxiliary Corps
Raised in **1917**

Woman's
Army Auxiliary Corps

1918
Redesignated
Queen Mary's
Auxiliary Army Corps

Queen Mary's
Auxiliary Army Corps

1919
Disbanded

Note : 'Army Schoolmistresses' were formed in 1848 to support the Army Schoolmasters.
They became the Queen's Army Schoolmistresses in 1928. Disbanded 1970.

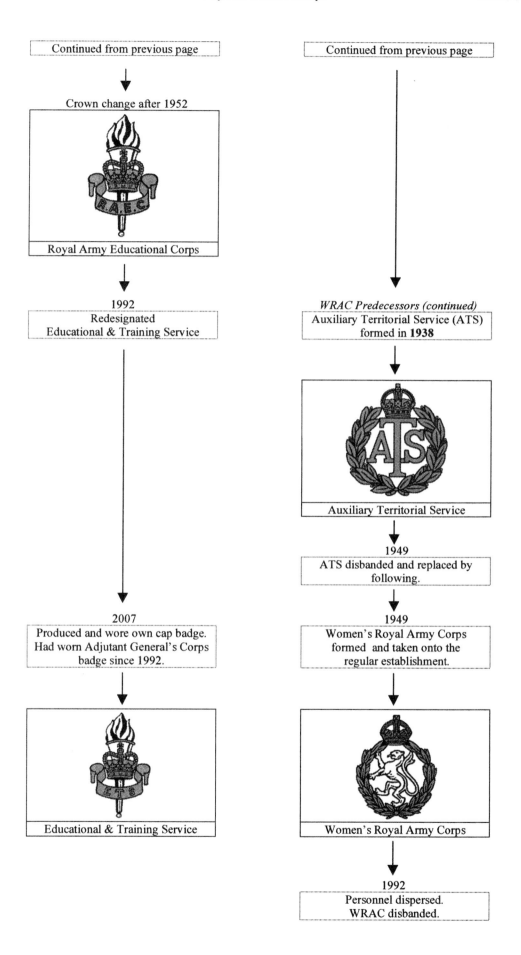

Continued from previous page

Crown change after 1952

Royal Army Educational Corps

1992
Redesignated
Educational & Training Service

2007
Produced and wore own cap badge.
Had worn Adjutant General's Corps
badge since 1992.

Educational & Training Service

Continued from previous page

WRAC Predecessors (continued)
Auxiliary Territorial Service (ATS)
formed in **1938**

Auxiliary Territorial Service

1949
ATS disbanded and replaced by
following.

1949
Women's Royal Army Corps
formed and taken onto the
regular establishment.

Women's Royal Army Corps

1992
Personnel dispersed.
WRAC disbanded.

5. ARMY LEGAL CORPS

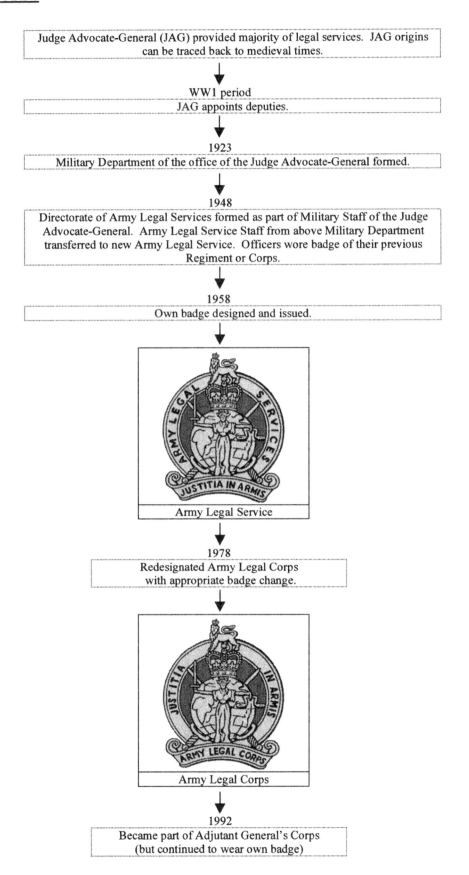

Judge Advocate-General (JAG) provided majority of legal services. JAG origins
can be traced back to medieval times.

WW1 period
JAG appoints deputies.

1923
Military Department of the office of the Judge Advocate-General formed.

1948
Directorate of Army Legal Services formed as part of Military Staff of the Judge
Advocate-General. Army Legal Service Staff from above Military Department
transferred to new Army Legal Service. Officers wore badge of their previous
Regiment or Corps.

1958
Own badge designed and issued.

Army Legal Service

1978
Redesignated Army Legal Corps
with appropriate badge change.

Army Legal Corps

1992
Became part of Adjutant General's Corps
(but continued to wear own badge)

ADJUTANT GENERAL'S CORPS ASSOCIATES

1. ASSOCIATE LIST

The following are independent units but all are relatively small. Their general (but not professional) administration has therefore been taken over by the Adjutant General's Corps (AGC) in the interest of efficiency. This is in line with the primary function of the AGC – the management of the Army's human resources (it's soldiers).

Royal Army Chaplains
Department (Christian)

Royal Army Chaplains
Department (Jewish)

Royal Army
Veterinary Corps

Small Arms
School Corps

Army
Physical Training Corps

Intelligence
Corps

General
Service Corps

Note: The Royal Army Veterinary Corps is also part of the Army's Medical Service. It thus features in that section as well as here.

2. ROYAL ARMY CHAPLAIN'S DEPARTMENT

The above is designated a Department rather than a Corps because it is entirely staffed by officers.

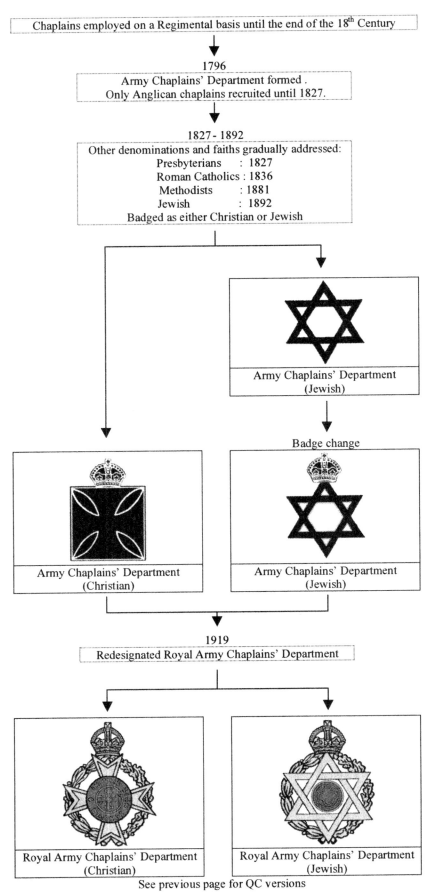

See previous page for QC versions

3. ROYAL ARMY VETERINARY CORPS AND SMALL ARMS SCHOOL CORPS

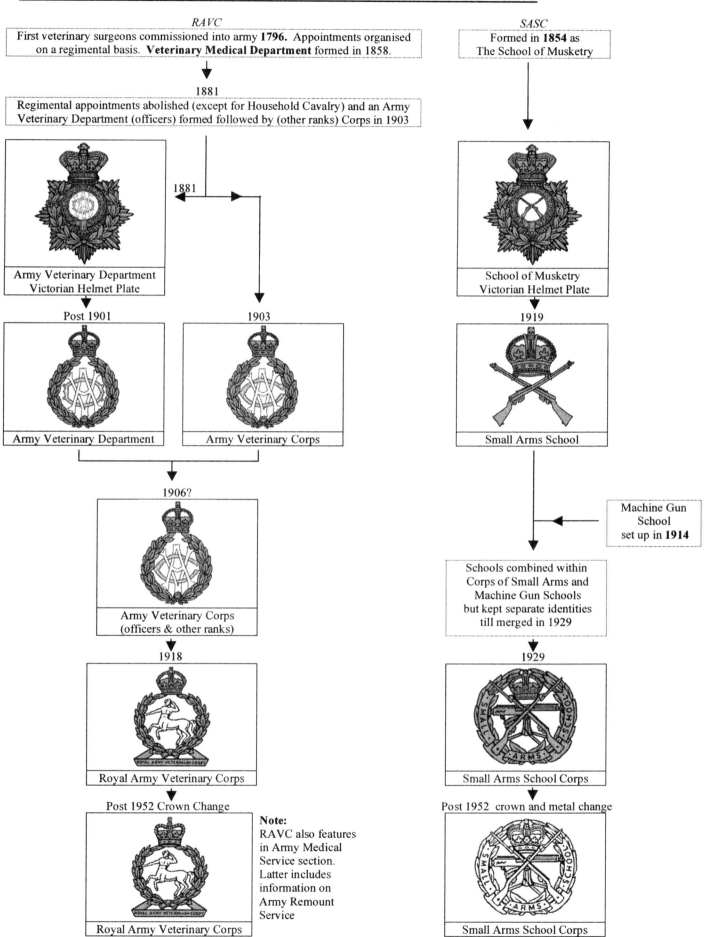

RAVC

First veterinary surgeons commissioned into army **1796.** Appointments organised on a regimental basis. **Veterinary Medical Department** formed in 1858.

1881
Regimental appointments abolished (except for Household Cavalry) and an Army Veterinary Department (officers) formed followed by (other ranks) Corps in 1903

1881

Army Veterinary Department
Victorian Helmet Plate

Post 1901

Army Veterinary Department

1903

Army Veterinary Corps

1906?

Army Veterinary Corps
(officers & other ranks)

1918

Royal Army Veterinary Corps

Post 1952 Crown Change

Royal Army Veterinary Corps

Note:
RAVC also features in Army Medical Service section. Latter includes information on Army Remount Service

SASC

Formed in **1854** as
The School of Musketry

School of Musketry
Victorian Helmet Plate

1919

Small Arms School

Machine Gun
School
set up in **1914**

Schools combined within
Corps of Small Arms and
Machine Gun Schools
but kept separate identities
till merged in 1929

1929

Small Arms School Corps

Post 1952 crown and metal change

Small Arms School Corps

4. ARMY PHYSICAL TRAINING CORPS , INTELLIGENCE CORPS AND GENERAL SERVICE CORPS

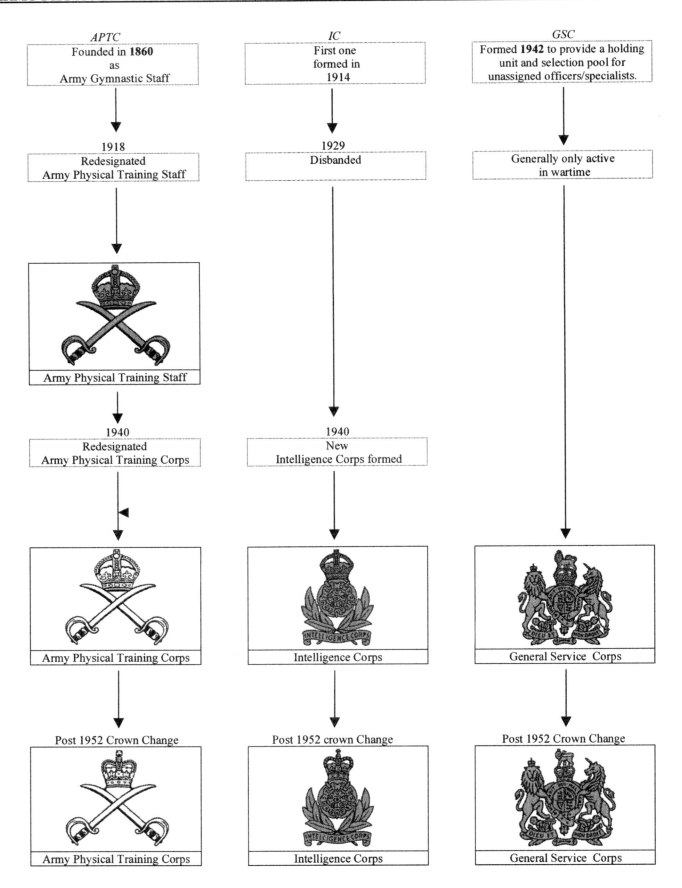

APTC
Founded in **1860**
as
Army Gymnastic Staff

IC
First one
formed in
1914

GSC
Formed **1942** to provide a holding
unit and selection pool for
unassigned officers/specialists.

1918
Redesignated
Army Physical Training Staff

1929
Disbanded

Generally only active
in wartime

Army Physical Training Staff

1940
Redesignated
Army Physical Training Corps

1940
New
Intelligence Corps formed

Army Physical Training Corps

Intelligence Corps

General Service Corps

Post 1952 Crown Change

Post 1952 crown Change

Post 1952 Crown Change

Army Physical Training Corps

Intelligence Corps

General Service Corps

Corps of Army Music

CORPS OF ARMY MUSIC

A relatively new Corps, formed in **1994** to oversee all our military bands.
The Corps is centred around the Royal Military School of Music, whose badge is shown below.
The Corps of Army Music has it's own insignia which is also shown below. However, individual bands wear their own cap badges and uniforms, usually the ones of the Corps, Regiments or Divisions to which they are affiliated.
Cap badges of the King's Division Band and the Queen's Division Band are shown as examples.

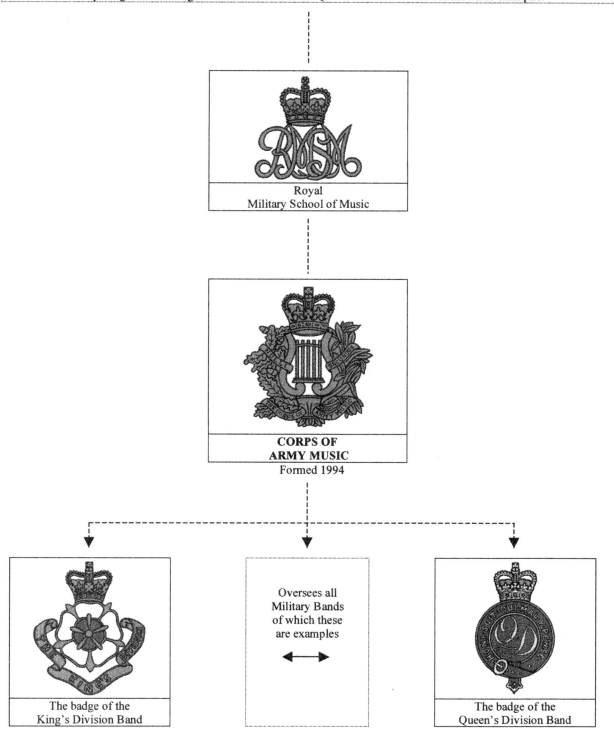

Royal
Military School of Music

CORPS OF ARMY MUSIC
Formed 1994

Oversees all
Military Bands
of which these
are examples

The badge of the
King's Division Band

The badge of the
Queen's Division Band

ROYAL MILITARY ACADEMY SANDHURST BAND CORPS

This Corps was, in it's time, the smallest regiment in the British Army. It consisted of one bandmaster and fourteen musicians when mentioned in the records in 1815 and it's numbers hadn't even reached forty when it was finally **disbanded in 1984**.

It was officially designated a Corps in **1923** and given the title **The Royal Military College Band Corps.** It changed it's name to **The Royal Military Academy Sandhurst Band Corps** in 1947 when the Royal Military College, Sandhurst merged with the Royal Military Academy, Woolwich. The 'Sandhurst' family tree, for this period, is given below.

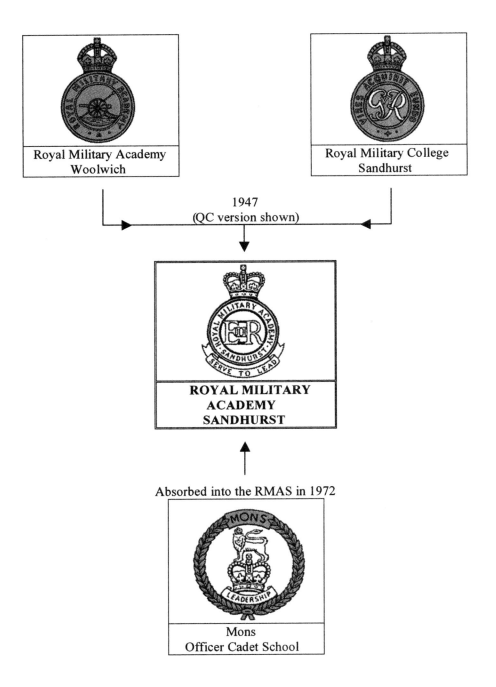

Woolwich trained Gunners, Engineering and Signals officers. Pre-1947 Sandhurst trained Cavalry, Infantry and officers of other Arms. Mons trained short-service commission officers.

OTHER DISBANDED 20TH CENTURY CORPS

Royal Defence Corps

Non-Combatant Corps

Formed in **1917**.
Took soldiers from Garrison Battalions (i.e. those too old or unfit for frontline service) and used them for internal security and guard service. Began to fade away after going thro' name and badge changes in 1936. Companies were briefly resurrected during WW2 but were gradually assimilated into territorial battalions of existing line regiments.

Formed in **1916** to accommodate conscientious objectors **within the army**. Corps members did not carry weapons or take part in battles but carried out tasks such as loading and unloading in support of the military. **Disbanded after WW1.** Resurrected for WW2. **Disbanded again after WW2.**

Badge modified

Royal Defence Corps

Name and cypher change in 1936

National Defence Company

Reformed 1939 with modified name

Non-Combatant Labour Corps

Badge and cypher change in 1936

National Defence Company
Finally faded away by end of WW2

Reverted to old name in 1940

Non-Combatant Corps
Finally disbanded after WW2

Other Disbanded 20th Century Corps (continued)

Mobile Defence Corps

Formed in **1955** during the Cold War to provide Civil Defence training within the Army. The Phoenix presumably represents us rising again from the ashes of conflict.
Disbanded in 1959.

Mobile Defence Corps
Disbanded 1959

APPENDICES

1. BRITISH ARMY ORDER OF PRECEDENCE 2008

Household Cavalry
  The Life Guards
  The Blues and Royals
Royal Horse Artillery
Royal Armoured Corps
  1st The Queen's Dragoon Guards
  The Royal Scots Dragoon Guards
  The Royal Dragoon Guards
  The Queen's Royal Hussars
  The 9th / 12th Royal Lancers
  The King's Royal Hussars
  The Light Dragoons
  The Queen's Royal Lancers
  The Royal Tank Regiment
Royal Regiment of Artillery
Corps of Royal Engineers
Royal Corps of Signals
Infantry
  Foot Guards
    Grenadier Guards
    Coldstream Guards
    Scots Guards
    Irish Guards
    Welsh Guards
  Line Infantry
    The Royal Regiment of Scotland
    The Princess of Wales's Royal Regiment
    The Duke of Lancaster's Regiment
    The Royal Regiment of Fusiliers
    The Royal Anglian Regiment
    The Yorkshire Regiment
    The Mercian Regiment
    The Royal Welsh
    The Royal Irish Regiment
    The Parachute Regiment
    The Royal Gurkha Rifles
  The Rifles
  The Special Air Service
Army Air Corps
Services
  Royal Army Chaplains Department
  Royal Logistics Corps
  Corps of Royal Electrical and Mechanical Engineers
  Adjutant General's Corps
  Royal Army Veterinary Corps
  Small Arms School Corps
  Royal Army Dental Corps
  Intelligence Corps
  Army Physical Training Corps
  General Service Corps
  Queen Alexandra's Royal Army Nursing Corps
  Corps of Army Music
  Royal Gibraltar Regiment

The Royal Marines used to be included in the Army's order of precedence as descendents of the old Army marine regiments of the 17th and 18th centuries. They were originally listed after the 49th Foot and it's subsequent descendents, because the 49th were the last regiment formed prior to the formation of the Royal Marines in 1755. The order of precedence only came into play when the Royal Marines were **not** on parade with the Royal Navy, in which case, like the Navy, they would take precedence over the Army. This dual precedence situation came about because the Royal Marines were considered a separate arm of the Royal Navy. This changed in April 2008. Since then, they have become an integral part of the Royal Navy and take precedence over the Army even if Royal Navy contingents are absent.

2. COLONELS NAMES - CROSS REFERENCES

Regiments were usually identified by their colonel's names before 1751. After that date, regiments were identified by their official number. The following tables allow you to cross-refer colonel's name with numbered regiment. The index can then be used to find that regiment within this guide. Colonels involved in the raising of particular regiments **after 1751** have also been included.

The following letter abbreviations have been used :

LG : Life Guards   RHG : Royal Horse Guards   D : Dragoons   H : Hussars   DG : Dragoon Guards   L : Lancers

Colonel's Name	Regiment	Colonel's Name	Regiment
Abercromby, Robert	75th Foot	Borthwick, William	26th Foot
Abercromby, James	50th Foot	Bowles, Phineas	6th DG
Albermarle, William, Earl of	29th Foot	and	8th H
Albermarle, George Monck, Duke of	Cold Gds	and	12th L
Ancran, William, Earl of	24th Foot	Bradford, Sir Thomas	94th Foot
Anglesey, Marquis of - see Paget, Henry, Lord		Bragg, Philip	28th Foot
Angus, James Douglas, Earl of	26th Foot	Brewer, Robert	12th Foot
Anselemne, Col	5th Foot	Bridges, Sir Matthew	17th Foot
Anstruther, Philip	26th Foot	Brown, John	4th DG
Anstruther, Robert	58th Foot	and	9th L
Arabin, John	57/59th Foot	Buchan, Thomas	21st Foot
Argyll, James, Duke of (was J Campbell)	3rd Foot	Burgoyne, John	16th L
and	9th Foot	Bury, George, Viscount	20th Foot
and	21st Foot	Byerley, Robert	6th DG
Argyll, John, 2nd Duke of	2nd DG	**Cadogan, William, Earl of**	5th DG
and	54/56th Foot	Cadogan, Lord Charles	6th D
Armiger, Robert	63rd Foot	Cambridge, Duke of – see Ulster, Earl of	
and	65th Foot	Cameron, Alan	79th Foot
Armstrong, John	18th Foot	Campbell, Sir Archibald	74th Foot
Arran, Charles, Earl of (later Duke of Hamiltion)	4th DG	Campbell, Duncan	91st Foot
and	5th DG	Campbell, Sir James (later Duke of Argyll)	2nd D
Ashley, Thomas	6th Foot	and	9th Foot
Babbington, William	6th Foot	and	21st Foot
Barrell, William	22nd Foot	Campbell, John (Earl of London / Duke of Argyll)	39th Foot
and	28th Foot	and	54/56th Foot
Barrington, Hon. John	64th Foot	and	60/62nd Foot
Barrymore, James, Earl of	13th Foot	Cannon, Alexander	3rd H
Bath, John Granville, 1st Earl of	10th Foot	Carney, Sir Charles	10th Foot
Beauclerk, Lord George	19th Foot	Carpenter, George	3rd H
Beauclerk, Lord Henry	31st Foot	Castleton, George, Viscount	30th Foot
and	48th Foot	Cathcart, Lord Charles	6th DG
Beaufort, Henry Somerset, 1st Duke of	11th Foot	and	31st Foot
Beaumont, James	8th Foot	and	9th Foot
Bellasis, Sir Henry	2nd Foot	Cathcart, George	8th H
and	6th Foot	Caulfield, William – see Charlemont, Viscount	
and	22nd Foot	Cavendish, Lord James	34th Foot
Berkely, Lord John	3rd DG	Cavendish – also see Devonshire, Earl of	
and	4th H	Charlemont, William Caulfield, Viscount	36th Foot
Bernard, George	84th Foot	Chesterfield, Philip, Earl of	3rd Foot
Bertie, Albermarle	81st Foot	Chichester, Arthur – see Donegal, Earl of	
Berwick, James, Duke of	8th Foot	Cholmeley, John	16th Foot
Beverage, William	14th Foot	Cholmondely, James	6th DG
Bissett, Andrew	30th Foot	and	12th L
Blakeney, Sir W.L.	27th Foot	and	34th Foot
Blackwell, Leigh	6th DG	and	48th Foot
Bland, Humphrey	3rd H	Cholmondely, Hon. John	6th D
and	13th H	Chudleigh, Thomas	34th Foot
and	36th Foot	Churchill, Charles	10th H
Bland, John	2nd DG	and	3rd Foot
Bligh, Thomas	5th DG	Churchill, Lord John	1st D
and	12th L	and	7th Foot
and	20th Foot	Churchill, Josiah	31st Foot
Blood, Holcroft	17th Foot	Clare, Viscount (Daniel O'Brien)	5th Foot
Bocland, Maurice	11th Foot	Clement, Neville	14th H
Borr, Jacob	32nd Foot	Clifton, Sir William	15th Foot

Colonel's Name	Regiment	Colonel's Name	Regiment
Cobham, Viscount Richard (was Sir R Temple)	1st DG	Dubourgay, Charles	32nd Foot
and	4th H	Dumbarton, Earl of	1st Foot
and	10th H	Duncanson, Robert	33rd Foot
Colchester, Richard, Viscount (was 'Rivers')	3rd DG	Dunmore, Charles, Earl of	2nd D
Columbine, Francis	10th Foot	Durell, Henry	16th Foot
Columbine, Ventris	6th Foot	Duroure, Alexander	38th foot
Conway, Henry S	13th H	Duroure, Scipio	12th Foot
and	34th Foot	**Echlin, Robert**	6th D
and	48th Foot	Edgeworth, Sir John	18th Foot
Conran, Henry	98th Foot	Elliot, George	15th H
Coote, Richard	39th Foot	Effingham, Francis, Earl of	20th Foot
Cope, Sir John	7th H	Egerton, William	20th Foot
and	9th L	and	36th Foot
and	5th Foot	Erle, Thomas	19th Foot
and	39th Foot	Erskine, Charles – See Mar, Earl of	
Cornwall, Henry	9th Foot	Essex, Augustus, Earl of	4th H
Cornwallis, Stephen (later, Lord)	11th Foot	Evans, William	2nd DG
and	34th Foot	and	4th H
Cosby, William	18th Foot	**Fairborne, Sir Palmes**	2nd Foot
Cotton, Stanhope	13th Foot	Fairfax, Lord Thomas	3rd H
Coy, John	5th DG	and	5th Foot
Crawford, John Lindsay, Earl of	2nd D	Farrington, Thomas	29th Foot
and	42nd Foot	Fenwick, Sir John	3rd DG
Crofts, James	9th L	and	5th Foot
Crook, Unton	RHG	Ferguson, James	26th Foot
Crosbie, William	89th Foot	Ferrer, Lord Robert	8th Foot
Cunningham, Sir Albert	6th D	Ferrer, Thomas	17th Foot
Cunningham, Henry	8th H	and	39th Foot
Cunningham, Robert	7th H	Fielding, Edmund	41st Foot
Cunningham, Thomas	9th Foot	Fitch, William	83rd Foot
Cuyler, Cornelius	86th Foot	Fitzcharles, Charles – see Plymouth, Earl of	
Dartmouth, George Legge, 1st Lord	7th Foot	Fitzhardinge, John, Viscount (also Lord Berkely)	4th H
Dalrymple, Lord James	26th Foot	Fitzpatrick, Edward	7th Foot
Dalrymple, Lord John (later Earl of Stair)	2nd D	Fleming, James	36th Foot
Dalway, Robert	13th H	Folliott, John	18th Foot
and	39th Foot	Forbes, Lord Arthur	18th Foot
Dalyell, Thomas	2nd D	Forrester, Lord George	30th Foot
Dalzell, Robert	33rd Foot	Forfar, Archibald, Earl of	3rd Foot
and	38th Foot	Fowkes, Thomas	2nd Foot
Dalzell, Thomas	2nd D	and	43rd Foot
De Burgh, Hon J. T.	88th Foot	Fox, Edward	32nd Foot
De Grangue, Henry	7th DG	Frampton, Charles	30th Foot
and	9th L	Francis, Alexander	38th Foot
and	30th Foot	Freake, George	19th Foot
Dejean, Lewis	6th DG	Fuller, Francis	29th Foot
and	37th Foot	Fuller, Jospeh	96th Foot
De Lalo, Sampson	21st Foot	**Gardner, James**	13th H
and	28th Foot	Gibson, John	28th Foot
Deloraine, Henry, Earl of	6th DG	Glayton, Jasper	14th Foot
and	16th Foot	Godfrey, Charles	4th DG
De Puizar, Lewis, Marquis	24th Foot	Godfrey, Francis	16th Foot
Dering, Sir Edward	24th Foot	Gordon, 4th Duke of	92nd Foot
Descury, Simon	32nd Foot	Gore, Humphrey	10th H
De Sybourg, Charles	7th DG	Gorges, Richard	35th Foot
Devonshire, William Cavendish, Earl of	7th DG	Goring, Sir Harry	31st Foot
Disney, Henry	29th Foot	Graham, Thomas – later Lord Lynedoch	90th Foot
and	36th Foot	Graham, William	11th Foot
Donegal, Arthur Chichester, Earl of	35th Foot	and	43rd Foot
Dormer, James	14th H	Granard, Earl of	18th Foot
Dormer, Richard	6th Foot	Grangue – see De Grangue	
Douglas, Sir Archibald	16th Foot	Granville, Sir Bevil	10th Foot
Douglas, James – see Angus, Earl of		Granville, John – see Bath, 1st Earl of	
Douglas, Sir Robert	1st Foot	Grove, George	19th Foot
Douglas, William	32nd Foot	Grove, Henry	10th Foot
Doyle, John	87th Foot	Guise, Sir John	6th Foot

Colonel's Name	Regiment	Colonel's Name	Regiment
Hale, Sir Edward	14th Foot	Huntingdon, George Hastings, Earl of	33rd Foot
Hale, John	17th L	Huntingdon, Theophilus, Earl of	13th Foot
Halkett, Sir Colin	95th Foot	Huske, John	32nd Foot
Halkett, Sir Peter	44th Foot	**Inchiquin, William, Earl of**	2nd Foot
Hall, Gage John	99th Foot	Ingoldsby, Richard	18th Foot
Hamilton, Archibald	14th H	and	23rd Foot
and	27th Foot	Irwin, Viscount Richard	1st DG
Hamilton, Duke of (was Earl of Arran)	4th DG	and	16th Foot
Hamilton, Frederick	18th Foot	Irwine, Alexander	5th Foot
Hamilton, Lord George (later Earl of Orkney)	1st Foot	Isla, Archibald, Earl of	36th Foot
and	7th Foot	**Jacob, Sir John**	13th Foot
Hamilton, Gustavus (later Viscount Boyne)	20th Foot	Jedburgh, Lord	7th H
Hamilton, Hans	16th Foot	Jocelyn, George	4th DG
and	34th Foot	Johnson, John	33rd Foot
Hamilton, Richard	5th DG	Jones, Edward	38th Foot
Hammer, Sir John	11th Foot	Jones, James	38th Foot
Handasyd, Roger	16th Foot	Jordan, John	15th Foot
Handasyd, Thomas	22nd Foot	**Kane, Richard**	9th Foot
Handasyd, William	31st Foot	Kellum, George	5th DG
Hargrave, William	7th Foot	Kennedy, James	43rd Foot
and	9th Foot	Kerr, Lord John	31st Foot
and	31st Foot	Kerr, Lord Mark	11th H
Harrington, William, Earl of	13th H	and	13th Foot
Harrison, Harry	15th Foot	and	29th Foot
Harrison, Thomas	6th Foot	Kerr, William	7th H
Harvey, Daniel	2nd DG	Killigrew, Robert	8th H
Harwich, Charles, Marquis of	7th DG	Kirke, Piercy	2nd Foot
Hastings, Ferdinando	13th Foot	**Lambton, Hedworth**	52nd Foot
Hastings, George – see Huntingdon, Earl of		Lambton, John	68th Foot
Hawley, Henry	1st D	Langdale, Lord Marmaduke	5th DG
and	13th H	Langston, Francis	4th DG
and	33rd Foot	Lanier, Sir John	1st DG
Hay, Lord John	2nd D	Lascelle, Peregrine	47th Foot
Hayes, Robert	34th Foot	Lee, John	44th Foot
Hepburn, Sir John	1st Foot	Legge, George – see Dartmouth, Lord	
Herbert, Arthur – see Torrington, Earl of		Leigh, Charles	82nd Foot
Herbert, Charles	23rd Foot	Leigh, Henry	33rd Foot
Herbert, Lord Henry	23rd Foot	Leinster, Duke of	7th DG
Herbert, William	14th Foot	Leighton, Francis	32nd Foot
Hertford, Algernon, Earl of	15th Foot	Lenoe, Charles	8th Foot
Hess, d'Armstadt, Prince George	6th Foot	and	36th Foot
Hewett, Viscount	6th DG	Leslie, Sir James	15th Foot
Hill, John	11th Foot	Leven, David Melville, Earl of	25th Foot
Hitchinbroke, Edward, Viscount	37th Foot	Leveson, Richard	2nd DG
Hodges, Robert	16th Foot	and	3rd H
Holmes, Henry	31st Foot	Ligonier, Francis	13th H
Honeywood, Sir Philip	1st DG	and	48th Foot
and	3rd H	Ligonier, Sir John (later 'Earl')	2nd DG
and	11th H	and	7th DG
Hopson, Peregrine Thomas	29th Foot	Lillingston, Luke	6th Foot
Hotham, Sir Charles	8th Foot	and	38th Foot
and	18th Foot	Lindsay, John – see Crawford, Earl of	
and	36th Foot	Linlithgow, George, Earl of	Scts Gds
Houghton, Sir Adolphus	8th H	Litchfield, Edward, Earl of	12th Foot
Houghton, Daniel	24th Foot	Livesay, John	12th Foot
and	45th Foot	Livingstone, Sir Thomas	2nd D
Howard, Sir Charles	3rd DG	Londonderry, Thomas, Earl of	2nd DG
and	19th Foot	and	3rd Foot
Howard, George	3rd Foot	Long, James	44th Foot
Howard, Henry – see Norfolk, 7th Duke of		Loudoun, George, Earl of	30th Foot
Howard, Thomas	3rd Foot	Loyd, Edward	5th Foot
and	24th Foot	Loyd, William	3rd H
Howe, Emanuel	15th Foot	Lucas, Richard	38th Foot
Howe, William, Earl	48th Foot	Lucas, Lord Robert	34th Foot
Hunsdon, Lord Robert	12th Foot		

Colonel's Name	Regiment	Colonel's Name	Regiment
Lumley, Henry	1st DG	**Naison, Philip**	13th H
Lumley, Richard, Viscount (Earl of Scarborough)	6th DG	Napier, Robert	5th DG
Lutterell, Alexander	31st Foot	and	51/53rd Foot
Lutterell, Francis	19th Foot	Neville, Clement	5th DG
Lynedoch, Lord – see Graham, Thomas		and	8th H
Macartney, George	6th DG	and	14th H
and	21st Foot	Newton, John	20th Foot
Macleod, Lord John (Mackenzie)	71st Foot	Newton, William	39th Foot
Mackay, Robert	21st Foot	Nicholas, Oliver	9th Foot
Mackenzie, Francis (later Lord Seaforth)	78th Foot	Norfolk, Henry Howard, 7th Duke of	12th Foot
Mackenzie, John – see Macleod, Lord		and	22nd Foot
Mackenzie, Kenneth – see Seaforth, Earl of		North & Grey, Lord William	10th Foot
Manningham, Coote	Rifle Bgde	Northwood, Henry	2nd Foot
Manners, Lord Charles	56th Foot	Nugent, George	85th Foot
Manners, Lord Robert	36th Foot	**O'Brien, Daniel – see Clare, Viscount**	
Mar, Charles Erskine, Earl of	21st Foot	O'Farrell, Francis Fergus	21st Foot
Marsh, James	77th Foot	O'Farrell, Richard	22nd Foot
Marlborough, Charles, Duke of	38th Foot	O'Hara – see Lord Tyrawley	
Marlborough, John, Earl of	24th Foot	Oglethorpe, Sir Theophilus	3rd Foot
Maxwell, Thomas	4th H	Onslow, Richard	8th Foot
Meath, Edward, Earl of	18th Foot	and	39th Foot
Meinhardt, Count	7th DG	Orkney, Earl of – see Hamilton, Lord George	
Melville, David – see Leven, Earl of		Orrery, Charles, Earl of	21st Foot
Meredith, Thomas	20th Foot	Osborn, Sir George	73rd Foot
and	21st Foot	Otway, Charles	35th Foot
and	37th Foot	Otway, James	9th Foot
Middleton, Charles, Earl of	2nd Foot	Oxford, Aubrey, Earl of	RHG
Middleton, John	13th Foot	**Paget, Henry Lord, (later Marquis of Anglesey)**	80th Foot
Molesworth, Richard, Viscount	5th L	Paget, Thomas	22nd Foot
and	9th L	and	32nd Foot
and	27th Foot	Palmes, Francis	6th DG
Monk, Thomas	5th Foot	Panmure, William, Earl of	25th Foot
Monck, George (later Duke of Albermarle)	LG	Pearce, Thomas	4th DG
and	Coldst Gds	Pembroke, Henry, Earl of	1st DG
Montagu, Sir Charles	59th Foot	Pepper, James	8th H
Montague, Edward	11th Foot	Perry, George	55th Foot
Montague, John, Duke of	2nd DG	Peterborough, Henry Mordaunt, Earl of	2nd DG
Montgomery, William, Visc't (Marquis of Powis)	11th Foot	and	2nd Foot
Mordaunt, Sir John (later Viscount)	7th DG	Peyton, Sir Robert	20th Foot
and	10th H	Phillips, Richard	12th Foot
and	12th L	and	38th Foot
and	18th Foot	and	40th Foot
and	21st Foot	Pierce, Richard	5th Foot
and	28th Foot	Plymouth, Charles Fitzcharles, 1st Earl of	3rd DG
and	47th Foot	and	4th Foot
Morduant, Henry – see Earl of Peterborough		Pocock, John	8th Foot
Morgan, Thomas	3rd Foot	and	36th Foot
Morgan, Sir John	23rd Foot	Pole, Edward	10th Foot
Morrison, Henry	8th Foot	Polwarth, Lord Patrick	7th H
Mostyn, John	7th Foot	Ponsonby, Henry	37th Foot
Moyle, John	22nd Foot	Portmore, David, Earl of	2nd D
and	36th Foot	and	2nd Foot
Mulgrave, John, Earl of	3rd Foot	Powlet, Sir Charles A	13th H
Munden, Richard	8th H	and	9th Foot
and	13th H	Pownall, Thomas	30th Foot
Munro, Andrew	26th Foot	Powis, Marquis of – see Montgomery, William	
Munro, Sir Robert	37th Foot	Preston, George	26th Foot
Murray, Lord John	42nd Foot	Price, Nicholas	28th Foot
Murray, Hon. Robert	37th Foot	Price, John	46th Foot
and	38th Foot	Price, Joseph	14th Foot
Murray, T	46th Foot	Primrose, Gilbert	24th Foot
Musgrave, Thomas	76th Foot	Pulteny, Henry	13th Foot
		Purcell, Toby	23rd Foot

Colonel's Name	Regiment	Colonel's Name	Regiment
Read, George	29th Foot	**Talbot, Sir John**	6th DG
Reade, George	9th L	Tatton, William	3rd Foot
and	9th Foot	and	24th Foot
de Reda, Henry, Marquis	6th Foot	Temple, Sir Richard (later Viscount Cobham)	1st DG
Rich, Sir Robert	6th DG	and	4th H
and	4th H	and	10th H
and	8th H	Teviot, Andrew, Earl of	2nd Foot
and	13th H	Teviot, Viscount (Sir Thomas Livingstone)	2nd D
Richard, Solomon	17th Foot	Tidcomb, Thomas	14th Foot
Richbell, Edward	39th Foot	Tiffin, Zachariah	27th Foot
Rivers, James	6th Foot	Tollemache, Thomas	5th Foot
Rivers, Richard (later Viscount Colchester)	3rd DG	Torrington, Arthur Herbert, Earl of	15th Foot
Rose, Alexander	12th L	Torrington, George, Viscount	48th Foot
and	20th Foot	Trelawney, Edward	49th Foot
Rothes, John, Earl of	2nd D	Tufton, Sackville	15th Foot
and	6th D	Tyrawley, Lord James (was J. O'Hara)	4th
Rowe, Archibald	21st Foot	and	14th H
Russell, John	Gren Gds	and	7th Foot
Sabine, Joseph	23rd Foot	and	10th Foot
Sackville, Lord George	6th DG	Tyrawley, Lord Charles (was Sir Chas O'Hara)	7th Foot
and	12th L	Tyrrell, James	17th Foot
and	20th Foot	**Ulster, Earl of (Duke of Cambridge)**	97th Foot
Sandforth, Edward	66th Foot	**Vane, Sir Walter**	3rd Foot
Sankey, Nicholas	39th Foot	and	6th Foot
Saunderson, Thomas	30th Foot	Venner, Samuel	24th Foot
Schomberg, Count	1st Foot	Villiers, Edward	2nd DG
Seaforth, Kenneth Mackenzie, Earl of	72nd Foot	Villiers, George	31st Foot
Selkirk, Charles, Earl of	4th DG	**Wade, George**	3rd DG
Selwyn, John	3rd Foot	and	33rd Foot
Selwyn, William	2nd Foot	Waldgrave, Hon. John	9th Foot
and	22nd Foot	Warburton, Hugh	45th Foot
Semphill, Lord Hugh	42nd Foot	Wardour, Thomas	41st Foot
Seymour, William	24th Foot	Waring, Richard	6th DG
Shannon, Richard, Viscount	6th DG	Webb, John Richard	8th Foot
Shirley, Robert	8th Foot	Wemyss, William	93rd Foot
Shrewsbury, Charles, Earl of	5th DG	Wentworth, Thomas	5th DG
Skelton, Henry	12th Foot	and	24th Foot
Skelton, John	32nd Foot	and	39th Foot
Somerset, Charles Seymour, Duke of	3rd H	Wentworth, Lord	Gren Grds
Somerset, Henry – see Beaufort, Duke of		Westmoreland, John, Earl of	37th Foot
Southwell, William	6th Foot	Wharton, Hon. Henry	12th Foot
Sowle, Robinson	11th Foot	Whetham, Thomas	12th Foot
Stair, John, Earl of	2nd D	and	27th Foot
and	6th D	Whiteford, Sir John	12th L
Stanhope, James, Earl of	11th Foot	Whiteman, James	17th Foot
Stanley, Hon. James	16th Foot	Whitshed, Samuel Walter	12th L
Stanwix, Thomas	2nd D	and	39th Foot
and	12th Foot	Wills, Charles	3rd Foot
and	30th Foot	and	30th Foot
St Clair, James	1st Foot	Windsor, Andrew	28th Foot
and	22nd Foot	Windsor, Thomas, Viscount	3rd DG
Stearne, Richard	18th Foot	Windress, William	37th Foot
Steuart, William	9th Foot	Wisely, Henry	5th Foot
St George, Sir George	17th Foot	Wolfe, Edward	8th Foot
St George, Richard	8th H	Wolfe, James	67th Foot
and	20th Foot	Wood, Cornelius	3rd DG
Strode, William	62nd Foot	Wood, Sir James	21st Foot
Sutton, Richard	19th Foot	Worcester, Charles, Marquis of	11th Foot
Sybourg – see De Sybourg		Wyndham, Hugh	6th DG
Sydney, Hon. Robert	3rd Foot	Wynne, Owen	4th DG
		and	5th L
		and	9th L
		Wynyard, John	17th Foot

3. REGIMENT OF FOOT CROSS-REFERENCES

3.1 Cross-Reference By Number

Most numbered Regiments of Foot had an additional territorial (or other) designation prior to 1881. Many kept that designation (or something similar) when the use of identifying numbers was discontinued in that year. However, some did not. The 2nd Warwickshires (24th Foot) for example, eventually became the South Wales Borderers.   The following list therefore addresses both sides of the 1881 divide.

Pre-1881 Territorial (or other) Designation	Regt No.	Post-July 1881 Territorial (abbreviated) Designation	Pre-1881 Territorial (or other) Designation	Regt No.	Post-July 1881 Territorial (abbreviated) Designation
Royal Scots	1	Royal Scots	West Essex	56	Essex Regt
Queen's Royal	2	Queen's (R West Surreys)	West Middlesex	57	D of C's Own (Middlesex)
East Kent (Buffs)	3	Buffs (East Kents)	Rutlandshire	58	Northants
King's Own Royal	4	King's Own (R Lancs)	2nd Nottinghamshire	59	East Lancashires
Northumberland Fusiliers	5	Northumberland Fusiliers	King's Royal Rifle Corps	60	King's Royal Rifle Corps
Royal Warwickshires	6	Royal Warwickshires	South Gloucestershire	61	Gloucestershires
Royal Fusiliers	7	Royal Fusiliers	Wiltshire	62	D of Ed's (Wiltshires)
The King's	8	King's (Liverpool)	West Suffolk	63	Manchester Regt
East Norfolk	9	Norfolks	2nd Staffordshires	64	P of W's (North Staffords)
Lincolnshire	10	Lincolnshires	2nd Yorkshire, North Riding	65	York and Lancasters
North Devonshire	11	Devonshires	Berkshire	66	Ps C of W's (Berks Regt)
East Suffolk	12	Suffolks	South Hampshire	67	Hampshires
1st Somerset (P Albert's LI)	13	P A's LI (Somersets)	Durham LI	68	Durham LI
Buckinghamshire	14	PofW's Own West Yorks	South Lincolnshire	69	Welsh Regt
Yorkshire, East Riding	15	East Yorks	Surrey	70	East Surreys
Bedfordshire	16	Bedfordshires	Highland (LI)	71	Highland LI
Leicestershire	17	Leicesters	D of Alb''s Own H'l'ders	72	Seaforth Highlanders
Royal Irish	18	Royal Irish Regt	Perthshire	73	Black Watch
Yorkshire, North Riding	19	PofW's Own (Yorkshires)	Highlanders	74	Highland LI
East Devonshire	20	Lancashire Fusiliers	Stirlingshire	75	Gordon Highlanders
Royal Scots Fusiliers	21	Royal Scots Fusiliers	Regt of Foot	76	D of Well's (West Riding)
Cheshire	22	Cheshires	East M'sex, D of Cambs	77	D of C's Own (Middlesex)
Royal Welsh Fusiliers	23	Royal Welsh Fusiliers	Ross-shire Buffs, H'l'ders	78	Seaforth Highlanders
2nd Warwickshires	24	South Wales Borderers	QO Cameron Highlanders	79	QO Cameron Highlanders
King's Own Borderers	25	King's Own Borderers	Staffordshire Vols	80	South Staffordshires
Cameronians	26	Cameronians	Loyal Lincoln Volunteers	81	Loyal North Lancs
Inniskilling	27	Royal Inniskilling Fusiliers	P of Wales's Volunteers	82	P of W's Vols (S Lancs)
North Gloucestershire	28	Gloucestershires	County of Dublin	83	Royal Irish Rifles
Worcestershire	29	Worcestershires	York and Lancaster	84	York and Lancaster
Cambridgeshire	30	East Lancashires	King's LI	85	King's LI (Shropshire)
Huntingdonshire	31	East Surreys	Royal County Down	86	Royal Irish Rifles
Cornwall LI	32	D of Cornwall's LI	Royal Irish Fusiliers	87	Ps Vic's (R Irish Fusiliers)
Duke of Wellington's	33	D of Well's (West Riding)	Connaught Rangers	88	Connaught Rangers
Cumberland	34	Border Regt	Princess Victoria's	89	Ps Vic's (R Irish Fusiliers)
Royal Sussex	35	Royal Sussex	Perthshire Vols (LI)	90	Cameronians
Herefordshire	36	Worcestershires	Ps L's Argyllshire H'l'ders	91	Ps L's (Suth & Argyll H's
North Hampshire	37	Hampshires	Gordon Highlanders	92	Gordon Highlanders
1st Staffordshire	38	South Staffordshires	Sutherland Highlanders	93	Ps L's (Suth & Argyll H's
Dorsetshire	39	Dorsetshires	Regt of Foot	94	Connaught Rangers
2nd Somersetshire	40	P of W's Vols (S Lancs)	Derbyshire	95	Sh Foresters (Derbyshires)
The Welsh	41	Welsh Regt	Regt of Foot	96	Manchester Regt
Black Watch	42	Black Watch	Earl of Ulster's)	97	QO R West Kents
Monmouthshire LI	43	Oxfordshire LI	Prince of Wales's	98	P of W's (North Staffords)
East Essex	44	Essex Regt	Lanarkshire	99	D of Ed's (Wiltshires)
Notts, Sherwood Foresters	45	Sh Foresters (Derbyshires)	P of W's Royal Canadian	100	P of W's Leinsters (R Can's)
South Devonshire	46	D of Cornwall's LI	Royal Bengal Fusiliers	101	Royal Munster Fusiliers
Lancashire	47	Loyal North Lancs	Royal Madras Fusiliers	102	Royal Dublin Fusiliers
Northamptonshire	48	Northants	Royal Bombay Fusiliers	103	Royal Dublin Fusiliers
Hertfordshire, Ps Charlotte's	49	Ps C of W's (Berks Regt)	Bengal Fusiliers	104	Royal Munster Fusiliers
Queen's Own	50	QO R West Kents	Madras LI	105	KOLI (S Yorkshire)
King's Own LI	51	KOLI (S Yorkshire)	2nd Bombay LI	106	Durham LI
Oxfordshire LI	52	Oxfordhire LI	Bengal Infantry	107	Royal Sussex
Shropshire	53	King's LI (Shropshire)	(Madras Infantry	108	Royal Inniskilling Fusiliers
West Norfolk	54	Dorsetshires	Bombay Infantry	109	P of W's Leinsters (R Can's)
Westmoreland	55	Border Regt	Rifle Bde (P Con's Own)	-	P Con's Own (Rifle Bde)

3.2   Cross-Reference by Territorial Name (alphabetically using July 1881 name)

Name	Regt of Foot.	Name	Regt of Foot.
Argyll, Sutherland &, H'landers (Ps Louise's)	91st & 93rd	Norfolk Regiment	9th
		North Staffordshire Regiment	64th & 98th
Bedfordshire Regiment	16th	Northamptonshire Regiment	48th & 58th
Berkshire (Princess Charlotte of W's)	49th & 66th	Northumberland Fusiliers	5th
Black Watch (Royal Highlanders)	42nd & 73rd		
Border Regiment	34th & 55th	Oxfordshire Light Infantry	43rd & 52nd
Buffs (East Kent Regiment)	3rd		
		Prince Albert's LI (Somersetshire Regiment)	13th
Cameron Highlanders (Queen's Own)	79th	Prince Consort's Own (Rifle Brigade)	Unnumbered
Cameronians (Scottish Rifles)	26th & 90th	Prince of Wales's Volunteers (South Lancs Regt)	40th & 82nd
Cornwall's (Duke of) Light Infantry	32nd & 46th	Prince of Wales's (North Staffordshire Regiment)	64th & 98th
		Prince of Wales's Own (West Yorkshire Regiment)	14th
Derbyshire Regiment (Sherwood Foresters)	45th & 95th	Princess Charlotte's of W's (Berkshire Regiment)	49th & 66th
Devonshire Regiment	11th	Princess Louises's (Sutherland & Argyll H'landers)	91st & 93rd
Dorsetshire Regiment	39th & 54th	Princess of W's Own Yorkshire Regt (Green H's)	19th
Dublin Fusiliers (Royal)	102nd & 103rd	Princess Victoria's (Royal Irish Fusiliers)	87th & 89th
Duke of Cambridge's Own (Middlesex Regt)	57th & 77th		
Duke of Edinburgh's (Wiltshire Regiment)	62nd & 99th	Queen's (Royal West Surrey) Regiment	2nd
Duke of Wellington's (West Riding Regiment)	33rd & 76th	Queen's Own (Royal West Kent) Regiment	50th & 97th
Durham Light Infantry	68th & 106th	Queen's Own Cameron Highlanders	79th
East Surrey Regiment	31st & 70th	Rifle Brigade (Prince Consort's Own)	Unnumbered
East Yorkshire Regiment	15th	Rifle Corps, King's Royal	60th
Essex Regiment	44th & 56th	Ross-shire Buffs (Seaforth Highlanders)	72nd & 78th
		Royal Scots	1st
Fusiliers, Royal (City of London Regiment)	7th	Royal Scots Fusiliers	21st
		Royal Sussex Regiment	35th & 107th
Gloucestershire Regiment	28th & 61st	Royal Welsh Fusiliers	23rd
Gordon Highlanders	75th & 92nd	Royal West Surrey Regiment (Queen's)	2nd
Green Howards (Ps of W's Own Yorkshire Regt)	19th	Royal Warwickshire Regiment	6th
Hampshire Regiment	37th & 67th	Seaforth Highlanders (Ross-shire Buffs)	72nd & 78th
Highland Light Infantry	71st & 74th	Sherwood Foresters (Derbyshire Regiment)	45th & 95th
Highlanders, Royal (Black Watch)	42nd & 73rd	Shropshire Regiment (King's Light Infantry	53rd & 85th
		Somersetshire Regiment (P Albert's Light Infantry)	13th
Inniskilling (Royal) Fusiliers	27th & 108th	South Wales Borderers	24th
Irish (Royal) Regiment	18th	South Staffordshire Regiment	38th & 80th
Irish Fusiliers (Royal) (Princess Victoria's)	87th & 89th	South Yorkshire Regiment (King's Own)	51st & 105th
Irish Rifles (Royal)	83rd & 86th	Staffordshire (North) Regiment (P of Wales's)	64th & 98th
		Staffordshire (South) Regiment	38th & 80th
Kent, East (Buffs)	3rd	Suffolk Regiment	12th
Kent (Royal West) (Queen's Own)	50th & 97th	Surrey (East) Regiment	31st & 70th
King's Light Infantry (Shropshire Regiment)	53rd & 85th	Surrey, Royal West, Regiment (Queen's)	2nd
King's (Liverpool) Regiment	8th	Sussex (Royal) Regiment	35th & 107th
King's Own (Royal Lancaster Regiment)	4th	Sutherland & Argyll H'landers (Ps Louises's)	91st & 93rd
King's Own (South) Yorkshire Light Infantry	51st & 105th		
King's Own Borderers	25th	Wales (South) Borderers	24th
King's Royal Rifle Corps	60th	Warwickshire (Royal) Regiment	6th
		Welsh (Royal) Fusiliers	23rd
Lancashire Fusiliers	20th	Welsh Regiment	41st & 69th
Lancashire (East) Regiment	30th & 59th	West Riding Regiment (Duke of Wellington's)	33rd & 76th
Lancashire (Loyal North) Regiment	47th & 81st	West Yorkshire Regiment (P of Wales's Own)	14th
Lancashire, South (Prince of Wales's Vols)	40th & 82nd	Wiltshire Regiment (Duke of Edinburgh's)	62nd & 99th
Lancaster, Royal (King's Own)	4th	Worcestershire Regiment	29th & 36th
Leicestershire Regiment	17th		
Leinster, Prince of Wales's (Royal Canadians)	100th & 109th	York & Lancaster Regiment	65th & 84th
Lincolnshire Regiment	10th	Yorkshire (East) Regiment	15th
Liverpool (King's) Regiment	8th	Yorkshire Regt (Ps of W's Own) (G Howards)	19th
London Regiment, City of (Royal Fusiliers)	7th	Yorkshire (South) Regiment (King's Own)	51st & 105th
Loyal (North Lancashire) Regiment	47th & 81st	Yorkshire (West) Regiment (P of Wales's Own)	14th
Manchester Regiment	63rd & 96th		
Middlesex Regiment (Duke of Camb's Own)	57th & 77th		
Munster Fusiliers, Royal	101st & 104th		

INDEX

Cavalry

Regular Infantry (including Guards and Gurkhas)

Argyll & Sutherland Highlanders   31 & 40

Bedfordshire &
  Hertfordshire Regiment   71 & 76
Berkshire Regiment, Royal   117
Black Watch   31 & 40
Border Regiment   54 & 56
Border Regt, King's Own Royal   53 & 55

Brigades:
  East Anglian   71
  Foresters   130
  Fusilier   65
  Green Jacket   120
  Highland   33
  Home Counties   43
  Lancastrian   54
  Light Infantry   123
  Lowland   32
  Mercian   89
  Midlands   130
  North Irish   103
  Welsh   97
  Wessex   114
  Yorkshire   81
Brigades – General Comments   26

Buffs, (East Kents)   43 & 46

Cameron Highlanders   33 & 38
Cameronians   32 & 36
Cheshire Regiment   89 & 90

Devonshire Regiment   114 & 115
Devonshire & Dorset Regt/LI   113 & 114
Dorset Regiment   114 & 115
Durham LI   123 & 126
Duke of Cornwall's LI   123 & 124
Duke of Edinburgh's
  Royal Regt (B& W)   117
Duke of Lanc's Regiment   53
Duke of Wellington's
  Regiment (West Riding)   81 & 84

Essex Regiment   71 & 76

Gloucestershire Regt   117 & 118
Gloucestershire, Berkshire
  & Wiltshire Regt/Li, Royal   113 & 117
Gloster & Hampshires   52
Gordon Highlanders   33 & 38
Green Howards   81 & 84
Green Jackets, Royal   113 & 120

Guards (all)   27

Gurkha Rifles (all)   109

Hampshire Regiment, Royal   43, 50 & 114
Highlanders, The, (S, C & G)   31 & 33
Highland LI   32 & 34
Highland Fusiliers, Royal   31 & 32

Irish Fusiliers, Royal   103 & 106

Inniskilling Fusiliers, Royal   103 & 104

Irish Rangers, Royal   103
Irish Regt, Royal   103, 131 & 132

Kents, East   43 & 46
Kents, West   43 & 46
King's Regiment   53 & 55
King's (Liverpool) Regiment   54 & 60
King's Own Royal Regiment   54 & 56
King's Own Scottish Borderers   31 & 36
King's Royal Rifle Corps   120

Lancashire Fusiliers   65 & 68
Lancashire Regiment, East   54 & 58
Lancashire Regiment, Queen's   53 & 55
Lancashire Regiment, South   54 & 58
Lancashire Regiment, The   54
Leicestershire Regiment   71 & 78
Light Infantry, The   113 & 123

Lincolnshire Regiment, Royal   71 & 74
Loyal Regiment   54 & 62

Manchester Regiment   54 & 60
Marines, Royal   148
Mercian Regiment   89
Middlesex Regiment   43 & 48

Norfolk Regiment, Royal   71 & 72
Northamptonshire Regiment   71 & 74
Northumberland Fusiliers   65 & 66
Notts & Derby Regiment   89 & 92

Oxfordshire &
  Buckinghamshire LI   120

Princess of Wales's Royal Regt   43

Queen's Lancashire Regiment   53 & 55
Queen's Regiment, The   43
Queen's Royal Regiment
  (West Surrey)   43 & 44
Queen's Own
  Highlanders (S&C)   33
Queen's Own Royal
  West Kents   43 & 46
Queen's Royal Surrey Regt   43

Rifles, The   113
Rifle Brigade   120
Royal Anglians   71
Royal Fusiliers   65 & 68
Royal Highland Fusiliers   31 & 32
Royal Regiment of Scotland   31
Royal Regt of Fusiliers   65
Royal Regt, Duke of Edinburgh's   117
Royal Regt, King's Own   54 & 56
Royal Regt, Princess of Wales's   43
Royal Regiment of Wales   97
Royal Scots   31, 32 & 34
Royal Scots Fusiliers   32 & 34
Royal Welch Fusiliers   97 & 98
Royal Welsh   97

Scottish Borderers,
  King's Own   31, 32 & 36
Scots Fusiliers, Royal   32 & 34
Scots, Royal   32 & 34
Seaforth Highlanders   33 & 38
Sherwood Foresters   89 & 92
Shropshire LI, King's   123
Somerset LI   123
Somerset & Cornwall LI   123
South Wales Borderers   97 & 98
Staffordshire Regiment   89
Staffordshire Regt, North   89 & 94
Staffordshire Regt, South   89 & 94
Suffolk Regiment   71 & 72
Surrey Regiment, East   43 & 44
Surrey, West   43 & 44
Sussex Regiment, Royal   43 & 48

Ulster Defence Regiment   103 & 106

Ulster Rifles, Royal   103 & 104

Wales, Royal Regiment of   97
Wales Borderers, South   97 & 98
Warwickshire Regiment   65, 66 & 130

Welch Fusiliers, Royal   97 & 98
Welch Regiment   97 & 100

Wiltshire Regiment   117
Worcestershire Regiment   89 & 92
Worcester &
  Sherwood Foresters Regt   89

York & Lancaster Regiment   81 & 86
Yorkshire LI, King's Own   123
Yorkshire Regiment   81
Yorkshire Regiment, East   81 & 82
Yorkshire Regiment, West   81 & 82
Yorkshire, Prince of Wales's   81
  Own Regiment of

Regular Infantry (continued) - Regiments of Foot (plus pre-1881 territorial title)

Air, Sea and Special Forces

Arms and Services

OTHER TITLES FROM PARTIZAN PRESS

15 The Life and Campaigns of Alexander Leslie	Charles Sanford Terry
16 German Artillery in the Franco Prussian War	E. Hoffbauer
17 Suchet's Memoirs of the War in Spain Vol I	Marshall Duke Suchet
18 Suchet's Memoirs of the War in Spain Vol II	Marshall Duke Suchet
19 Battles of Frederick the Great	Cyril Ransome
20 Oxford & Cambridge During the English Civil War	F.J. Varley
21 The Geat Civil War in Lancashire 1642 - 1651	Ernest Broxap
22 The Adventures of Dunsterforce	Major-General Dunsterville L.C.
23 The Great War in England in 1897	William Le Queux
24 The Siege of Chester 1643-1646	Canon R.H. Morris
25 Memoirs of the American Revolution	Maj. A. Leggett & Col. M. Willett
26 Memoirs of Marshal Oudinot	Marshall Oudinot
27 The German Cavalry in Belgium and France 1914	M von Poseck
28 Strategy of the Franco-German War	Brev-Maj WD Bird
29 My Zeppelins	Hugo Eckener

PARTIZAN CLASSICS TITANIC SERIES:

1 The Civil War in Hampshire 1642 - 1645	Rev G.N. Godwin
2 The Williamite Wars	Col C O'Kelly
3 Bibliotecha Gloucestrensis Vol I & II	
4 Bibliotecha Gloucestrensis Vol III	
5 The Navy in India 1763-1783	Admiral Sir HW Richmond

PARTIZAN PRESS WARGAME RULES: & SUPPLEMENTS

Warlord - Ancient & Medieval	Trevor Halsall & Richard Harper
DBMM - Ancient & Medieval	Phil Barker
DBMM List 1: 3000BC - 500BC	Phil Barker
DBMM List 2: 500BC - 476AD	Phil Barker
DBMM List 3: 476AD - 1071AD	Phil Barker
Forlorn Hope - ECW	Pete Berry & Ben Wilkins
Wargaming ECW Cavalry Actions	Stephen Maggs
Wargaming ECW Sieges	Stephen Maggs
ECW Scenarios 1	Stephen Maggs
ECW Scenarios 2	Robert Giglio
ECW Scenarios 3	Robert Giglio
ECW Scenarios 4	Robert Giglio
To the Banners - Pike & shot era	Stephen Danes
Lace Wars - Horse and Musket era	Stephen Danes
Lace Wars Scenarios 1: The Wars of Glory	Stephen Danes
Lace Wars Scenarios 2: The Wars of the Grand Alliance	Stephen Danes
Lace Wars Scenarios 3: The Great Northern & Turksih Wars	Stephen Danes
Lace Wars Scenarios 4: The Wars of teh Spanish Succession	Stephen Danes
Lace Wars Scenarios 5: The Wars of Austrian Succession	Stephen Danes
Warlord II - Medieval, Renaissance & 18th Century	Trevor Halsall & Richard Harper
Evolutionary War - Seven Year's War	T Kubik
A Severn Years Wargame Campaign - Volume 3	James Woods
The Raid on St Michel - 18th C scenarios	Charles Grant & Phil Olley
British Grenadier - American War of Independence	'Eclaireur'
American War of Independence Scenarios 1	'Eclaireur'
American War of Independence Scenarios 2	'Eclaireur'
L'Aigle - Napoleonic Wars	J. Delannoie
Champs de Mars - Napoleons Battles 1: 1806 The Campaign Against Prussia	Johan Delannoie
General de Brigade - Napoleonic Wars	David Brown
Napoleonic Scenarios 1	Dave Brown
Napoleonic Scenarios 2	Dave Brown
Napoleonic Scenarios 3	Dave Brown
Napoleonic Scenarios 4: Against the Ottomans	'Eclaireur'
There Are Your Guns - 19th Century	Dennis Williams
Esprit de Corps: A House Divide - ACW	Trevor Halsall & Chris Smith
Guns at Gettsburg - American Civil War (GdB variant)	David Brown
GaG Scenarios 1: Heartland - Kentuck & The Tennessee	Paul D. Stevenson
GaG Scenarios 2: Frontier - Early Battles for the Trans-Mississippi	Paul D. Stevenson
GaG Scenarios 3: On to Richmond - The Peninsula and the Severn Days	Paul D. Stevenson
The Gatling's Jammed	Stephen Danes
Warfare in Egypt and the Sudan	Stuart Asquith
Bloody Picnic - 1901-1925	Dillon Browne
Great War Scenarios 1: 1918 - The War in France & Italy	Dillon Browne
Battlegroup Panzer-Grenadier 2nd Edition - WWII	David Brown
Battles for the East	Dave Brown
Battles for the West	Dave Brown
Contact! - Post-WWII to modern	'Big Sid'